Handbook of
Therapeutic Life Story Work

The Rose Model

Karla Burley & Suzanne McGladdery

Foreword by Professor Richard Rose

Grosvenor House
Publishing Limited

Licensed Material on p.184-6 from S. Lloyd (2016)
'Improving Sensory Processing in Traumatized Children'
reproduced with the permission of the Licensor,
Jessica Kingsley Publishers Ltd, through PLSclear.

All rights reserved
Copyright © Karla Burley and Suzanne McGladdery, 2024

The right of Karla Burley and Suzanne McGladdery to
be identified as the authors of this work has been asserted in
accordance with Section 78 of the Copyright, Designs
and Patents Act 1988

The book cover is copyright to
Karla Burley and Suzanne McGladdery

This book is published by
Grosvenor House Publishing Ltd
Link House
140 The Broadway, Tolworth, Surrey, KT6 7HT.
www.grosvenorhousepublishing.co.uk

This book is sold subject to the conditions that it shall not, by way of
trade or otherwise, be lent, resold, hired out or otherwise circulated
without the author's or publisher's prior consent in any form of
binding or cover other than that in which it is published and
without a similar condition including this condition being
imposed on the subsequent purchaser.

A CIP record for this book
is available from the British Library

ISBN 978-1-80381-828-3

'Without a life story, a child is adrift, disconnected and vulnerable.'

(Perry, in Rose 2012, p.10)

List of Figures

Figure 1: Squiggle Drawing Example 1 — 70
Figure 2: Squiggle Drawing Example 2 — 70
Figure 3: Squiggle Drawing Example 3 — 71
Figure 4: Hands of Interests — 75
Figure 5: Hands of Support and Safety — 75
Figure 6: Working Agreement Example 1 — 77
Figure 7: Working Agreement Example 2 — 77
Figure 8: Session Chart example — 78
Figure 9: Air Balloon — 81
Figure 10: Air Balloon Happy Place — 81
Figure 11: Air Balloon Safe Place — 82
Figure 12: Corridor of my Mind — 82
Figure 13: Preoccupation Bar Graph — 84
Figure 14: Anger Iceberg — 88
Figure 15: Hand Model of the Brain — 90
Figure 16: How Trauma Affects the Nervous System — 92
Figure 17: Tangle of Feelings — 94
Figure 18: Three Mountains Imagery — 99
Figure 19: Adapted from Kuypers' (2011) 'Zones of Regulation' — 102
Figure 20: Finding the Warrior Within — 106
Figure 21: Suitcase Exercise — 109
Figure 22: Treasure Chest — 109
Figure 23: Feelings, Actions and Behaviour Tree — 112
Figure 24: Timeline — 119
Figure 25: Adapted from Nicholls 'The Parent Thing' — 121
Figure 26: Development of Nicholls 'The Parent Thing' — 122
Figure 27: Adapted from Golding and Hughes (2012) Shield of Shame — 131
Figure 28: SHANARRI Assessment Chart – Child Age 9 – Parent — 160
Figure 29: SHANARRI Assessment Chart – Child Age 9 – School — 162
Figure 30: SHANARRI Assessment Chart – Child Age 9 – Child's View — 164
Figure 31: SHANARRI Assessment Chart – Child Age 15 – Parent — 165
Figure 32: SHANARRI Assessment Chart – Child Age 15 – School — 167
Figure 33: SHANARRI Assessment Chart – Child Age 15 – Child's View — 169
Figure 34: Use of Play for Communicating Internal World — 194
Figure 35: Use of Squiggles for Communicating Internal World — 195
Figure 36: Use of Lego for Information Sharing — 204
Figure 37: The Fish of Anger — 205
Figure 38: Collier's Five Pillars of Protection — 244
Figure 39: Adapted from Rogers Person-Centred Core Conditions — 249
Figure 40: Umbrella of Support — 252
Figure 41: The Supervision Triangle — 266
Figure 42: Re-drawing of Morrison's Supervision Cycle — 268
Figure 43: Hill's Model of Non-Managerial Clinical Supervision — 269

Contents

Foreword	vii
Acknowledgements	x
Feedback	xi
Introduction	xii

PART ONE: Beginning Therapeutic Life Story Work 1

Chapter 1: Where, When and How to Start as a Therapeutic Life Story Work Practitioner 3
    What is Therapeutic Life Story Work? 3
    Therapeutic Life Story Work Training 7
    How and Why We Began Therapeutic Life Story Work 11

Chapter 2: The Referral Process and Initial Meeting 18

Chapter 3: First Practical Steps 29
    Preparation Sessions with Parents 29
    Information Gathering 31
    Working with Birth Families 35
    The Complexities of Contact 45

PART TWO: Therapeutic Life Story Work: The Sessions 53

Chapter 4: Therapeutic Life Story Work Sessions 55
    The Importance of Beginnings 55
    Preparing and Planning Sessions 60
    1. Connecting and Creating Containment 62
    2. Working with Emotions 79
    3. Building Self-Confidence 98
    4. Exploring a Sense of Self 103
    5. Creating a Timeline 115
    6. Exploring Hopes and Dreams 138
    7. Ending Session 139

Chapter 5: Creating a Record of the Sessions: The Life Story Book 142

Chapter 6: The Importance of Endings	149
Chapter 7: Measuring Outcomes	156
PART THREE: Considerations for the Practitioner	177
Chapter 8: Working with Complex Needs, Sensory Processing Needs and Neurodiversity	179
Complex Medical, Physical and Learning Needs	180
Sensory Processing Needs	184
Neurodiversity	193
Chapter 9: Creativity	199
Chapter 10: Creating Therapeutic Stories	207
Chapter 11: When Things Go Wrong – and What to Do!	222
Challenges During Sessions	222
Challenges with Parents and Birth Families	228
Challenges with the Organisations Holding Records for the Child	236
PART FOUR: Practicalities for the Practitioner	241
Chapter 12: Self-Care and Supervision	243
Self-Care	243
Peer Supervision and Clinical Supervision	245
Safety and Containment	251
Connection and Relationship	261
Reflection in Supervision	267
What Makes a Good Supervisor?	272
Becoming a Supervisor	274
Practicalities of Supervisory Contact	276
Chapter 13: Authenticity and Working Online	280
Chapter 14: Therapeutic Life Story Work and Beyond	287
Appendices	293
References	309
Subject Index	317
Author Index	322

Foreword

This wonderful book is a journey of sorts, as told at the very beginning as Karla and Suzanne thank those that have inspired and supported them. I am always intrigued by dedications and thanks, and wonder how, what it was and what is remembered. I am lucky as I have a mention, for the model they have so engaged with and the support for their book, but in truth, they were always going to write their stories and the main thing I did was to recognise their potential.

Karla and Suzanne were on the Professional Diploma on separate years, but I felt that there may be a cooperation of practice and put them together, not realising what I had started. Since this time, they have both achieved great outcomes for children and young people, drawing on their skills and the model that they had presented to them.

They supported me and others in developing a truly international professional body of practice and raised the profile of the intervention. I can say that they have often been the difference between successfully navigating the space and falling between the lines, between them and a few others, we have developed a lovely approach.

Such a contrast from my humble beginnings in 1997, when I was asked to do life story work and to get on with it. About 20 years ago, I was asked to present at a National Health Conference in Leeds, UK – it was my first conference, and I was very excited that the life story work had been recognised. I delivered a good workshop and afterwards a very experienced psychologist said how amazing the work was, and that it could only be done by me as it was so personal and individual. On the one side, I was quite honoured, but the other, saddened that this was a personality approach and not a wider professional practice. I decided there and then that I would try and teach as much of my practice as I could, whether life story work – that became Therapeutic Life Story Work, or investigation, trauma and attachment thinking. This led to my commitment to share practice and encourage the development of the approach and those seeking to learn and widen the application.

Today we train across the world and the Rose Model of Therapeutic Life Story Work is widely adopted, Karla and Suzanne have been on this journey for the last few years, they have worked with many children and young people and now contribute to the development of the model through their tireless support of TLSWi (therapeutic life story work international). A perfect journey which, this book is their first published step into the narrative world.

Having had the opportunity to read their manuscript and experience the thought and the passion that gives it gravitas, I was then asked if I would write this Foreword; it was and is an honour for me to do so. Both have put their heart and soul into each page and agonised over each character, and with so much thought contained in this handbook of Therapeutic Life Story Work, they have provided a rich guide to the Rose Model of TLSW, and this will be a valuable addition to the practitioner's toolbox.

Stories are who we are, and in writing this short piece, I kept reflecting on the stories of the last 26 years of developing, arguing, championing and sometimes demanding the authorities to invest in and support this amazing intervention. Now that I am coming towards the end of my working life and handing over to those who,

I am sure will develop it, Karla and Suzanne have set the way forward.

With genuine honesty, refreshing clarity and a clear intention for the reader to learn and to develop their practice, the handbook does exactly what it sets out to, a guide and a support for those on their Therapeutic Life Story Work journey.

The Rose Model of Therapeutic Life Story is now practised in countries such as Australia, New Zealand, Japan, Portugal, Norway, Denmark, UK, Ireland, the USA, and Canada. Now evidence based, and subject of four more research projects as well as applying the model not just for traumatised children and young people, but for care experienced adults, adult adoptees, parents who are grieving through the loss of their children to the care system and those where their past defines their present. We know that this model of Therapeutic Life Story is a recovery intervention, and Karla and Suzanne's contribution will further establish this wonderful approach.

When I wrote Life Story Therapy in 2012, I was fortunate to have Bruce Perry write a foreword, and it was amazing. I often refer to it as the best bit in the whole book, and I, in pure honesty, still believe that. I can confidently say that this foreword cannot overshadow this well thought out, and well-structured guide to delivering recovery for children and young people, read on and enjoy.

> *'We are all a collection of stories, if left unheard, who are we and how can we be?'*

Richard Rose
November 2022

Acknowledgements

We would like to thank the many children we have had the privilege to work with and who, alongside their parents, have taught us so much. Especially thanks to those children who have agreed to assist the learning of others by sharing examples of their work in this book.

We want to thank Professor Richard Rose for sharing his Therapeutic Life Story Work model with us, for continuing to teach us so much and for supporting us in getting our book published.

Karla: I would like to thank all those who have supported me along the way: Vanessa and Pete Szcerbicki for their continued motivation, Karen Capuano, Roberta Cameron and Lou Jones-Sullivan for their inspiration and encouragement, post adoption support teams for their confidence in my work, and Suzanne for being my co-author and sharing the journey.

Suzanne: I would like to thank my parents, Marie and Maurice McGladdery, for their support, especially in helping create some of my direct work tools, my sister Julia Thompson for drawing the umbrella image in our chapter on self-care and supervision, Alison Keith for guiding and informing my therapeutic practice. To my university tutor for the self-fulfilling prophecy that I would write a book one day, Leon Fulcher for encouragement and editorial feedback, Afshan Ahmad for introducing me to life story work, and Karla for the many days of sharing and sparking ideas together.

We may only work with a handful of children each but, with the growth of Therapeutic Life Story Work there are increasing numbers of practitioners and together we are making a difference to more children's lives.

Feedback

We feel the power of Therapeutic Life Story Work is demonstrated by the feedback we have received from those who have benefitted from this intervention.

Feedback from parents:

'I have seen my son grow, become stronger, honest and trusting in how he feels and, with us, more open about his past and present thoughts and feelings. He is like a tree growing and reaching for the sky, knowing more of where his roots are and that he has his family to support and hold him when needed. He never liked talking or sharing what was going on with him until he met you Karla; he felt safe with you and it was your accepting manner that enabled him to go through this process. We have our son back!'

'The boys were angry, destructive and confused; the eldest blamed himself. They are now able to confidently manage the emotions they have and understand fully why they now live with me. They are now able to talk about the past. They understand and feel no blame.'

Feedback from children:

'I know I didn't want to do this life story work at the start and I gave you and Mum a tough time, yet you hung in there and I am happy that I have done it. I know more of me and I don't hold a lot of stuff in my head anymore.'

'I did not talk much when we first met and now I talk a lot. I found my voice. Thank you. Things are better at home, school and with my friends ... yes, I have friends now. I was worried when I first met you and now I can see you never judged me. Thank you.'

Introduction

Life Story Work is something we do all the time, be it reminiscing with friends or family about a particular event or period of our lives, or keeping memorabilia, photographs, and written records. Reflecting on and re-examining past events and experiences helps us to make meaning of them in the present.

In this book we focus on our Therapeutic Life Story Work with children and their parents using The Rose Model of Therapeutic Life Story Work which is a specific intervention, developed by Professor Richard Rose (2012), designed to help children understand and make meaning of their lives. The model, ideas and principles can also be transferred to many settings where a person is wanting help in reflecting on and making sense of their lives.

In addition, in Chapter 10 we outline the unique model of creating therapeutic stories that Suzanne has developed to tell a child's narrative through a favourite character or area of interest. Richard Rose has endorsed this as sitting within his model of Therapeutic Life Story Work as well as being a model in its own right. Suzanne and Karla have designed and deliver a 3-day training course on creating therapeutic stories.

We are independent Therapeutic Life Story Work practitioners with many years' experience of direct work with children, as a certified play therapist and a qualified social worker. In 2016/7 we completed Richard Rose's Diploma in Therapeutic Life Story Work and began providing Therapeutic Life Story Work in England, mostly funded by the central government Adoption Support Fund (ASF). This book offers a reflection of our practice and is the result of hours of work, exploring our experiences and the challenges we have faced, and a hope that it will prove beneficial to other Therapeutic Life Story Work practitioners.

While nothing can beat training, experience and good supervision for learning and developing practice, we hope this book may be of additional support and guidance to those undertaking this important area of practice. It acknowledges our journey alongside that of the families we support. You may find it helpful to dip in and out when looking for inspiration or ideas that may help in a particular situation.

We aim to build on existing literature in this field, with insights from our own experiences, ideas and theories, including activities that we have found helpful. Please keep in mind that our views and practices may differ from those of others. This is not a prescriptive 'how to' manual; our intention is rather to provide additional strategies and resources for you to create your own 'toolkit'. We feel it is important to bring your own creativity to the process, as we discuss in Chapter 9.

We use the term 'parent' to refer to those providing the day-to-day parenting for the child, including any primary carers, such as adoptive parents, wider birth family members or connected people, foster carers and house parents. We use the term 'child' to refer to all children and young people, and 'maternal/paternal brother/sister' to refer to children who do not share both birth parents. We seek to use 'brother' or 'sister' in place of 'sibling' where possible. We recognise that this work is equally valid and helpful in many situations: these could include working with care-experienced adults, in prisons, with birth parents who have had their children removed, and those in end-of-life care. In these circumstances, the terms could be changed to 'adult' and 'supporter'.

Black lives matter, and particularly in our work black children's lives matter. Therapeutic Life Story Work is an intervention that is tailored to each child's needs which includes supporting cultural safety and inclusivity. It is about identity and knowing your history and birth family culture. Consideration is given to matching a practitioner to a family. Wishes and needs must be taken into account for all children, but especially for children from a minoritised ethnic background. As white women we are committed to this in our work and in this book. We honour the child's choice of practitioner where possible, as it is imperative that they feel comfortable, knowing the practitioner has an insight into and knowledge about their culture or belief system. This enhances the child's experience and, therefore, their self-identity.

We refer to unconscious (or implicit) bias to describe the associations we hold outside our conscious awareness that lead to automatic judgements and assessments. Our attitudes and behaviours, especially towards others, are influenced by our experiences, background, society and culture, and can lead to inequality. We feel that we all have a responsibility to increase our awareness, recognise our own biases and enter into discussion with others in order to mitigate against it.

The Rose Model of Therapeutic Life Story Work refers to using 'wallpaper' as a way of recording the content of sessions, ideally with the child contributing the most in terms of drawing or writing thoughts and feelings. In direct work sessions this tends to refer to rolls of lining paper: a long strip of plain paper designed to be pasted onto a wall to provide a smooth surface for painting. Here we use the term wallpaper broadly to include any form of recording sessions, such as digital recordings made when providing online sessions.

We continue to feel enthused about our work. These families teach us so much and it is a privilege to guide them through this experience. It has become apparent that as Therapeutic Life Story Work evolves, so do we alongside the family.

Part One

Beginning Therapeutic Life Story Work

Chapter 1
Where, When and How to Start as a Therapeutic Life Story Work Practitioner

What is Therapeutic Life Story Work?

So, what do we mean by the term Therapeutic Life Story Work?

Life story work was developed to support children who are unable to live with their birth families. It helps them to gain an understanding of and helpful narrative about their birth family history. It is trauma-informed and guided by theories of attachment, separation and loss, identity, and child development, as found in the works of writers such as Brodzinsky et al. (1984) and Fahlberg (1994).

A Therapeutic Life Story Work intervention can help a child make sense of their past and understand how this impacts their present. It can help them to build healthy relationships and make positive changes for the future. The focus is not on telling the child's story to them, but rather on the therapeutic process which facilitates and contains the child's exploration of information about their past, making sense of it and creating a narrative from their view.

How did Therapeutic Life Story Work develop?
In the UK, legislation such as The Adoption and Children Act 2002 and The Children Act 2004 acknowledged the importance

of attachment and the need for access to therapeutic interventions and core practices, such as life story work, to help children in forming attachments and developing a secure emotional base. Following this legislation, life story work practitioners, such as Nicholls (2005), Rees (2009) and Baynes (2008), began writing about their practices. Rose and Philpot (2005) advocated a therapeutic approach as part of the recovery process from trauma, based on psychodynamic principles of considering not just the information but the impact of past experiences and relationships on the present. More recently, Rose (2012) and Wrench and Naylor (2013) have developed trauma-informed therapeutic models.

The Rose Model of Therapeutic Life Story Work is an approach based on attachment and child development theories. It provides a holistic way of healing trauma through processes of internalisation and integration and is based on principles of psychodynamic and attachment theory. Writers such as Perry (2001) and Van Der Kolk (2014) further developed early theories of attachment and child development, such as Bowlby's (1969 and 1988) internal working model, to show the impact of the child's relationship with their primary caregiver and adverse childhood experiences on their developing brain. The Rose Model of Therapeutic Life Story Work enables children to explore, question and understand the past events of their lives. It aims to secure their future through strengthening attachment with their parents and providing the opportunity to develop a healthy sense of self and feelings of wellbeing.

How does it work?
The Rose Model of Therapeutic Life Story Work seeks to provide children with a narrative of their life, to enable healing from the trauma of abuse, abandonment and neglect, through talking, play and art activities. Thoughts and feelings are usually recorded

on wallpaper; if working online the recording can also be done in a variety of ways, such as creating a document as a continuous sheet of paper (working online is explored in detail in Chapter 13). The aim is to support the child in externalising their thoughts and feelings in order to investigate and internalise them in a potentially new and more helpful way.

The Rose Model of Therapeutic Life Story Work has three main stages (Rose 2012):

Stage One: The Information Bank
The child's pre- and post-birth history is gathered from social work files, health records and interviews, including with the birth family. It is collated chronologically and can help identify gaps, questions and where to source further information, as well as informing session plans. The aim is for this information to be considered from the child's perspective to facilitate exploration of their own story and make meaning of their lives.

Stage Two: Internalization
The focus is on the process of externalization and internalization through direct work sessions, conducted over several months with the child and their parents, to support emotional security and strengthen attunement and attachment. The aim is for the child to externalise wishes, thoughts, feelings and emotions, using various techniques, which are usually examined and recorded on wallpaper to enable the child to reach new understanding and meanings that are internalised as their own story.

Stage Three: The Life Story Book
The focus is on creating a book which reflects the process of the work, the meanings made, and celebrates the child's journey. In this way the books differ from the more traditional life story

books made for a child at the point of adoption, such as those using the Rees (2009) model, which are designed as a tool to support the child's future journey of understanding their story.

The most significant benefit of The Rose Model of Therapeutic Life Story Work is that it offers the child a better sense of self, identity and belonging, and an opportunity to heal emotional ruptures from the past. There will be many challenges to address throughout. It begins the process of healing the trauma experienced, releasing difficult feelings and emotions in a safe environment. The child, their primary carer and the practitioner collaborate to increase the communication of intense emotions, and deepen the understanding of each other's thoughts and feelings, with the outcome of enhancing and strengthening the attachment between the child and their parent.

Adopted and fostered children are likely to have experienced the trauma of abuse and neglect as well as separation and loss of their birth family. Trauma affects development of the brain as well as future attachments (Howe 2009) and can lead to emotional, behavioural, and educational difficulties (Pennington 2012). Howe (2009) and Cairns (2002) both suggest that successful care requires emotional attunement, creativity, and a willingness to understand how the world feels from the child's perspective, all of which are key principles of The Rose Model of Therapeutic Life Story Work.

For children who have been removed from their birth family, an understanding of their life history can be fragmented. They often have a sense of loss and not belonging which creates a vulnerability to future adversity. The Rose Model of Therapeutic Life Story Work gives these children a voice and an opportunity to explore their past and their feelings about it, in relation to their feelings today. It helps them to answer their questions about the past; with a greater understanding, their behaviour tends to become calmer and more focused.

Greater opportunities to undertake this kind of work have been created by the Diploma in Therapeutic Life Story Work which is now offered by Therapeutic Life Story Work International (TLSWi) in several countries around the world. In 2014, in England, life story work was included as a requirement of the National Institute for Health and Care Excellence Guidance. Also, the subsequent introduction of the Adoption Support Fund in England in 2015 enabled local authority adoption and friends and family teams to commission extensive therapeutic life story work for children who had previously been in care but were now adopted or living with family members or connected persons under a special guardianship order. Together these factors have served to transform both the status and practice of Therapeutic Life Story Work in England.

Therapeutic Life Story Work Training

We feel it is important for the practitioner to have a background in working directly with vulnerable children and families, an understanding of trauma and attachment, and to have completed training in life story work. The Diploma in Therapeutic Life Story Work directed by Professor Richard Rose is an excellent foundation for undertaking this work (further information is available on Professor Richard Rose's Therapeutic Life Story Work International website: www.tlswi.com).

Karla: *I am a qualified and experienced play therapist and psychotherapist with over 20 years' experience in working with children from the age of 18 months, young people and families. My work has included managing a practice of counsellors* *and play therapists, providing support tailored to the specific needs of individual children and families, delivering training for parents, foster carers, adoptive parents, professionals in education and other fields that support children on an emotional, psychological or behavioural level. The training I offer encompasses a wide variety of areas, such as therapeutic play skills and techniques, counselling young people, child protection and child development. I aim to provide a safe environment and place of agreed confidentiality, mutual trust, and respect, professional growth and development, grounding experiences, supervision and peer learning, an understanding of how vital this therapeutic process is for children, outcomes which are as unique as each individual.*

Suzanne: *I am an experienced senior social worker and have worked for over 30 years with children and families in child protection, adoption, and fostering settings in public, private and charitable sectors. My experience has included direct work with children in taking action to protect children, family assessment, preventative work with families, child witness support, presenting evidence at family and criminal courts, recording in casework files and life story work. All this has provided a strong foundation for my Therapeutic Life Story Work practice which includes designing and delivering training in the UK and internationally and offering supervision and consultation to therapeutic Life Story Work Practitioners and agencies.*

Completing the Diploma in Therapeutic Life Story Work served to consolidate our learning and provided us with a good foundation, and the structure, tools and techniques for the work that followed. We found that the days of being taught, the additional reading, research, and assignments, together with the skills and experience we brought, equipped us with an invaluable basis from which to adapt the interventions to both the child and our own styles.

Karla: *The Diploma in Therapeutic Life Story Work presents a process which supports children and their parents in building attachment, improving communication and trust and achieving clarity about the circumstances which caused the child to be placed for adoption or long-term care.*

For me personally it enhanced my processing abilities around the impact of trauma and my understanding of how this and child development are so inter-related. My work has always been concerned with the stages of child development and how a child's emotional and psychological wellbeing is affected if these stages are not fulfilled. When parents wanted their child to receive play therapy, I would always ask, 'Could you tell me when you noticed your child's behaviour changing and what was happening at that time?' This would grant me insights into when the child had experienced a life trauma, and how it had affected their emotional growth.

One nine-year-old boy was referred to me for play therapy before being considered for Therapeutic Life Story Work. His parents were perplexed and concerned as to why their son would not eat meat all of a sudden; they could not think of anything that might have caused this change of behaviour.

When I first met him we reflected upon his situation and discussed why he was seeing me. Within 40 minutes he revealed that a young family member had died a year earlier from choking on meat. The family had been traumatised by this but had not seen the connection between the trauma and their son's change of behaviour; this boy had become frightened of eating meat as he worried he too would die like his family member. He also disclosed a memory of being told that his father had been taken to hospital once for eating something that caused an allergic reaction (he had survived); this had heightened the child's fear.

I have learnt to notice how, through sharing their experiences, children can reveal the connections between family life events and developmental challenges, and this example underlines the importance of exploring and locating the child's trauma.

Suzanne: *Prior to undertaking the Diploma in Therapeutic Life Story Work, I worked as a life story work coordinator in an international independent fostering agency. The diploma confirmed that I was working in line with the key principles and concepts of The Rose Model of Therapeutic Life Story Work. It enhanced my practice by providing clearer guidance through the process of assisting a child to explore, question and understand the past events of their lives. A key element in my learning was developing a greater range of creative and therapeutic techniques. I found I was able to communicate with the children and connect with their emotions at a deeper level through listening, noticing and wondering more in the sessions, responding to and focusing on what the child was bringing to the sessions* and *not simply rigidly following the session plan.*

As a social worker I had been used to having an agenda and being directive; using The Rose Model of Therapeutic Life Story Work guided me towards being more child-led. I became more mindful of allowing the child's story rather than my own interpretation, working at the child's pace, ensuring them the space to process the information, and guiding them towards making their own meaning.

My learning from the Therapeutic Life Story Work Diploma course, together with reflective supervision, equipped me to better use opportunities presented during the sessions to notice and respond to the child's thoughts and feelings, as well as reflect on the impact of experiences on current feelings and behaviours. It became clear that working on wallpaper to explore and record thoughts and feelings allowed for a new narrative to be created and the resulting life story books became less formulaic and more reflective of the child and the process of the work.

Clinical and peer supervision have been vital in our learning, allowing us to stay grounded and to manage, reflect upon and make meaning of our work. They have enabled us to develop our practice and grow within the process of undertaking the work, allowing valuable room for creativity and flexibility. We consider the importance of good supervision and peer support in more detail in Chapter 12.

How and Why We Began Therapeutic Life Story Work

Suzanne: *I have long held a strong belief in the need for children to feel listened to, heard and helped to understand their past and present life events. I was struck, however, by how little support the children received with understanding their lives.*

When I supported children who were giving evidence in criminal courts, for the National Society for the Prevention of Cruelty to Children (NSPCC), I was given a questionnaire to use. It consisted of a list of worries for the child to rate as '1, not worried', '2, a little worried' and '3, really worried'. I designed a set of 'worry pots': bright coloured beakers for each level of worry and a set of cards with the worries on (including some blank ones). They were read out, discussed, and put into the beaker of the child's choice. The 'not worried' cards were discarded, and we looked at the remaining worries in a tangible way, some, such as 'going to prison myself', could be torn up or thrown out straight away with an explanation of how the criminal courts work and a reassurance that this could not happen. When I suggested the child could leave their worries with me until the next session, the relief was visible. The worries reduced over the course of the sessions and we considered strategies to support any remaining worries.

Later in my career, while working for an international independent fostering agency supporting foster carers, I had the opportunity to work alongside Afshan Ahmad (co-creator of My Life Story CD-ROM 2003 and co-author of a chapter on Digital Life Story Work in Ryan and Walker 2007) as a life story work coordinator. At this time there was no qualifying life story work training and we considered setting this up.

I later became aware of Richard Rose's Diploma in Therapeutic Life Story Work which had been launched in 2014, and that this work could now be carried out independently in England with funding from the Adoption Support Fund which had been set up in May 2015. I jumped at the chance to obtain the qualification and began to work as an independent practitioner. I am so pleased I took that leap of faith. One of our motivating factors in writing this book was to share our experiences to encourage and support others to take the same steps.

Karla: *I first became aware of Richard Rose when I received a referral for one young person. Richard had recommended art and play therapy for this child while he was carrying out Therapeutic Life Story Work with their siblings. I was inclined to wait until Richard's work was completed, but the local authority informed me that he wanted me to provide the play therapy work while he was carrying out the Therapeutic Life Story Work.*

I did not feel that two therapeutic interventions would be beneficial for any child or young person. We spoke for the first time on the telephone and shared each other's reasoning and points of view. It was agreed that I should go ahead and start the sessions but hold off until the Therapeutic Life Story Work was completed, if it became apparent that this was ineffective.

Richard had asked me if I had ever done life story work; I informed him that I had not and would not do so without any training. He was pleased to hear this and shared a little bit about his work. He had a course starting in October of that year; I applied, was accepted, and have not looked back since!

The Therapeutic Life Story Work process has enriched my passion for providing children with a safe and accepting space where they can express their thoughts, feelings, and ideas. When I started to learn about it, I felt it would be difficult to transition from non-directive to more directive work. It was tricky at first, but I made the transition through my understanding of the process involved and its effectiveness. I now work in and support Therapeutic Life Story Work full time in various ways.

We both started out as independent practitioners during our diploma course by advising our local authority adoption and friends and family teams that we would be available to offer Therapeutic Life Story Work. Where we were not well known to and already undertaking work for an organisation we were interviewed and required to submit evidence of our qualifications. These teams have been the main source of referrals for work, mostly funded by the Adoption Support Fund in England but also by local authorities. One independent fostering team whom Suzanne previously worked for funds several pieces of Therapeutic Life Story Work a year.

We do not accept work funded privately by a parent as we feel that, as independent workers, we require all safeguarding matters to be considered. This includes professional self-care and managing all aspects of the work with the support and protection of an official regulatory board, such as the Office for Standards in Education and Children's Services in England (Ofsted).

Karla: *I was known to my local post adoption support team through my work as a play therapist and filial therapist with adopted children, and adoptive parents and families. I introduced myself to the assistant team manager to obtain a placement for my Therapeutic Life Story Work course. Since then I have continued to receive referrals from this team. I had to go through the vetting process again, as my work was changing from play therapy to Therapeutic Life Story Work, and this process took a few months. However, it was required, and it enabled the families to feel safe knowing I had been approved.*

We consider our approach with each child from multiple angles, placing importance on being realistic about our own ability and skills. We stress that it is okay to say no to referrals if you do not feel confident or that you have the appropriate learning and experience to take them on. We continually re-evaluate our abilities, required skills, experience and understanding of the complexities that are involved in our work, particularly within clinical supervision. As a result, we have found ourselves having to say no to some referrals where it would be inappropriate, either for the child or ourselves, to accept. Working with a non-verbal child, for example, can be challenging; one practitioner may feel able to do this piece of work while another may not, depending on their work and life experience. However, do also bear in mind that you will be working alongside the parent who will be the expert on their child's unique needs and can guide you.

When deciding whether to accept a referral, you need to consider your understanding of the child's development, the trauma, attachment and loss they have experienced, possible existing abuse and the level of safety within their current environment.

This will enable you to assess whether the child is capable of being present within the Therapeutic Life Story Work process. These areas are examined in more depth later in the book, as well the importance of considering the impact the work can have on you as the worker.

Once you feel equipped for this work, ensuring you are well supported and guided, you can approach agencies, as we did, such as local authority adoption or friends and family teams and independent fostering agencies who are able to commission your services.

Things to consider before you start
You will need to have the time to meet with the child on a consistent basis. Ryan and Walker (2007) suggest aiming for weekly sessions for the first 8-10 sessions. The Rose Model of Therapeutic Life Story Work suggests fortnightly sessions to give the child time to process information between sessions. The number of sessions can vary in relation to the needs of the child as well as the funding available. We have found this is often between 16-22 sessions, though we have at times undertaken many more. You need to be able to create a safe and secure relationship with the child and parent and to be able to sit with and hold their powerful feelings; this is what we mean by connection or connecting.

It is vital to have good support and supervision given the challenges of this work and the emotional impact it can have. We explore this in more detail in Chapter 12, Self-Care and Supervision.

You need to be able to work in an anti-discriminatory way, and to be committed to examining and being aware of any of your own unconscious biases. Consider your own skills and needs, areas for development and whether you have what is needed for each family, and what you may need to prepare for the work.

Approaching Organisations
You may already be working for an agency who will provide you with work. If you are seeking referrals elsewhere, once you have the relevant training, the next step is to approach the organisations you wish to work for to let them know of your availability. This can be done initially by a phone call to ascertain the person to contact and followed up by an email or another phone call.

We, and those we supervise, have found it useful to create a booklet which includes an outline of the Rose Model, the way we work and an introduction of ourselves, outlining our qualifications and experience. You may want to commission this professionally or design it yourself. We use a graphic design platform called Canva, who are an Australian based company providing a helpful and easy to use tool for self-designing and printing booklets, flyers and brochures.

As you may be working with several organisations it is helpful to understand what your referring agency requires from you to get started. In our experience the process of being approved as an external service provider can take anything from a week to as long as two months.

As an independent provider you are likely to be interviewed and required to provide a copy of your CV/résumé, qualifications, insurance certificates, references, and Enhanced Disclosure Barring Service (DBS) Check or other relevant police check in your area; in Australia this is called a Working with Children Check. It is good practice to keep all your personal and professional information up-to-date and available.

At the time of writing, to practice as an independent Therapeutic Life Story worker in the UK, you needed:

- To register with Her Majesty's Revenue and Customs (HMRC) as self-employed, usually as a sole trader
- Professional indemnity and public liability insurance to the level required by the commissioning agency
- A DBS check.

To practice independently in Australia at the time of writing you needed:

- An Australian Business Number (ABN)
- Professional indemnity and public liability insurance which includes the Privacy Act, Health Act, and your state child protection related act.
- Cyber security insurance
- A privacy policy
- A services agreement
- A Working with Children's Check
- A diploma in Therapeutic Life Story Work.

For children living in England, organisations may require you to complete an accreditation questionnaire for the provision of services accessible under the Adoption Support Fund. This is a form provided by the Adoption Support Fund and is likely to be the same form for each local authority you are commissioned by, but with their logo added. If you are commissioned by more than one organisation, keeping a copy will save time.

Once approved as a service provider you can receive referrals. We look at the referral process in Chapter 2. When we started out in 2016/7 there were few Therapeutic Life Story Work practitioners and many referrals, so obtaining enough work has not been an issue.

Chapter 2
The Referral Process and Initial Meeting

A decision to seek Therapeutic Life Story Work for a child is usually made by the local government department for children's services. The need may be identified because a child has increasing questions or unrest about their family of origin and how they came to live in their present situation.

While the work can strengthen the relationship between the child and parent and have a stabilising effect, we see Therapeutic Life Story Work in relation to an identity need rather than a crisis intervention. In our experience the child needs to feel a sense of safety in their present in order to be able to look back at the past.

You need to assess the referral and consider whether it is appropriate and something you can take on.

We also suggest you consider who is being referred to you, and if there may be unconscious bias in relation to disadvantaged children. For example, black children are overrepresented in the looked-after population; is this reflected in your referrals? Are children who have complex needs being considered for Therapeutic Life Story Work? Consider how you reflect diversity in the service you offer and keep these issues in mind.

When you receive your first referral you may be so pleased that you just want to jump right in and say yes!

However, we have found it helpful to consider the following areas at the point of referral:

Checklist for Therapeutic Life Story Work Referrals

> Location
> Reason for Referral
> Who is requesting Therapeutic Life Story Work?
> Current situation regarding safety and stability
> Child's ethnicity, age and level of understanding
> Child's view
> Therapeutic Parenting Capacity
> Background History
> Birth parents' current situation
> Allocated worker and other brothers and sisters
> Initial Meeting

Location Is the location for the sessions a feasible distance for travel? This may seem obvious, but we have learnt that this is the first thing to consider as, however appropriate the referral may be, the meeting place for the sessions needs to be a manageable distance for you or the family to travel. If costs such as mileage and travel time are high there is likely to be less funding available for your work, which may mean fewer sessions or less time spent information gathering or compiling the life story book, and you may not be able to claim travel time.

Reason for referral At the point of inquiry, a discussion with the referrer is helpful in ascertaining why the referral is being made now, and what the understanding and expectations of the referrer and possibly the family are. If the child is in crisis Therapeutic Life Story Work may not be the most appropriate intervention. As previously stated, we believe that to feel safe enough to look back at the past, the child needs to feel a sense of safety in their present. While it may be possible to create adequate safety in the sessions and work around trauma such as helping the child to regulate their feelings, which is important and valuable work, this can potentially take up all your sessions, leading to a greater number of sessions being needed which may require additional funding, which is not always available. If you are self-employed, it is up to you to decide if you want to take on this work.

For some children it may be beneficial prior to engaging in Therapeutic Life Story Work to provide interventions such as a sensory processing assessment or Just Right State programme (as detailed in Chapter 8), referral for child and adolescent mental health services, dyadic developmental psychotherapy, play, art, movement, or drama-therapy. Where practitioners have this training, the work can be incorporated into their sessions.

Who is requesting Therapeutic Life Story Work?
Identifying who is asking for the intervention can help further your understanding of the reasons for the referral. For example, has the parent requested the intervention and if so, why? Is it because a parent wants to change the child's behaviour, or are they wanting to help their child to understand their past, assist in knowing their identity, increase their confidence, self-esteem, self-worth, and sense of belonging? Therapeutic Life Story Work is not aimed at behaviour modification, though changes may be seen. The primary aim is to assist a child in understanding

their past and present so they can have a more positive view of possibilities for their future, as well as developing a positive sense of identity.

Current situation regarding safety and stability Is the child's environment safe and stable? If not, as previously suggested, it may not be appropriate for Therapeutic Life Story Work to commence. It may be better to wait until they have a greater sense of safety and stability, and an adult with whom they feel safe. The following issues need to be addressed: if a child is not feeling safe within their home because of neglect or abuse, they are likely to not be stable enough to fully engage in Therapeutic Life Story Work. If the parents are unable to work together the child may not receive the support they require throughout the experience. Until the situation is secure it is not in the child's best interests to proceed with direct work sessions. Consideration can be given to the support parents need and whether the practitioner can offer a number of parent preparation sessions. Where a child's behaviour shows that they do not have a sense of safety in their present a sensory processing assessment by a specialist occupational therapist may be of benefit. Similarly, play therapy may be of benefit before receiving Therapeutic Life Story Work. Is the child struggling on an emotional, psychological or behavioural level? Play therapy can provide the child with a space to express difficult emotions, allowing them to be more available for Therapeutic Life Story Work.

Child's ethnicity, age and level of understanding Are there any cultural considerations to take into account? What is the child's ethnicity, are there any particular areas to consider, and do they have a preference for a practitioner?

A younger child (6/7 years old) may yet have to learn how to process feelings and self-regulate. In this situation a therapeutic story has proved helpful for the child as detailed in our Chapter 10. Fewer sessions may be needed focused on giving the child a narrative in the form of a More About Me book (Rose 2012).

It is helpful if a child has the cognitive ability to read and write and is emotionally and psychologically available to engage in the process of undertaking extensive Therapeutic Life Story Work.

If they are below the level of understanding that is needed to process and make meaning of the information shared, a shorter piece of work, such as All About Me sessions (Rose 2012), or an individually tailored therapeutic story for the child may be more helpful.

Child's view Have the child's views been sought? What did they say? Do they know and agree? It may be that they are asking a lot of questions, suggesting they are needing help with making sense of themselves and their past; this is when Therapeutic Life Story Work can be most helpful for them. Some children want to know, 'Why could I not live with my birth parents?' or 'Why am I the way I am?' We give opportunities for hearing and recording the child's questions and exploring them in the first session. Does the child have a particular preference of practitioner in terms of race, gender, and style? If so, this should be taken into consideration and met wherever possible.

Therapeutic Parenting Capacity Do the child's parents have the capacity and support to be alongside their child during the time the sessions are taking place? The parent will need support throughout the Therapeutic Life Story Work process, and our modelling of therapeutic nurturing may enable them to offer this to their child. Parents can feel overwhelmed for various reasons; this may mean they are not in a position to support their child therapeutically within the work. It may be helpful to discuss this with the social worker, parent, and network.

Background History Ask the referrer what they know of the child's history, such as the circumstances leading to their current situation. Are there reports and summaries that can be made available to you? Are there existing life story books, memory books or later life letters that have been compiled for the child? For adopted children in England, the Child Permanence Report, social worker's assessment of need, or chronology may be good documents to request to help you determine whether this referral is appropriate for you, or whether it may require another worker or intervention. (For example, there may be a number of reasons why you might choose not to take on a piece of work such as a conflict of interest or an area that you have identified would be difficult for you personally to work with).

A child may have been clear they would like a worker who reflects their ethnic background, or a particular specialism may be needed, such as experience of selective mutism. This information is relevant to your consideration of the referral and the subsequent work with the child and their family. It will also inform the questions and discussion you have during the initial meeting with the parent and social worker.

Having sight of this information at the outset is important. It will help you plan how to gather your information and how best to support the family appropriately concerning past events. This in turn will ensure that the child gains as much information and understanding of their past and themselves as possible, taking into account the importance of connection and relationship. However, we recognise that not all countries allow access to official records, and you will need to follow procedures in your jurisdiction.

Birth parents' current situation Contact with birth parents can be discussed at the initial meeting, but it can be helpful to know beforehand if birth parents' current status is known. You need to consider the following factors: Is there any contact with the birth family and are they known to the local authority? Are they alive, for example? Where do they live? Do they have letterbox contact and is it felt appropriate? What is the parents' view of birth parents and wider birth family members, such as grandparents, being contacted and interviewed as part of the information gathering stage? If contacting birth parents is a possibility, are there structures in place for contacting them? Who will assist with this, and is it known if they want to be contacted? Are there any safety risks for the worker, child, or family? What is the child's view and will it cause them concern if contact is made? It is important to note that the legal parent for the child must agree to you contacting birth family members.

Allocated worker and other brothers and sisters It is most helpful to clarify who the allocated social worker is for the child, for all future correspondence, meetings, reviews, and any difficulties that may arise within the work. They may be able to offer information about other children born to the birth parents, and if there is any other information that is important to have. For instance, has the parent had subsequent children? Who are these children living with? Do they have contact with or know about this child, and do they want to meet them?

Initial Meeting After reading the background information that is available to you and deciding to take on the referral we arrange a meeting, usually with parents and the social worker. The initial meeting provides an opportunity to start to get to know the family and their culture in preparation for working together. It may be appropriate for the child to be involved, especially if they are older.

The aim is to further discuss much of the above, as well as considering the parents' support needs, identifying desired outcomes, and planning where and when the sessions will take place. It is important to investigate further and consider whether a Therapeutic Life Story Work intervention is right for this child at this time, taking into consideration the information you have gathered in relation to the above areas.

We find the referral checklist is a helpful guide for taking new referrals. It enables us to maintain good record keeping, ensures we follow our procedures and avoid missing important elements during the information gathering process, as well as having everything in place before the initial meeting. An initial meeting checklist containing prompts for discussion is provided (Appendix A) which you may find helps you to structure this meeting. It is intended as a guide for you to use and adapt to your own requirements.

When receiving a new referral inquiry, it is important to consider the time you have available, to prevent overload and to maintain self-care. The number of families you work with can vary greatly depending on individual capacity, complexity, and the location of each piece of work. From our experience in starting out it has been helpful to start gradually, with a few referrals to gain experience and develop your skills and confidence. We recommend a discussion with your supervisor about new referrals to support you in taking stock of the needs of the child and ensure you are making the appropriate decision in accepting or declining.

To proceed with the referral, you can use a referral form, such as the TLSWi Referral Form available on TLSWi.com, or a self-designed or agency one, for the person requesting the intervention to complete and sign. This can be used to process the referral according to your procedures. If you are self-employed it may be advisable to check if the referrer requires you to sign a contract for each piece of work and if a purchase order is also required for your invoicing purposes, as this may delay you receiving payment if not clarified.

Consent may be required from the legal parent for information to be shared with you. If you are self-employed an adoptive parent may need to write a letter of consent to the agency that will be providing you with access to information.

If you are undertaking the work as a self-employed practitioner, you will be required to submit a quote for the referring agency to agree funding or apply for funding approval. Include all aspects of the work, keeping in mind any funding restrictions or the amount available for work with each child and, not to state the obvious, be sure you have calculated your costs and totals correctly. Incorrect calculations can cause later complications when any additional funding required may not be available.

An initial meeting can then be held, either before or after receiving written confirmation that any funding required has been approved. Sometimes it may be appropriate to meet before submitting a referral to gather further information, check the referral is suitable, and to allow the parent and possibly the child, if older, to decide if they would like you to be the person they work with.

At the initial meeting you can consider who to be involved in the sessions. Where there are two parents, we have found it valuable to include both of them in some of the sessions, as each will have a different relationship with the child. As a minimum, a working parent taking time off to attend the final session works well in connecting them with the process and the work accomplished. Consistency in the parents' attendance is vital in maintaining the therapeutic work and the child's wellbeing; it upholds the child's sense of safety and feeling that they matter and enables us to provide continuity of support to the parents.

The initial meeting provides an opportunity to agree the day, time and venue for the sessions, making it clear how important it is to ensure consistency of attendance. If the child is not present at the initial meeting, this can be discussed with them in the first session. When maintained, consistency can provide the child and parents with a different experience: one that will enhance their ability to trust and gain confidence in another professional and reassure the child that they are the priority and that they matter.

An outcomes measure, such as the Therapeutic Life Story Work Needs Assessment provided as a phone application by a company called Supportive Hands, can be completed at this beginning stage. Usually this is completed by the parent, child and school, if appropriate. Outcomes measures are examined in further detail in Chapter 7. If an outcomes measure has been completed prior to the initial meeting it can be helpful to inform and review at the meeting. The assessment tool can then be completed at the midway stage and the end of the work.

Chapter 3
First Practical Steps

Preparation Sessions with Parents

We like to have a preparation session with parents to gain a better understanding of the child from their perspective. It is an opportunity for us to establish communication, relationship and form a mutual understanding with the parent, which is invaluable in the weeks to come when emotions can be triggered. We take time to ask and learn about the family's customs and culture, as well as what is known about the birth family culture. This gives us some understanding of the religious or cultural beliefs, celebrations and ways of being that are important to each family. Respect and acknowledgement of diversity is essential to secure a good working relationship.

Some parents may require further support before the work begins, to help them process the information. We need to ensure they are equipped to fully support the child through the sessions. We find it helpful to offer as many as six parent support sessions where, for instance, a parent has high levels of anxiety about the work, their own history of trauma, or where stability is not present in the current relationships. They can run alongside or prior to the Therapeutic Life Story Work, either with the same or a separate practitioner.

Where attachment is the main issue, it may be helpful for the family to have an another intervention before the Therapeutic

Life Story Work sessions begin, such as Dyadic Developmental Psychotherapy, a model of therapeutic practice developed by Dan Hughes, 2011, which is undertaken with the child and parent/s and is based on attachment, intersubjective relationships and the impact of developmental trauma aimed at helping and strengthening the child parent relationship. Or Theraplay, a dyadic child and family therapy developed for any professional working to support healthy child/caregiver attachment may be of benefit. Theraplay utilises playful activities using face to face reciprocal interactions aimed at enhancing trust and joy between a child and their parent. It uses the senses, including movement, touch, and rhythm. Filial therapy, a form of parent only play therapy that helps parents develop skills to address their child's concerns and affect change in the family unit, may also be helpful for parents prior to a Therapeutic Life Story Work intervention. Similarly, Therapeutic Parenting training, a highly nurturing parent approach, with empathy at its core, aimed at increasing parents therapeutic parenting skills may also be considered.

During the preparation sessions you can share an outline of the way you work to familiarise the parents with the process. You may wish to show them your prepared session plans (Rose 2012 p. 101) or discuss what activities you will be introducing and the purpose of these. You can also explain to them how you will support them within and between sessions, how you will be modelling listening, wondering, reflecting and sharing feelings and thoughts. An activity such as creating a behaviour tree (Rose 2012 pp.129–35) can help parents connect their child's current feelings, actions and behaviours with past experiences and can be carried out either at the initial meeting or a preparation session.

It is important to create safety and containment at the outset and maintain it throughout. In the initial meeting we explore the reason for the referral, discuss expectations and ensure that the parent is fully informed and has a clear understanding of what the work entails. We speak with them between sessions to review and reflect upon the previous session and to agree a plan for the next. This helps to further develop the relationship with the parent and keep them fully informed.

We can often learn a great deal about a family's daily life and struggles during our first meeting with them. There may be tensions within their relationships or signs of the impact the child's past trauma has had upon them and their family. We may also learn how the parents' own past experiences may be triggered. It is imperative to build a stable foundation which will keep everyone safe; emotionally, psychologically, and physically.

Information Gathering

The Rose Model of Therapeutic Life Story Work establishes information gathering as the first stage. The aim is to put together written and verbal accounts of birth parents' and grandparents' lives and events leading to the child's current situation. This information provides the basis for co-creating a narrative for the child in the sessions. There is not just one story, and it is important to gather information from as many perspectives as possible. Make sure you read through the files available, including sources of anecdotal information such as foster carer or residential workers recording and any messages they may have written to the child, and meet with people who have known the child. Listen to their accounts and recollections, including anecdotes, opinions and stories. We find it helpful when recording information to use different colours to identify the source of information gathered. For example, social workers comments might be in purple, the birth mothers in green, and so on.

Access to Social Work Case Files

Social work case files can be a valuable source of information about the who, what, where, why and how of decisions made, support offered and action taken. However, they should be seen in the context of reflecting a view rather than a truth, and bear in mind that they can contain errors and unconscious bias. Keep in mind the importance of anecdotal information and photos; for children who have been in out of home care the files should contain recording from any previous carers or key workers, see if there are any copies of cards and letters the birth family have written either with the casework file or in the UK these may be held with the letterbox co-ordinator for adopted children.

Access to information will vary between countries, depending on data protection legislation and policies. In the UK it is generally accepted that a Therapeutic Life Story worker can be given jurisdiction to read social work case files for the purpose of informing their work, but it can take a great deal of time to gain access to files which are held by a different area children's department to the one you are working for or commissioned by. It is, therefore, important to request access to files at the earliest opportunity. If you are working independently, Richard Rose suggested to us including the following wording, sent by secure email by the commissioning social worker or from the therapeutic life story work practitioner with the commissioning social worker copied in:

> 'In order to fully inform this work, it is important for [the worker] to gain a clear understanding of the historical events leading to the child's current situation. I would therefore be grateful if [the worker] could view the casework files for [name and date of birth of the young person]. I make this request in the belief that it is in the child's best interest for [the worker] to have access to this information'.

We sometimes encounter barriers to gaining access to files. Some UK local children's departments state they require the allocated worker to sit with us throughout viewing the records, which can prevent us from having a full day to study them. Generally, however, we are allocated a desk where we can be observed and supported by an office-based worker. During the worldwide pandemic of 2020, it was easier to obtain permission for electronic casework records and documents to be emailed securely to the referring social worker; they in turn gave us access to the information, either via email or printed copies.

Consider what information the legal parents have: do adoptive parents have later life letters, life story and memory books that have been compiled for the child at the point of adoption? What other information do they hold that they are able to share with you?

Please remember that any confidential information that is held by you must be safely and securely stored, for example, in a locked cabinet or on a password protected computer.

The Rose Model of Therapeutic Life Story Work recommends that the information gathering is carried out prior to starting the Therapeutic Life Story Work sessions, as delays in viewing files can cause difficulties in completing the work. For one child there was a delay of 12 months which meant having a long break in the sessions. The effect of this waiting can have a detrimental effect on the child emotionally, psychologically, behaviourally and in some cases medically. It can also put a strain on the family and could potentially cause a breakdown in the family unit.

To prepare for reading files we recommend compiling a list of documents you may wish to view. If these can be sent to you securely beforehand it will save you valuable time when visiting an office to read files. For adopted children in the UK, the child permanence report can be a good place to start. A chronology compiled by the organisation who were responsible for safeguarding the child can be used as a starting point for adding information, questions you may have and identifying gaps.

You will probably develop ways of collating the information from files that work best for you. The Rose Model of Therapeutic Life Story Work recommends separating the information into a series of boxes; this can assist in generating questions and identifying gaps. We have found this to be a lengthy process and prefer to make a chronological record of information gathered, perhaps as a Word document. It is important to ensure you record the source of the information gathered; as previously mentioned, we have found using different colours for information assists this process. It can also be helpful to note the document from which the information was obtained, particularly when information may need double checking at a later stage.

Adopted children are likely to have a later life letter, but the quality and accuracy of these may vary. We feel Nicholls, (2005 p.72–81) provides an excellent example of a later life letter. In some instances, a 'team-around-the-child' decision may have been made not to share the later life letter with the child at this point. It may have been agreed that some of the information within it is not deemed suitable or appropriate at this time.

We find it is a good idea to produce a narrative account from the chronological information that we have gathered, as preparation for starting the timeline and information-sharing part of the work. The narrative can be shared with the parents and social worker first. Ideally this is discussed at the midway meeting and agreement is made about what information to share.

We find it helpful to take the narrative we create from information gathering into sessions, either in electronic or paper form, as a guide. We may add questions in red to prompt us to pause for reflection during information sharing. The narrative, with the questions taken out and the thoughts and wonderings from the sessions added, forms the basis of the information added to the life story book alongside photographic copies of the wallpaper used.

It may be of help at the information gathering stage to bear in mind the sorts of questions we are often asked by children, such as does my sister or brother know about and ask about me? Do they think of me? Do they want to see me? Do we have anything in common? Do we look alike? Am I like my birth parents? Why couldn't they look after me? Why do they keep having children and keep making the same mistakes?

Working with Birth Families

Gathering information from birth or 'born to' parents is a significantly important part of the process.

We use the term birth parents to refer to the child's biological parents. Fahlberg (1994) identifies three parts of parenting: the born to, legal and parenting parts. Nicholls (2005) has presented these as an exercise which we have incorporated into our Therapeutic Life Story Work sessions, as outlined in Chapter 4.

It is important for a child to be aware that there are qualities and characteristics their birth parents have given them which remain constant, such as physical characteristics and often their names. The stories and information around the born to parts of parenting are of great value in Therapeutic Life Story Work.

The first step is deciding who to contact and in what order. This is not a lone decision by the Therapeutic Life Story Work practitioner, but an important part of the initial planning process. It is important at the initial meeting to discuss the views of the legal parent about potential contact with birth family members.

Reading the casework files and speaking with children's services can assist with making decisions about seeing birth family members. Where there are past concerns of violence and the birth parents' current situation and mental health is unknown, a telephone, video, or face-to-face meeting in the organisation's offices can provide greater safety for you.

Parents and other professionals may be concerned about the impact of contacting a birth parent. The worry may be that it will result in the birth parent seeking to initiate unwanted contact, which they may feel is best left unexplored. There might be concerns about safety: for example, the practitioner's contact could identify the geographical location of the family where, for safety, this has not previously been disclosed. It is important to consider the concerns and information held, in order to make a sound decision about who to contact. However, in our view, Therapeutic Life Story Work sessions can offer a safe environment to share information from birth parents or their families in a containing and sensitive way. The child can be prepared for hearing the information and their thoughts and feelings explored in the sessions in an informed way, rather than finding out later in an unplanned and unsupported way.

You must make it clear to birth family members at the start of the interview that you cannot give them any information about the child that has not been agreed with the legal parents and child. This includes where the child lives or goes to school or college. However, it can be helpful for the birth family member and the interview if you can tell them a little about the child, for example if they are doing well in a school subject or growing well. Extreme care must be taken where there are safety concerns and the birth family member has no current contact, letterbox or otherwise.

Where a birth parent has been unable to break the cycle of repeated harmful behaviour or lifestyle, due to their own mental health issues or trauma, it may be felt that it is not in their best interests to have communication, as it could cause further distress and harm to their mental health. The network can consider putting in place therapeutic support for the birth parent around the likely impact of talking with the practitioner about their past experiences.

In other situations, it may be decided that contact with the birth family could put the child and their adoptive family at risk due to the birth family members' aggressive and abusive behaviour. There may be a serious concern that if contacted the birth family might try to trace where the child is living and cause distress, possible trauma, and disruption to the child's overall wellbeing and that of their adoptive family. Such decisions are not made lightly: they are made to ensure the safety of the child and their family. Although the opportunity to hear directly from the birth parents about their thoughts, feelings, and experiences will be lost, the child's safety is paramount. The danger of replicating a child's early experience of trauma while in the care of their birth family is not tolerable or acceptable and, therefore, not in the best interests of the child. The importance of the child's emotional and physical safety and security is something we continue to model throughout our Therapeutic Life Story Work, to enable the child to trust the adults around them and for appropriate decisions to be made.

Karla: *If there are safety concerns, we sometimes make use of peer support and give each other's contact details to protect our identity and location. One adoptive family I worked with had a high-profile public position; there were concerns that their child might be located, and their public position jeopardised. After serious thought and consideration within peer supervision, and with the permission of the parents, I gave the birth parent a peer's contact number and a different name. I was able to make contact with the birth parent without any risk that the location of the family could be identified through my details, maintaining confidentiality and safety for all concerned. There are times when situations such as this arise where you need to be creative. It is imperative to considering all aspects of our work to ensure safety and confidentiality.*

Where possible we meet with birth parents to hear their account of their lives. An outline of things to consider for birth parent interviews is included in Appendix B.

Contacting birth family members needs careful consideration for each family and, as previously suggested, how best to contact birth family members can be discussed and agreed at the initial meeting.

It can help if initial contact is made in writing by someone who is already known to the birth parent, such as a letterbox coordinator, social worker, or family support worker. Where there is no current contact, a request can be made to check if the family are currently known to any other parts of the organisation such as mental health services, to help inform the decision making.

A letter can be sent with very brief details or perhaps a request for the person to contact you in relation to a relative of theirs. Where there is certainty about the address, more detail can be included. You can stress how important it is to hear their views; there will be things only they may know, which may be helpful for their child. An example of a letter to a birth parent is included in Appendix C and can be adapted to the situation.

If the referring agency has no current contact details an electoral register search may provide information. In the UK a search can be done through 192.com, for which there is a charge. You may be able to locate a birth family member through searching social media profiles, though this needs to be done with caution as the person may see who has visited their profile. We recommend this is only done when other avenues have been exhausted. Ideally find an address and write to the person to give them the opportunity to digest and respond to the letter at a suitable time.

We find it is fruitful to follow up the letter with a phone call, or other communication. Some birth parents have commented that they had been unsure how to respond to the letter and agree to be interviewed as a result of the follow up call.

Suzanne: *We received no response from one family to a letter sent by the family support worker who was known to them. As I was passing, I called at the homes of the maternal and paternal grandparents. Both households said they had not been sure how to respond to the letter but were willing to meet me. The maternal grandmother arranged a visit the following week, with the birth mother attending. The paternal grandparents invited me in and, as luck would have it, while I was there the birth father arrived to visit his parents. He also agreed to meet with me.*

These meetings were of great benefit in settling the adopted child's unrest about his birth parents. I was able to give him current photos and information about their present lives which allayed his worries. Turning up on people's doorsteps, of course, needs to be done with caution, and safety measures need to be set up. However, if I had not made the follow-up visits, it is likely that these opportunities would have been missed.

It seemed particularly helpful for the child to see a photo of his birth mother as an adult, smiling, with her mother's arm around her. This replaced his image of her as a very troubled and isolated teenager at the time of his adoption. When the birth mother was about to have her second child, she asked me to help her write a letter to her son, to apologise for not looking after him well enough as a baby. This letter was extremely helpful for the child and seemed to go further in resolving his concerns; he seemed satisfied that she was happy in her life and he no longer felt the need to meet her at this time.

On hearing he had a new birth brother he asked me if she was giving him the right milk (as she had not done this for him). I was able to reassure him that I had spoken to the specialist health visitor who would be keeping an eye on this. The parent and I thought this would be very big information to give him, but at eight years of age he just needed to know that his birth mother was in a better situation and that there would be safeguards for her new baby.

Visiting unannounced

Suzanne: *This does, of course, need to be done with caution and sensitivity. I learnt an important lesson when I knocked on the door of one birth family member without prior letter or phone contact. It was a big shock for the maternal grandmother, who was visibly angry. The lesson learnt was that it is respectful and necessary to contact the birth family member in advance and seek their permission for a visit. We often find that a birth parent is willing to meet with independent workers like* *ourselves, as we are not connected to the organisation who removed their child.*

Interviews with birth family members

Hearing the views and stories of birth parents and wider family members provides a multi-perspective overview. For adopted children this work generally takes place several years post-adoption. Care and sensitivity are essential, and it should be acknowledged beforehand that meeting you is likely to bring up painful feelings for the birth family member or connected person. Suggest they arrange to have some support, possibly before, during and after the interview. If they choose to have a support person present, get in touch before the interview to confirm whether they would like the person to stay for part or the whole of the interview.

Acknowledge again at the beginning of the interview that this is likely to trigger painful feelings for them and check that they have support in place. We suggest that you allow plenty of time for the interview and prepare the person for this. It sometimes takes around two to four hours for you to create safety and go through their family history and their own childhood experiences, as well as those of their child. Make it clear to the birth parent or person that they will not be pushed to talk about anything they do not feel comfortable discussing. Permission questions are important to use, such as, 'Is it okay to ask you about …?' or 'It's okay to say if you don't wish to talk about …'

It is important to be respectful of any photographs or other memorabilia the birth parent has. Taking relatively good copies is possible by using the camera on a smartphone or tablet without the risk of damaging an older photo by taking it out of its frame. Looking at photos in sessions can be invaluable for prompting discussion and giving insight into the situation the child was in.

It is imperative to let the birth parent know that any photos taken will be deleted from the device they are taken on and used solely for the work you are doing with the child.

Many of the birth parents we have seen report that they found it a helpful and therapeutic experience to revisit their past and have someone listen and validate their views and experiences. This is especially so when they connect the impact of their own childhood experiences on the choices they made and the events that happened. The interview may enable them to express and let go of feelings of guilt, anger and blame. There is sometimes a visible physical change during the interview where the person has perhaps been able to accept for the first time that things went very wrong and has gained insight into why this was so. As a consequence they have been able to let go of some of the shame and guilt they have been carrying.

Where the birth parent does not see their child, or perhaps finds it hard to talk about their feelings with the child, it can be beneficial to support them in writing a letter to express those feelings. They may wish to let the child know they are sad they were not able to look after them but pleased that they are with someone who can. Many birth parents wish to write to their child but feel unable to do so, not knowing where to start or what to write. There may be local organisations who can support them in this task and in maintaining the agreed communication with their child.

An exciting area of development in Therapeutic Life Story Work has been the idea of offering this intervention to birth parents who have had previous children removed. This could promote wellbeing and provide insights for the birth parent, supporting any future communication and relationship with their child, and has the potential to inform and transform any future parenting.

A key part of Therapeutic Life Story Work is helping the child to understand why their birth parents could not provide them with the care they needed. We see clear benefits when we are able to hear first-hand accounts from birth parents in relation to their own childhood, their reflections on the events and circumstances leading to their child being placed in alternative care, and hear about their current situation. A letter from the parent can be extremely helpful and consideration can be given to making a short video of the birth parent for their child, such as a wish for the future and/or saying they are sorry for what happened. This needs careful thinking through with the network and would need permission from the child's legal parent, as well of course informed consent from the birth family member/s being videoed.

It proved extremely helpful for one young person who was in foster care to be involved in the interviews with his birth family, he regularly saw his birth mother and maternal family but not his birth father. The joint visit to birth father included a video interview where he accepted responsibility and apologised for walking out on his partner and young children. Editing the video with the child was an extremely healing process for the young person, and also enabled maternal family members to forgive him and allow two younger brothers who had remained living with maternal grandparents to have family time with their father.

It can be extremely powerful for the children we work with to have their birth parents' current views, in their own words, especially where the birth parent is able to say for the first time that they are sorry for what happened. It can also help settle a child's unrest to know that their parent is alright. For instance, if a parent has been homeless, it helps the child to know that they now have a place to live and access to the things they need.

Hearing from the birth parent about their current situation can also help the child understand what may have changed in their birth parent's life, such as where the birth parent has been able to adequately parent subsequent children. For example, they may now be in a more loving, stable, and secure relationship and/ or they may no longer be mis-using alcohol or drugs.

One birth parent interview gave the birth mother a chance to reflect on the past and express her feelings of guilt and blame for abandoning her daughter. She was able to acknowledge that things had gone very wrong and that she had been unable to parent her child safely, due to her own traumatic childhood experiences and her unhelpful coping strategy of misusing drugs. Her view had changed from a position of opposing the adoption at the time it was made, to currently viewing it as having been in her child's best interests.

The insights she gained in relation to her own childhood were helpful to her child's understanding; they explained how not getting the parenting she needed as a child got in the way of being a parent herself. The birth parent expressed her wish for her child to be happy and have a good life, recognising that her children were in a nurturing family and were now having a better experience of childhood than she had. She poignantly said she wished that she had been similarly removed from her own birth mother's care during her childhood. This was helpful for her child to hear in our sessions.

The birth mother felt that the interview had provided her with a sense of release from the burden of guilt she had been carrying. Her acceptance of the current parents had the settling effect of giving the child permission to be happy in her new family, which was also helpful for the parenting parent.

This is something we have witnessed repeatedly. Such outcomes in birth parent interviews are extremely helpful for the children with whom we are working. Another meeting with a birth parent enabled a child to see current photos of his birth mother as an independent adult with supportive people around her. This served to replace his previous image of her as a vulnerable teenager who needed him to be with her. This in turn contributed to a decrease in the unrest and aggression he was displaying at home.

The Complexities of Contact

The term 'contact' is often raised in discussion when considering the use of language. Contact is the term that has traditionally been used to refer to any communication between the child and their birth family, or time they spend together. We prefer to use the term 'family time' to refer to visits with the birth family, as suggested by the late Yusef McCormack, a care experienced foster parent, adopter and youth worker, who regularly attended the Independent Life Story Work Forum in the UK and shared with us his great wisdom. Family time is a term that has now generally been adopted in the UK, we feel if this term is used by a child in their peer group it is less likely to identify them as different or as being in care. It is important for children to have a choice of language, to be able to use a term that fits with how they feel. Here we use 'birth family communication' as an umbrella term to include all contact.

Birth family communication raises complex issues and needs to be carefully considered when providing Therapeutic Life Story Work to children who are fostered and adopted, especially where there may not have been any communication for many years. It is important to consider each situation individually.

> 'The meaning of contact from the birth parent needs to be carefully explored with each individual child and re-evaluated as they grow and change in order to even stand a chance of getting it right. And those explorations should now probably also consider planning for the potential of internet interaction.'
>
> (Maddox 2012)

Many adoptive parents will have great concern regarding the impact of birth family communication on their child. Grotevant and Von Korff (2011) suggest research contradicts key concerns that birth family communication unsettles adoptees, increases birth mother's grief and exacerbates adoptive parent's fears of losing their child.

Information obtained from the Therapeutic Life Story Work practitioner's interviews with the birth family can help the child and the network around them to be better informed when it comes to making decisions around future communication between the child and birth parents. Knowing where and in what circumstances birth parents now live, whether they acknowledge past concerns, what they say and how they present can all have implications for any future communication.

Where a parent can accept responsibility for their past actions it suggests that meeting in the future may be positive for the child. Conversely, where a parent is in denial and blames others, it may become clear that any communication could be emotionally unsafe for the child. There may be some situations which cause the child to decide to cease communication with the birth parent. Such cases could be when a birth parent cannot accept that the child has experienced abuse and trauma.

Knowing that a birth parent remains unable to accept responsibility for their actions can help the child to understand the decisions that were made at that time. If the parent was unable to see what changes were needed, they would have been unable to make them. It can also enable the child and network to re-evaluate the relationship and communications between the child and birth parent. If the birth parent cannot accept or acknowledge the abuse the child suffered, it can be extremely hard for the child to have ongoing communications with them. The early sessions around feelings gave one young person permission to express their view in relation to this. They revealed how anxious they felt prior to family time and at the midway review they told their social worker that they wanted to suspend family time with their birth mother.

Social media can increase the possibility and likelihood of unplanned and unpredictable communication. A child who is undertaking Therapeutic Life Story Work will be prepared for information that is known about their birth family and will receive it within the safety and security of the sessions. It is important for parents and children to be aware of the need to review privacy settings on their social media profiles, to ensure that only friends can see their photos and posts.

The possibility of unplanned, unsupported and unregulated social media communication makes the case for the Therapeutic Life Story worker to make the initial contact with birth parents, and for the child to undertake Therapeutic Life Story Work in order to make informed decisions about future family communication. Keefer and Schooler (2000) provide helpful guidance for adoptive and foster parents in relation to concerns around what and when to tell their children about their past. They powerfully demonstrate, through examples, why the truth, with all its details, can help towards healing the child's trauma and they consider the possible negative consequences of not telling the truth.

Suzanne: *I worked with one young person whose birth parents chose to place her for adoption at birth. Her birth family contacted her in an unplanned way via social media when she was 14 years old. Unlimited communication continued in an unregulated way via social media with the birth mother and other birth family members. The young person's fantasy about the relationship she would have with her birth mother did not match the reality of a birth parent with a different understanding of safety, boundaries and the mother-daughter relationship. At the age of 17, when reflecting on her experience, and at the point of deciding to put the communication on hold, this young person powerfully wrote:*

When deciding to terminate my relationship with my birth family, I described it as 'This is not me abandoning you, this is me simply doing what's best for me, like you did when you placed me for adoption.'

Before I had contact with my birth family, I knew minimal information about them. This felt as though there was a closed door in the corridor that is my life. During my contact with them, I felt the door open. I was hoping that the door would open slowly, and I would have the key to lock it whenever I needed, but instead it felt as though my birth family were a strong gust of wind that quickly opened my door without me being ready.

My birth family explained that they gave me up to give me a better life. I have learnt the importance of not letting them negatively impact the life that they were not able to give me, as it defeats the object. I also learnt that I do not owe them anything. I do not owe them contact, I do not owe them gratitude, I do not owe them a relationship.

Before I got to know my birth family, I had unrealistic fantasies and expectations of how our relationship would be and how they would behave. However, when I uncovered the reality it was a very long way to fall. I soon realised that I am very different to my birth family. Not knowing who my birth family were during my early teenage years meant I had a very weak sense of identity. This was not helped by contact with them, as I then had to process all of the difficult information I had received, and it led to me feeling torn between two sides of me – my nurture and my nature:

Not knowing = big, closed door
Knowing = birth family strong gust of wind opening door quickly without any control
Letter = me shutting the door but me holding onto the Key

The young person chose not to send the letter, but felt writing these words had been helpful.

Some adoptive parents do not agree to birth parents being contacted. It can be helpful in these cases to discuss the potential consequences of the child making their own contact with the birth family. For example, information about the past from birth parents may conflict with the information on the casework files. If the practitioner does not have access to the birth parents' views it can undermine trust within the working relationship. The possibilities of this arising and the difficulties it can create need careful consideration.

Karla: *I worked with a 14-year-old child, whose birth family contacted her through social media, without the knowledge or consent of her parents. Her parents were happy for her to have more information about her past and accordingly arranged for Therapeutic Life Story Work to take place. What they were not aware of was the emotional, behavioural and psychological difficulties this contact would have on their child.*

Previously the child had been doing well at home, in school and with her friends, but during our sessions she appeared troubled. She lacked engagement and concentration, and her behaviour towards her parents deteriorated. It began with verbal abuse, then she started stealing things from them and later became extremely aggressive and violent towards them, which required police involvement on several occasions. All of this was unusual for her. The contrast was clear, but the problem was not.

She had said she wanted to know as much as possible, but when the information sharing began she became distressed, held her head down and cried. She told us she thought she was in trouble and that, if she learnt the truth about her birth parents, her parents would be in trouble too. Concerned, - we sat with her - to review how best to move forward. It was at this point that she revealed she had heard from her birth parents, who wanted her to return to them and had threatened her that if she didn't 'there would be trouble'.

The birth parents had told the child that she was not being looked after properly by her 'so-called parents'. They told her not to tell her parents that they had contacted her and to call them from school so her parents would not know what was taking place. They feared that if the child heard what others views of the past were she would not want to see them again.

This unsupervised communication proved traumatic for the child and was detrimental to her overall wellbeing and that of her parents. She was not angry with her parents; she knew they loved her and would support her no matter what. But she took her anger, fear and worries about what her birth parents might do out on them.

This was a traumatic experience for the child to have, especially as she was neither prepared for nor aware of the impact it would have on her. Through the Therapeutic Life Story Work process, however, she was able to see that this was her birth parent's pattern of behaviour. She concluded that having no communication with them and not meeting them in the future would enable her and her parents to remain safe, secure and no longer at risk.

This experience frightened her so much that she decided she had learnt all that she needed to know about her birth parents at that time. We were unable to share with her all the information we had, but she was aware that her parents had it all; if she changed her mind in the future, they would be open and honest with her about the truth of her past.

Contact with birth families is full of complexities. We can all learn from our own experience as well as through the advice and experience of others. Listening to our peers and supervisors will also strengthen our understanding of these complexities and remind us of the sensitivity and care that is needed in this area of our work.

Part Two

Therapeutic Life Story Work:
The Sessions

Chapter 4
Therapeutic Life Story Work Sessions

In this chapter we explore how we implement the ideas and techniques from The Rose Model of Therapeutic Life Story Work, and incorporate other elements from our other disciplines and practices. So much can be achieved and so many insights revealed through creative activities and playful exercises, storytelling and discussion. There is a wealth of practical games, art activities and storytelling techniques to facilitate your Therapeutic Life Story Work. We hope you will find plenty of ideas here to enable you and the families you work with to have fun, to strengthen their bonds, to reflect upon and make meaning of past events in a safe and relaxed setting, and to provide them with a means of expressing their thoughts and feelings in a free and secure way.

We offer this outline for structuring sessions as a guide only. It is not set in stone as the process needs to be informed by the child and their pace, and you will bring your own creativity to it.

The Importance of Beginnings

How we begin the Therapeutic Life Story Work sessions is integral to the success of the intervention; it creates the foundation for the work and requires a great deal of thought and planning. Building a strong foundation will optimise the whole experience for the child and family. We need to have a solid structure in place to maintain the stability of our work no matter what stresses occur or challenges we face. Without that solid foundation the work will be compromised and everything to follow will be affected.

It is essential to be well prepared for our first communication with the family and child, as we are beginning an important relationship with them. We agree with Rose (2012) that it is best to work through the stages of Therapeutic Life Story Work, completing the information gathering before starting the sessions. We need to consider which things should be done first before jumping in too quickly as the consequences may cause disappointment, mistrust or just simply embarrassment. We consider beginnings to be a point of optimal potential; how we begin determines the choices we, the child and the family make along the way, which will impact on the end result. Following the Therapeutic Life Story Work stages will positively influence the way in which this process takes place.

Before meeting with the family we recommend exploring your first session with your supervisor, giving you time to examine your thoughts, feelings and thinking about your session plan. Consider the needs of the child and parents: for instance, are the parents struggling with behaviours relating to a new diagnosis of Attention Deficit Hyperactivity Disorder (ADHD), or a medication? Are there some areas that resonate for you personally?

If you are new to this work, we recommend having a plan A, B, C and D as you never know what the child is going to respond to. It is always good to have something else up your sleeve. If a child does not respond to an activity you have offered in a session you need to go to plan B. Have you thought about what plan B looks like? When a child does not want to do a particular exercise you can check what they want to talk about. You can offer to explore how they are feeling in that moment by writing the feeling word: draw a circle around it and investigate what this feeling means for them, in their past or present and in relation to any experiences that they have had. This is what we mean by 'working in the moment'. As you become more experienced this will become more of an automatic part of your mental toolkit.

How you begin your first session sets the tone for how you will work together. In those first few moments when you meet the child and parent you have an opportunity to make a connection. You can do this by noticing and naming something positive about the child that will reduce anxiety and invite them to begin interactive communication. Show them you are interested, by perhaps commenting on their smart trainers or the mobile phone they may be holding; you could ask them about the game they are playing on it.

Be mindful that you are a stranger coming into their home and that you will each have different expectations and anxieties about this first meeting. Acknowledging your own anxieties can be a big icebreaker and permit the family members to express how they are feeling. If the child seems reluctant to come into the room, they may feel reassured if you tell them you are there to help answer their questions about the past and their birth family. Explain to them that you hope by the end they will have a better understanding of themselves and like what they see, but that first you need to get to know each other.

Karla: *One family had arranged their room for the session and invited me to sit at the table. The child was moving all around the room, collecting things, and holding them close to her body. I noticed this out loud, saying to the child, 'I can see you are* *busy collecting things.' The child commented, 'Yes I am.' I responded, 'I'm wondering when you're ready if you would like to join us.' She replied, 'Okay'. Within a few minutes she came to sit at the table, showed the things she had collected and shared why they were important to her. Allowing her the time to do this enabled her to relax and engage in the session.*

Establishing safety starts from the moment the child first meets or speaks to you. The aim is to provide a safe, open and non-judgmental atmosphere where the child can feel accepted, comfortable and free to speak. This first session tells us so much about the family and the themes that are playing out for them. It is important to reflect on this as the work progresses as these themes will re-emerge and weave through future sessions.

Engaging in play is a great icebreaker in the first session and can help to establish safety and relationships. There are lots of games we find useful in the early sessions such as squiggles, boxes, noughts and crosses, Jenga, exercises such as drawing around each other's hands and writing or drawing various things about ourselves, such as likes and interests.

Another good activity to establish safety is to draw up a working agreement; we tend to do this in the second session. We describe some of these 'getting to know you' games and exercises in greater detail later in this chapter, under the heading 'Connecting and Creating Containment'.

Giving choice from the beginning and doing what feels comfortable for the child is important to support a sense of safety. The roll of wallpaper can feel overwhelming or daunting at the beginning for some children; giving them a choice of whether to start using the wallpaper straight away or to begin with an A3 art pad, or even A4 paper, may feel safer. When you first start putting things onto paper, take the opportunity to show the child that it is okay to make mistakes: the paper is a tool for working things out. Make it clear that there is no right or wrong. Whatever the child adds to the paper is valued and is not being judged.

Introducing a 'welcome book' in the first session creates a focus for discussion about 'the purpose, aims and objectives of the service' (Rose 2012 p.70–72) and can also feel more comfortable for the child than direct eye contact at this initial stage. It makes them feel involved and provides them with a tool for considering questions they may have. The book can be adapted for the child's age, interests and level of understanding. It is left with the family and can be a helpful reference, to remind them of what has been discussed and to add any further questions that may arise.

Similarly, you can create an 'All About Me' book (Rose 2012 p.112–19) for them to fill out. This is helpful in that it starts with the present and gives you and the child an insight into their current thinking and feelings. It can be done between sessions with the parent and can serve to strengthen their attachment. As Rose suggests, a disposable camera can be given for the child to take photos of their world and things that are important to them, to be added into their book. Many children have access to smartphone cameras which may be a preferable and easier way to capture and add images. You may choose to create the child's All About Me book after the initial session when you have gained a sense of their interests and level of understanding. Creating a page together in the session can also work well and be included in their life story book. We find the books work well for most children, but can be less of an interest to older children.

Beginnings offer us glimpses of the child and their family's internal world. How our work may be received, rejected or embraced by the family will make itself known in time. However, being as authentic as you can at the start enables the child and their family to relax, trust and become more open to what is about to take place over the next several months. They need to feel contained and held on an emotional and psychological level to trust the Therapeutic Life Story Work process and all that it offers. Creating a stable foundation will enable this to take place.

When you start to read a book, either the cover will draw your attention to open it up or you may read the first few pages and feel invited to continue the adventure of the story. This can be how it feels when you first meet a child and their family. It can also feel like this for them meeting you. How you present yourself and the Therapeutic Life Story Work is paramount to the success of the child's learning journey. For example, pay attention to your body language and aim to be relaxed, smiling, listening and engaged. On first meeting the child we let them know that their parents have checked us out and chosen us as someone they feel will be able to help answer their questions. Now it is their turn to see if they would like to go on this journey of exploring and making sense of the past with us. We add that first we will be getting to know one another and will aim to have some fun along the way. Beginnings are important; they can reflect the ending!

Preparing and Planning Sessions

Planning and preparation for sessions is vital. You need to allow time for creating a plan and discussing and reviewing it with the parent prior to each session. Here we aim to outline the stages of the sessions and activities we have found useful in each stage.

Wrench and Naylor (2013) identify the following stages of the Life Story Work process, which we have found helpful to use as a guide for our Therapeutic Life Story Work sessions:

- Building a Sense of Safety for the Child
- Developing Emotional Literacy
- Building Resilience and Self-Esteem
- Exploring Identity
- Information Sharing and Integration
- Looking to the Future

We have drawn the following headings from Rose (2012) and Wrench and Naylor (2013) to identify ideas and techniques that can be used in each stage of the Therapeutic Life Story Work sessions:

1. Connecting and Creating Containment
2. Working with Emotions
3. Building Self-Confidence
4. Exploring a Sense of Self
5. Creating a Timeline: witnessing the child's story, sharing information, making meaning
6. Exploring Hopes and Dreams
7. Ending

While the number of sessions may vary in line with the needs of the child, The Rose Model of Therapeutic Life Story Work suggests around 18 sessions are undertaken. The evidenced based research (Lucas et al., 2022) has led to the Rose Model identifying the following outline for the content of sessions which is essentially the same:

Sessions 1-6: relationship building, play and attunement (1-3) and witnessing the child's story (4-6)

Sessions 7-12 sharing family history and stories from grandparents to the present day.

Sessions 13-18 problem solving, making sense and endings.

1. Connecting and Creating Containment

It is important to connect with the child in order to create a safe and accepting environment for the work you will be undertaking. In the first session the focus is on building a connection between the child, parent and practitioner, and establishing a relationship which will support the child in making meaning of past experiences.

This early session provides the scaffolding and constructs the support which will enable the child to feel safe enough to consider and process information and feelings about the past. Levine (2015) is among writers who identify the need to create a sense of relative safety to enable just such an exploration. Hughes and Baylin (2012) suggest you have to feel safe to feel sad.

Connection and containment can be created through a variety of ways, namely building a relationship, creating a safe space, building routine and establishing ground rules.

Building a Relationship

When you meet, think about how you greet the child and parent; provide a welcoming atmosphere if you are meeting away from their home, or show respect to their home if visiting them there. The aim is to build rapport. This can be done by showing the child you have noticed and are interested in them, for example observing something positive about them.

Consider where you sit when entering the family's home, especially if the child or parent have limited mobility. Ask the child where they would like you to sit; sitting on the floor can help create safety by giving a signal of non-threat.

It is important to acknowledge that meeting with you for the first time may feel different and strange to them. You can sound out their thoughts and emotions by asking what it feels like meeting you, inviting them to write or draw any words, ideas or feelings that come to mind. Being curious about their understanding of why you are there demonstrates that you value their sensitivities and are interested in their views from the outset. Asking the child if their parent has told them why you are meeting provides them with an opportunity to say if they don't know, or don't want to be there. Let them know that you have met their parent so they could check you out, and now it is their turn to check you out and ask any questions, to see if they want to work with you.

Acknowledging differences between you is a useful part of creating safety. Having a conversation about the differences each of you see, such as power, race, age, gender, ability and so on, is important as well as stating your commitment to working in a non-discriminatory way with openness to learning and examining your bias.

Creating a Safe Space
Whether sessions are taking place in the child's home or somewhere else such as a school, it is essential that the child feels the space is private. When working in the child's home you can confirm with the child and parent whether there are any other people in the house and consider areas such as whether there are due to be any deliveries or phone calls that may interrupt the session and if so how this may be managed. Does the parent need to have a discussion with other members of the household, does the door need to be locked. You could agree whether you create a playful forfeit if someone comes into the room, such as doing star jumps, what will be done with the wallpaper or other materials, for example you might agree to roll it up and sit quietly until the person leaves the room. Will one of you be responsible for reminding the interrupter that it is a private session?

When working in a school, the staff need to understand that the sessions are not to be intruded upon as it will disrupt the child's process and impact their work.

Whatever the child's age, they may need time out during a session. It is a good idea to create a safe space for them to sit quietly, perhaps with a duvet or blanket, a favourite comforting drink or their family pet. This will allow the child to feel safe at the outset, knowing they can take time away and not feel on their own. For young children, their safe place might be on the sofa beside their parent, with a favourite soft toy. Older children might have a mascot they would like to bring into the room with them; you can support this by introducing your own mascot. The safe place can be discussed in sessions, or with the parent between sessions, to ensure everything is available in the room. How and when a child makes use of a safe place gives an indication of how they are feeling and can help you to judge when a game break or change of activity is needed.

Building Routine
Establishing routines helps to create a sense of safety and containment. It is important where possible to meet at consistent intervals and to start and finish on time. Dates and times for sessions can be agreed in advance and you can check and confirm at the end of each session when you will be meeting next. Of course, there may need to be changes, due to a change in after school activities, sickness or traffic delay for instance, but it is important that you all agree to any changes.

Establishing a routine can be supported by starting and/or ending with relaxation exercises; these can be of great benefit for grounding and calming. Exercises such as the Special Place from the Mindful Kids cards (Stewart and Braun 2017) guide the child and carer to sit comfortably and think of a special place where they feel calm and relaxed. Similarly, you can try out the Yoga Pretzels cards (Guber and Kalish 2005) to see if selecting one and doing the pose is something the child enjoys. Some children may benefit from regulating activities, such as bouncing on a trampoline, while others may need grounding activities like visualisation and breathing exercises. Wrench and Naylor (2013) outline several visualisation and breathing exercises: imagine blowing a bowl of soup, or doing a range of actions in slow motion, such as chopping wood with an axe.

The '5,4,3,2,1' exercise is very useful during periods of anxiety or panic. It helps to ground a child in the present when their mind or emotions are bouncing around between various anxious thoughts. Before starting this exercise, pay attention to their breathing: slow, deep, long breaths can help the child to maintain a sense of calm or help them return to a calmer state. Once they have found their breath, ask them to notice and name:

- Five things they can see
- Four things they can touch
- Three things they can hear
- Two things they can smell
- One thing they can taste

Some children may find it helpful to start each session with a calming and grounding exercise based on their sensory needs. Erin Jefferies, a complex needs worker recommended to Suzanne that a young person she was working with would benefit from beginning with blowing through a straw, Suzanne designed a game of using a straw to blow ping pong balls along the wallpaper into a goal made from a paper cup which worked well for the young person. For another child, an exercise of walking along a rolled-out piece of wool as if it were a tightrope had been working well in Erin's sessions and was continued in the therapeutic life story work sessions. It might be useful to have a sensory processing assessment carried out with the child, such as the Just Right State programme (sensoryattachmentintervention.com), which we discuss in Chapter 8.

Lloyd (2016) suggests practical ideas that can help improve sensory integration in traumatised children. These are helpful to bear in mind when working with children who have experienced early childhood neglect and deprivation of sensory stimulation, such as frequently being left alone in their cot or pram for long periods of time. For instance, if a child's neck muscles are underdeveloped as a result of not having had time lying on a rug on their front as a baby, lying on the floor to draw or write on the wallpaper can support that area of development. The sensory processing needs of children are explored further in Chapter 8.

Another good way of establishing routine is to end with a game of the child's choice. This assists in reconnecting to the present and having fun. Most adults and children enjoy playing games, but for older children who may not wish to play a game you can end with a conversation to bring them back to the here and now. For example, asking what they will be doing next, what events they are looking forward to or what they are planning to have to eat.

Establishing Ground Rules
A contract or working agreement which agrees ground rules supports a sense of safety and containment. It can be discussed and created in early sessions. The children often choose to call these their rules (for example, 'Jayden's Rules') and enjoy the sense of control they achieve from identifying the rules they want. It is made clear that everyone needs to agree each rule. Confidentiality and safeguarding should be included. Explain that what is shared in the sessions is private, but if there is something that suggests a child is not safe this will need to be

shared with others, such as the child's or the referring social worker. Examples of working agreements are shown later in this chapter.

Activities for Achieving Connection and Containment:
Here we consider activities that are helpful for connection and containment in sessions, namely using an introduction booklet, games, creating hands of interests, support and safety, a working agreement, session chart and session plans.

Introduction Booklet
Rose (2012) suggests using a welcome booklet which explains life story work to the child, parent and those around the child. The welcome booklet was originally designed by Rachel Oliver, life story therapist, at SACCS (the company formerly known as SACCS was established in 1987 and provided specialist residential care and therapeutic programmes for children with a history of trauma, neglect, and sexual abuse). The welcome booklet can be created in age and level of understanding appropriate language and images. Looking at the booklet in the first session can help create a more relaxed environment as direct eye contact is not required. The final page invites the child to say or write down any questions they may have, which can be a useful indicator of how comfortable they feel, how many questions they may have, and so on. We make it clear that they don't have to identify their questions at this point, and that this can be added to and revisited at any time.

Games
Dots and boxes is a fun and simple pen and paper game for two or more people. The game starts with creating an empty grid of dots. The grid can be any size. Each person takes their turn connecting two un-joined horizontally or vertically adjacent

dots. The person who completes the fourth side of a box adds their initial into the box and earns another turn. The game ends when all the lines are drawn and the boxes are claimed. The person with the most completed boxes wins.

This game offers the child, parent and practitioner time to learn about each other through playfulness. In later sessions the game can be played by adding something about yourself into claimed boxes. It can be an ice breaker, tension reliever, and can bring the child and parent closer together through communicating where they may draw their next line. It can also provide a way of helping the child relax during their session.

Squiggle drawings are a fantastic and easy beginning exercise to do together to create a sense of fun and safety. If the child particularly enjoys them you may wish to continue doing them throughout the sessions. Each person draws a squiggly line for the other, using pens and paper, or online whiteboard or tablet. They then add to the squiggle to create an image, either together or individually. You can use it as a 'chase game' where the child starts and the parent chases after them by following the child's lines. Its unstructured, child-led format allows a child who is feeling overwhelmed to become relaxed, playful and creative with no direction needed. It generates laughter and fun and enables the family to be free in their expressions, nonverbally, whilst strengthening the bond between them.

Winnicott (1971) used the squiggle drawing as a means of assessing a child's ability to engage on an emotional and psychological level before commencing therapeutic work. Children love being creative when communicating their thoughts and feelings. The child's drawings are about what they feel at that moment. Although we do not make interpretations, these questions can form a useful part of processing those moments:

What can you see? What do you feel is being communicated? What might the child be conveying in their Squiggle?

Squiggles are a powerful bonding tool. They give the parent and child the freedom to express themselves in the moment, without hesitation or instructions. The spontaneity is wonderful especially when it brings the child and parent together in a shared moment that leads to smiles, laughter and a very big hug afterwards!

Mirroring squiggles are where the child leads and the adult copies their pen movements. It can have a calming effect and create a greater sense of safety and connection. Often children will giggle with joy as they experience the adults mirroring their pen marks.

Karla: *The drawing in Figure 1 was created from a squiggle line by a child and parent together. It shows how one mirrored the other's image. The child explained that she did not feel she was much like her birth mother due to the differences in their life, experiences, likes and dislikes; she felt more like her mum, and felt happy about that. This occurred during the later stages of the Therapeutic Life Story Work. The child had become aware of how much she belonged and felt loved by her parents, something she had struggled with since being adopted. Without being intentionally created, the drawing indicates their closeness and the mirroring of one another in their lives.*

The child was incredibly pleased with their drawing and took a picture of it to remind her that when she felt bad, lost, lonely or unhappy, she had her parents alongside her, no matter what. She knew she mattered to them and felt for the first time that she had her family, at last.

Figure 1: Squiggle Example 1   Figure 2: Squiggle Example 2

We used this technique for one family at the end of each session as it offered them time to enjoy, laugh and communicate together while having fun and play time. On one occasion they discussed what they wanted to create and what colours to use, laughing together as they produced a picture of a smiling turtle. The child had led the creation, supported by the adult.

Figure 2 shows a further example of a squiggle drawing. Here the child drew a picture of a shark swallowing me up as I fell out of a boat. He was expressing his feelings about the information I had shared with him and what he had learnt about his birth family. The squiggle gave him an excellent means to express his angry emotions safely and in a playful manner. He knew it was okay to share what he felt, he just could not allow the words out verbally. The art of the squiggle is that it gives children permission to express themselves in a visual way.

Another child sat quietly drawing a squiggle that showed how calm she felt at the end of the session compared to how anxious she had been at the start.

This is an empowering technique to use for children to express themselves, however they may feel, in the moment. Two sisters used the squiggle drawing in Figure 3 to explore and express the mixed emotions and thoughts they experienced in their daily life at school and at home, while looking back at their past. They identified that school was confusing, and home could be tricky. It left them with thoughts and questions, such as, 'Stop being good, you get attention ...' and 'Why am I acting like I am?'

They spent time on their squiggle and felt relieved once they completed it. One said, *'There, I'm done. This is how it is for me!'*

The other sister said, 'I didn't realise this would be so calming.'

Figure 3: Squiggle Drawing Example 3

Wooden Stacking blocks such as Jenga blocks give the child, parent and practitioner the opportunity to collaborate. They build the wooden blocks together in a sturdy tower, building at the same time upon their relationship and attachment. Once you have agreed who is going first (no doubt the child!), each person takes a turn to pull out a block until the whole stack crashes down. Questions and challenges can be added to the blocks at a later stage, such as *'If I had a million pounds I would …'* or *'When I am sad I …'* or *'dance around the room like you are at a disco'*. Rose (2012) suggests Jenga can be used as an ice-breaker, an assessment, to explore the child's questions and feelings, and as a means of having fun. Children enjoy the many versions of this game. They may relish practising their power in winning, tripping and setting up or helping the parent or practitioner.

Dobble is a quick and fun card game that is popular with children and easy to play at the beginning or end of sessions. There are 55 cards, each printed with eight different symbols. Any two cards always share one, and only one, matching symbol. The objective of the game is to find the one matching symbol between two cards. This generates lots of communication, laughter, connection and playfulness. Each person is competing against the others. It can be played in several ways: the winner can be the first to get rid of all the cards they have been dealt if you are putting the cards down, or the person with the most cards when the deck runs out if you are picking the cards up. Children are very clever and quick to see the symbols, keeping the adults on their toes, which boosts their self-esteem and confidence.

Story Cubes, such as Rory's Story Cubes, is a game where the child, parent and practitioner take turns to be the narrator. You throw the dice, which have symbols on each of their four sides, and invent a story from the images, starting with *'Once upon a time …'* You never know what combination of images you will get when rolling the dice, or what ideas will inspire the child's imagination: there are no limitations. The game can help highlight how each person can create a different story from the same images.

If the game feels a bit daunting at first the story can be co-created, with each person taking turns to choose an image and add a part of the story. Once the child has co-created a story, the freedom of the game may give them the confidence to create their own stories. They may use this game to share other experiences they have remembered from their past or something that is occurring in the present. The story cubes can be a wonderful way to invite the child to use and give narration to their imagination.

You can introduce many other games into the sessions. The child may suggest ones they already know and enjoy, such as Uno, snap, beetle (an updated version of hangman), charades, or other games such as Connect 4. Ideally the games need to be short enough to be played for five minutes at the beginning and/or end of sessions, or when the child needs a break. Many board games require more time but could be played for a short time each session.

The games we have mentioned emphasise the importance of play in Therapeutic Life Story Work. Activities such as the squiggle drawings can create safety, assist the child in resolving stress, trauma or behaviour concerns, and encourage free expression. Games like Jenga provide a sense of control when making up the rules. Play offers the child, parent and worker a means to communicate and express difficult or intense emotions while feeling safe and contained. It enhances a child's problem-solving skills, encourages them to relate to others in a positive manner and promotes the healing that is vital to their continuing growth and development.

Our aim is to provide space for children to learn to express themselves in a healthier way, become more empathic, and to discover more of themselves through playful exploration. We invite the parents to enjoy the spontaneity of play and to use it to build on their attachment and trust.

Some children only have a short period of time or 'window of tolerance' (Siegel 1999) in each session during which they can engage in the work. Allowing the child to engage in play for the rest of the time can reveal a great deal about how they see the world as well as strengthening their relationship with the parent and practitioner. Play can also be incorporated into information sharing to increase the child's window of tolerance, which is explored further in Chapter 8.

Hands of Interests

'Hands of interests' (Rose 2012), illustrated in Figure 4, is a useful exercise to use for getting to know one another in the first session. This can be done on a large pad, wallpaper, tablet or a shared whiteboard if doing the session online. It can be done in lots of ways, for example, the parent and child draw around each other's hand (the practitioner can draw around their own hand) and add five things they like or are interested to their own hand, one in each of their fingers and thumb. Or you can each add three things into three of your digits, then put one thing in the other's hand that they have noticed they like, are good at or that they like about them. The child then chooses who shares their hand first. We have found that this can open up communication in a playful way. Writing the reasons why you are meeting in a think bubble adds clarity from the start and, literally, gets you all on the same page!

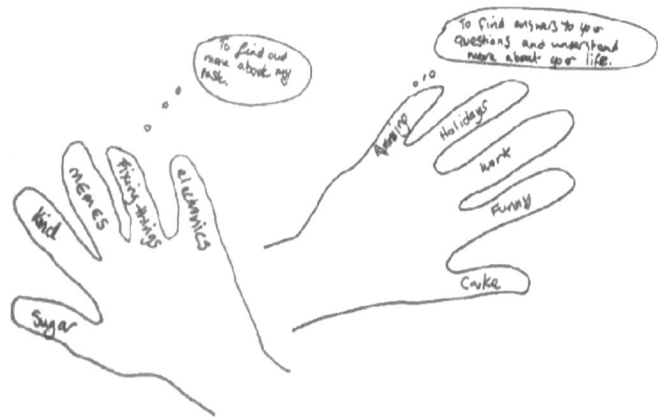

Figure 4: Hands of Interests

Hands of Support and Safety

A similar exercise is suggested by Wrench and Naylor (2013 p.30–31). The hands are drawn around in the same way as the hands of interests, but the names of people with whom the child feels safe are placed in the fingers. In Figure 5 a 'hand of support' has also been added, identifying the people who can offer the child support.

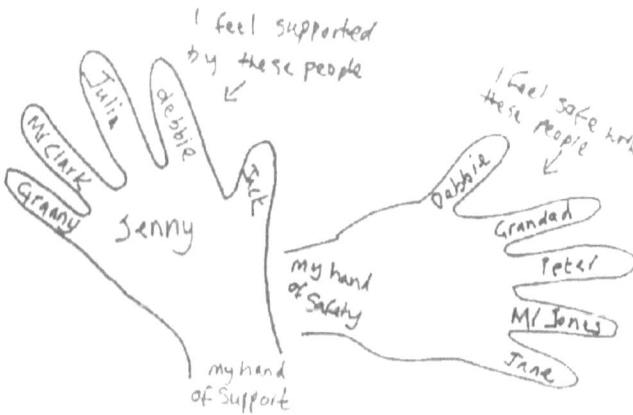

Figure 5: Hands of Support and Safety

Working Agreement

As we have already mentioned in this chapter, creating a contract or working agreement together (Rose and Philpot 2004) can promote the child's sense of safety, and we often do this in the second session. You can engage the child's creativity by giving a choice about the form this takes; it could be a star, map, scroll, spider graph or mind map, and working agreements can be drawn or written. You can call it the child's rules and make it official by each of you signing and dating it. The agreement can be reviewed, added to and referred to at any time during future sessions.

Points we suggest you could include are the time and day you will be meeting, how many times you plan to meet, having fun, expectations of each other (for instance, if delayed, who will be informed and how?), agreement about mobile phones, respect for each other: the purpose is not to judge others but to understand, confidentiality (who you will each speak to, agree no recording of session), okay to have feelings and be upset, okay to make mistakes (whether that be spelling, drawing or how you create something), okay to ask questions, okay to say stop (agree how the child can do this, for example putting hand up into stop sign or having a card), having a drink and snack, keeping everyone safe (explain what you will do if you have a worry about their safety), importance of listening to each other, starting and ending with a game.

You can find examples of working agreements in Figures 6 and 7.

Figure 6: Working Agreement Example 1

Figure 7: Working Agreement Example 2

Session Chart

Some children find it helpful to have a visual record to show how many times you will meet. They may enjoy adding a sticker at the end of each session, as shown in Figure 8. Here we used the child's favourite pirate theme. The child also used the chart to indicate that they felt happy meeting and thought they would feel sad when we came to the end of our sessions.

Figure 8: Session Chart example

Session Plan

It can help some children, such as those with additional needs or challenges, to have a clear outline of the session, and they may already have this structure in place at school. For them, agreeing and writing down a plan together on the wallpaper or separate sheet of paper at the start of each session works particularly well. It also benefits those children who are anxious about what you might tell them; having a plan gives them clarity about what will be covered.

A plan could look like this:

Plan: Tuesday 17th July

- Boxes game
- Drink and snack
- Balloon Journey
- Game of Dobble

2. Working with Emotions

Exploring feelings is an important part of the next few sessions. We have already illustrated how squiggle drawings can help the child to express their feelings in non-verbal ways and there are many more fun ways in which you can assess and develop their emotional literacy.

Working with a child and their parents grants you the privilege of learning about them, their hidden selves, and how they express themselves (or not!). Rose (2012 p.109) suggests 'Emotional regulation and emotional expression are all vital to the life story process'; this is the grounding of our work in every session. Not everyone knows how they feel or how to express the emotions that their life experiences have caused. It is, therefore, important to provide a safe environment that is accepting and non-judgmental, where a child can examine and process their emotions while feeling secure. Games and playful, creative activities allow a child to communicate their thoughts and feelings in a safe and comfortable way.

We can all have different emotions from one moment to another. For most children, mixed feelings cause emotional difficulty, which can show in their behaviour. Helping them to understand what these emotions are can be the start of unravelling what feels confusing and troublesome.

We have found the following games and activities useful for exploring feelings and developing emotional literacy.

Feelings charades is a game played with cards that represent a range of emotions. You can buy a set of emotions cards, such as Karen Treisman's *'A Therapeutic Treasure Deck of Feelings and Sentence Completion Cards'* *(Therapeutic Treasures Collection 2018c)*, or have fun making a set with the child or make your own set using emoji images.

Place all the cards face down and take turns in selecting one to act out for the others to guess. The child can consult or pair up with another player if they need to feel more secure. Observe what happens in this game: the child may be an expert who, for survival, has learnt to be highly attuned to recognising other people's feelings and therefore is good at identifying other's emotions, and may struggle to act out emotions having learnt to keep theirs in.

Feelings charades can encourage the child to consider their emotions in relation to events that have taken place. Once a feeling has been enacted and identified, the conversation can lead on to 'How I feel now … how I felt yesterday … when this happened', and so on.

This may seem like a slow process, but when we stay at the child's pace they can achieve a better understanding and are better able to make connections and express their feelings with clarity. They can unlock emotions that have been hidden from them but which have perhaps emerged in their behaviour, and begin to connect to them internally.

Feelings games present the child with an opportunity to explore and experiment with their experiences of these emotions, and they open up a dialogue between the child, parent, and practitioner.

Being open about your own feelings encourages the child to do the same and it models to the parent how they too can express themselves and continue to support the child outside the sessions.

Guided Fantasy: Oaklander (1978) describes guided fantasies as giving a 'window into a child's world'. You can acquire insights into the child's happy, sad and safe places by taking them on an imaginary adventure, such as the air balloon journey (Rose 2012). The child draws their balloon, or another image of their choice, on the wallpaper and then chooses a safe adult to accompany them on their imaginary journey (not the practitioner as you will be the narrator). Pets, friends, or favourite toys may also accompany them, as we can see in Figure 9.

Figure 9: Air Balloon   **Figure 10: Air Balloon Happy Place**

The journey begins with travelling across the land, over mountains and great seas. Invite the child to look down from the safety of their balloon and see the happiest place they can imagine. Then invite them to draw what they see. The child who drew the image in Figure 10 imagined a rainbow with a pot of gold. Inside the rainbow was an opening door with a sign which read 'Finding Hope in a Happy Place'. The child explained that the door led to finding out about her past.

The journey continues over mountains and across seas. Invite the child to look down from the safety of their balloon and think of the saddest place they can imagine. One child drew a bottomless dark pit, but with a ladder representing how they could use their imagination to get themselves out of the pit. Another child drew a house on fire and a graveyard that they wanted to run away from. Some children don't want to go to or draw their sad place but may be able to describe it. One child said it was the place where his favourite Disney character had died. This enabled a conversation about the loss and longing he felt for a significant birth family member who had died, and his fear that his parent might also 'disappear'.

The journey continues over the mountains and across the seas until you come to a place where the child looks down and can see their safe place. It is a good sign when the child's safe place is their current home, alongside their parenting parent, as Figure 11 shows. Here we have a view into the child's sitting room, portraying the sofa, television, and parent. This indicates their present security and safety, which can be drawn on when you continue the journey you are on together to look back at their past.

Figure 11: Air Balloon Safe Place

Figure 12: Corridor of my Mind

Imagery and metaphor are great ways to discover a child's inner world. One child, aged 14, drew the image shown in Figure 12 when we discussed how she felt about beginning her life story journey.

The image shows a long corridor with doors leading to all the things in her life; the larger door at the end of the corridor represents her birth family. She drew cobwebs to represent the feeling that the door had been shut for a long time but was now starting to open. The image was helpful to revisit during the work when her birth family instigated unplanned communication. She stated that the door had become a revolving one which she could comfortably go in and out of as much as she wanted. Later, aged 16, she envisaged a key in the door, as she had needed to put in some boundaries and take control of closing and opening the door. At 17, when she decided to stop the communication, she envisaged locking this door and keeping the key somewhere safe in order to get on with her life.

Preoccupation: Rose (2012 p.127–9) identifies how using the image of a bar chart, or beaker can be helpful in offering a child the means to explore, express and communicate what is taking place within their internal world. Figure 13 shows an example of a child's preoccupation beaker. The child identified outside the beaker what was taking up their thoughts and to what extent. The drawing showed Post-Traumatic Stress Disorder was taking up a good portion of the beaker, which the child identified as stemming from the separation from her birth family, being adopted and having so many questions about her past.

At the top of the beaker the child demonstrated, by the added drops, that her anxiety increased due to the pressures she felt in her daily life. The light-green area is not named. The child wanted to keep these thoughts to herself; she was not ready to share them as her parent was in the session and she did not want to upset them. Although the parent knew what it was about, they were not able to address the lack of communication between them at this time, especially when they were feeling upset with one another.

The preoccupation beaker was extremely helpful for this child. She used it each week to show how she was doing and whether her thoughts and feelings had shifted. It provided her with a way of measuring her wellbeing and seeing if she had been able to resolve some of her concerns.

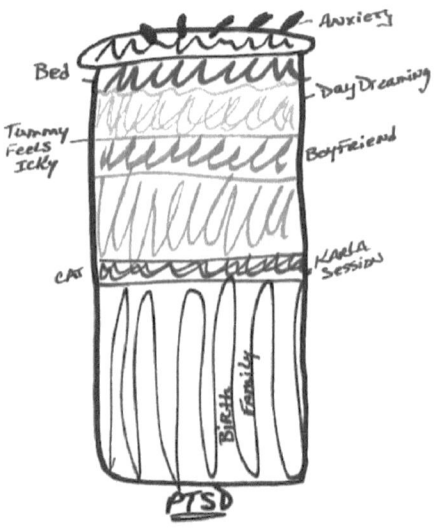

Figure 13: Preoccupation Bar Graph

A **Body Outline** has many uses, and we go on to examine some of them further in the section on exploring a sense of self. Here we are focusing on it as a great way to identify the child's emotions and where they notice feeling them in their body. The child lies on the wallpaper and the parent draws round them. The child can then indicate the location of the feeling on the image of themselves. One child described anxiety as feeling like they had a tightening knotted rope in their stomach, and that loss felt like barbed wire around their heart.

Encourage the child to use a visual image or colour to represent their feelings, as suggested by Rose (2012 p.111). You can create a 'feelings' theme chart which can include people, food, and travel. For example, lonely could be symbolically represented as one pea on a plate, frustrated could be a bowl of hot soup, happy might be the child's favourite food such as spaghetti Bolognese.

Suzanne: *I used a graph to help one child show the extent of his anxiety levels for the first time. We started with a preoccupation beaker, where he identified that anxiety was taking up 90% of his brain. He commented that it was different at different times of the day, so we drew a graph with 1–100% on the upright axis to show level of anxiety and the hours in the day along the bottom axis. The results showed that he had huge spikes of anxiety which were school-related, such as getting homework completed and making sure he had the right books. He indicated the extent of his anxiety by walking into the connecting room and going to the far end, which was approximately 15 metres away from the graph.*

We used the back of a previous roll of wallpaper to roll along the floor to him so he could place his mark and then joined this into the graph. This exercise enabled him to demonstrate the huge level of anxiety he was experiencing. He was able to talk about his preoccupation with these thoughts which were at times 'off-the-scale' and were causing anxiety-led repetitive behaviours, which he said worried him further.

The graph indicated low anxiety around mealtimes, suggesting he associated food with calm and safety. His grandparent's initial reaction was to offer solutions for his anxiety, but I guided them to look at the huge spike of anxiety and imagine how that must feel. This prompted them to offer him comfort and observe out loud that he was shaking. It was the first time the child had shown the extent of his anxiety, and we acknowledged what a big and brave thing it was to do.

From this session onwards, the child was able to identify when he was feeling anxious and seek support from his grandparents. They learnt to notice out loud his shaking, and while comforting him they helped him to find words to express what he was experiencing.

In later sessions we were able to link these high levels of anxiety to his experiences of trauma in the first year of his life when he been unsafe in his birth parents' care. I made him some emoji flip cards on a key ring, with emotions he had chosen. He carried them as a helpful tool, to help him notice and name his immensely powerful feelings, both at home and school. In subsequent sessions he identified strategies that helped him manage these strong emotions, and I added these to the back of the emoji cards. They included ideas such as, 'When I feel anxious I can tell someone like my Nan, class tutor, pupil mentor or scout leader'.

One child was unable to choose a single theme, so she combined all three to produce a 'symbolic representation of each feeling'. She was able to refer to her chart when she was feeling any of these emotions during her sessions. We discussed each of these feelings and symbols, what they meant for her at the time and how they related to her past. Previously, when her parents asked her 'How are you feeling?' or 'What are you feeling?' she could not answer as she either was not always sure how she felt, or she did not have the words to describe her feelings. This tool enabled her to show them how she felt by pointing to the feeling on her chart. It offered a new way of communicating with her parents and it supported her emotional awareness while enabling her to self-regulate.

Treisman (2018a) provides helpful worksheets for exploring emotions, which draw on narrative theory (White & Epston 1989). Feelings such as anxiety, sadness, fear and anger can be considered and externalised by drawing what they look like, identifying them and giving them a name and voice. For instance, the child might experience their anger as a monster, a tornado or a weight pushing down on them. Assigning a metaphor, persona or image to the feeling serves to externalise it and enables the child to think and talk about it in more helpful ways.

Scaling also provides a visual measure of emotions. We find it helpful to use a graph like the one outlined by Rose (2012 p.110) to show how we all can have many differing feelings during a day or week. We can feel up one moment and low the next. This rollercoaster feeling is likely to be familiar to the children we work with, caused by their environment, past experiences, traumas, and everyday life events. The children we work with may have learnt to survive their trauma by cutting off from their emotions. They may not know what they are feeling, let alone be able to name it.

As the sessions progress and deep feelings are triggered, you may see fight, flight, and freeze behaviour. The child may display tremendously powerful feelings, which can have a huge impact on you. You can share and reflect on this with the child. Remember to acknowledge the likelihood that you have only seen a glimpse of what they are feeling.

Many young people describe their persistent and frequent feelings of anger as a troublesome feeling that affects their lives and wellbeing, and as something they want to reduce.

One child described her constant anger as a pulsating, seething tangle in their head, which she then drew. In exploring this child's anger further, we used the imagery of an iceberg (Goleman 1995) to see how the feeling we see on the surface is fuelled by many emotions below. The image in Figure 14 powerfully illustrates the important feelings that were underneath the anger.

Figure 14: Anger Iceberg

This child had experienced years of extreme neglect in her early childhood, but on the day we did this work together the bullying she was experiencing at school was the greatest cause of her anger. She was able to express her feelings to a greater extent through the drawing than she could with words. It also provided a powerful image for her parent and social worker to take to a meeting with the school head.

An image of a volcano also provides a helpful metaphor for anger; the child can label the red-hot lava spilling out, and the space inside or underneath the volcano can be used to identify and contemplate the underlying feelings which are causing it to explode.

Hand Model of the Brain: Goleman (1995) identifies how anger causes blood to flow to our hands, making it easier for us to strike an enemy or hold a weapon. Our heart rate speeds up and a rush of hormones, such as adrenaline, gives us a surge of energy so we can physically protect ourselves. This is embedded in our brain as a survival mechanism. A child's life experience may mean that they are in a constant state of alarm.

We find a neurodevelopmentally-informed approach helpful in our sessions. Neuroscience is an ever-developing field that has a lot to offer us in terms of understanding the impact of trauma on the developing brain. Siegel and Bryson's (2011) hand model of the brain provides a child-friendly way of demonstrating what may be happening for the child when they experience survival responses such as fight, flight and/ or freeze.

By making your hand into a fist with your thumb tucked in you can show how we have an upstairs (fingers) and downstairs (thumb) part of our brains. Downstairs is the primitive or survival part which is triggered when we feel we are in danger; upstairs is the thinking part where we make good decisions and do the right thing, even when we are feeling really upset. The downstairs brain is where big feelings come from. It lets us care about other people and feel love. It also allows us to feel upset, angry or frustrated. This is the part of the brain that developed in early man to keep us safe from threat or danger: it helps us survive by choosing fight, flight or freeze. When the survival or animal part of our brain is triggered, it is like 'flipping our lid': the thinking part is disengaged.

When we flip our lid, our upstairs brain is no longer touching our downstairs brain and so can't help it to stay calm. When we have had very frightening experiences our brain can keep flipping into survival mode a long time after the danger has passed. It is a false alarm, like when the toaster makes the fire alarm go off. Our brains keep acting to protect us as if the trauma is happening right now.

Jeanette Yoffe has created a child friendly 'Hand Model of the Brain' video (https://www.youtube.com/watch?v=H_dxnYhdyuY) which you can show during a session or watch to develop your own way of explaining it. You can buy or make some finger puppets so you can all choose a representation of your animal brain – perhaps a meerkat, lion or tiger – and add some eyes (which can easily be sourced from craft outlets) to your fingers to represent the thinking part of your brain, as shown in Figure 15.

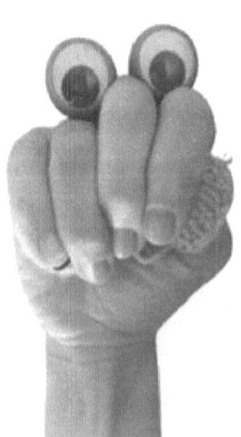

Upstairs/ Thinking Part　　Downstairs/ Survival Part
(makes good decisions)　　(Fight, Flight, Freeze, Faint)

Figure 15: Hand Model of the Brain

Siegel and Bryson (2011) advocate the value of noticing and naming feelings to tame them through increased awareness and understanding. You can model this in the sessions by starting and perhaps ending each session by noticing and naming three feelings you each have and exploring what events have led to these. The value is in conveying an understanding to the child of being in survival mode and the possibility of change: how we can 'rewire' our brains by noticing and naming our feelings.

As well as understanding what may be happening in our brains, we have also found it useful in sessions to notice and investigate what may be happening in our bodies as a result of trauma. Brain and trauma research draws attention to the need to process traumatic experiences through the body. Van Der Kolk (2014 p.101) writes *'In order to change, people need to become aware of their sensations and the way their bodies interact with the world around them. Physical self-awareness is the first step in releasing the tyranny of the past.'*

Drawn from Porges' (2011) Polyvagal Theory, Dana's (2018) ladder provides a useful metaphor to use in a session to show how trauma affects our nervous system. A strong reaction to something occurs when our autonomic nervous system tries to protect us from a perceived threat. This defensive position may lead us to becoming withdrawn (dorsal vagal state) or anxious and frantic (sympathetic state). People who cannot comfortably notice what is going on inside their bodies become vulnerable to responding to any sensory change by either shutting down or going into panic, as shown in Figure 16.

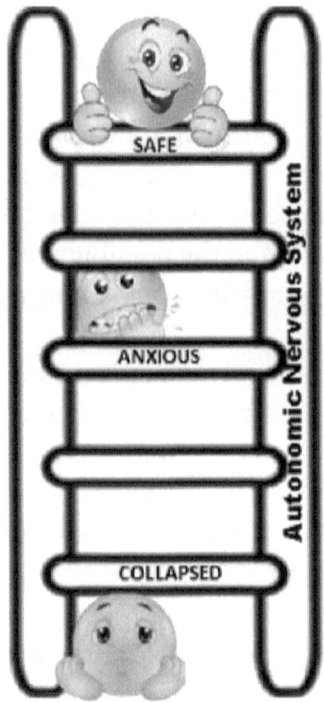

Ladder adapted from Dana's
The Polyvagal Theory in Therapy

Figure 16: How Trauma Affects the Nervous System

It may help an older child to practice Dana's (2018) four R's, as a way of climbing out of the agitated (sympathetic) and collapsed (dorsal) states and returning to feeling safe and connected (ventral vagal activation), where they can feel open to learning and social interaction:

Recognise the physical response you are having and identify what may have triggered it. Becoming aware and conscious of the survival response can help you to overcome it. For instance, notice if your heart is beating faster. Are you feeling hotter, are your hands sweaty, does your body feel tense?

Respect the survival response that your body unconsciously and automatically instigates to protect you. Instead of fighting it, consider that it has done a good job of protecting you at a time when you might have needed it. This can help you to be kind and compassionate to yourself.

Regulate or allow someone to help you regulate your feelings in order to return to a safe and connected state. Use your toolkit of strategies to help you, such as imagining your safe place or talking with an adult.

Re-story (reframe) what is happening and why. The narratives we create about our feelings and actions are powerful and self-fulfilling. They can keep us in a defensive and high alert state, but if we change our stories we can move towards connecting with and trusting others.

Dana (2018) suggests that following these four steps can enable us to move from being in the moment to a more conscious sitting with and understanding of our responses, as well as those of others. It can help us to recognise the physical nature of our responses and develop self-compassion.

A **Circle of Feelings** is a good starting exercise and provides a way of guiding the session, containing, hearing each person and identifying shared feelings. Draw a circle and divide it into sections for each person to write in words to describe their feelings and thoughts.

It is vital to practise active listening in our sessions, and to demonstrate this to the child by repeating their words. Children can, consciously or unconsciously, bring their own helpful metaphors to the session. One child said his feelings were in a tangle, so we created a **Tangle of Feelings** on the wallpaper by drawing the tangle and adding the words and feelings within. The child realised there was not just one tangle but several overlapping ones, so these were added to represent the tangle of feelings around his brother and sisters, school, friends, home and birth family, shown in Figure 17.

Figure 17: Tangle of Feelings

This was a powerful image for the child and conveyed so much more than words could do. The experience of drawing the separate tangles in itself led to some untangling!

Karla: *One child I worked with was unable to express how she felt. Instead, she would run away from her parents, or hide in the house where they could not find her. We needed to gently peel away the delicate layers of feelings she carried to get at the underlying cause.*

We considered what triggered her to run and how she felt when this took place by drawing different feeling faces on the wallpaper and using feelings cards to playfully act out the emotions. She recalled the list of feelings (Rose 2012 p.110) she had drawn out several sessions ago, using different symbols for each feeling. This enabled her to share some of the emotions she had experienced. I encouraged her parent to say how it felt for him when his daughter ran from him.

When she saw he had chosen a sad face with tears coming down the cheeks, and heard him say he felt hurt, confused, sad and desperate to help her, and that he did not want her to run away as he felt scared she might get hurt, she put her arms around his neck and said, 'I feel like that too'.

They were beginning to forge an understanding of one another. The playful approach we started with created a safe and secure place for her to explore her emotions and the result was a huge breakthrough for her in owning her feelings and being able to name them.

Towards the end of this session the parent said something that triggered the child to run away from him to the other side of the room. It was clear to see that she was upset. I reminded her that she was safe and that she did not have to say anything unless she wanted to. She sat quietly next to her dad for a few minutes. He appeared sad and confused not knowing what he had said that had triggered her to run away from him.

I could see their sadness and confusion and let her know that I wanted to help her and could see that her dad wanted to help her as well. The child looked at her parent and said, 'That is how I feel, but why do you feel like that?' He explained that he did not know what he had said to upset her and was confused and sad that she had gone away from him to be on her own. She then revealed that she did not like it when he said she was clever; she believed she was not, from earlier years of being told she was stupid. She was able to say how this confused her and became overwhelming.

Once she heard that her parents genuinely did believe she was clever, she was able to consider that it could be true! We reflected upon this further and then made an agreement that when things were said or done that upset her, she could try stopping and sharing her thoughts and feelings with her parents, so they could support her. She liked this idea and in every session since that time she applied it and stopped hiding or running away from her parents. She had gained a greater understanding of what was occurring internally for her and had learnt to express her thoughts, feelings, confusion, and disappointments when they occurred. She confirmed that she felt much better having her parents understand her needs.

Suzanne: Many of the children we work with can find it hard to manage conversations about their past, one child who said she could not remember her past added that she had no feelings. We used a session to wonder when and why her feelings might have stopped. She was able to identify that there were some very difficult feelings and memories from the first six years of her life when she lived with her birth parents through the **imagery of a rubbish bin and a treasure chest**.

She drew a bin with the lid securely glued shut. She said it contained some memories of 'bad things' to do with her birth parents; it was the first time she had been able to talk about this. She drew blobs around the lid to show the strong glue holding the lid tightly shut, and a spider's web to show that it had been shut for a long time. She was very clear that she did not feel ready to take the lid off, but she was able to identify the sorts of things that were inside such as the pain of having *decaying teeth and having 20 of them removed when she came into foster care. There were bad guys in the bin who she identified as her birth parents being naughty, angry and hurtful.*

We thought together about how having no feelings was a clever thing for her brain to do for survival, because at the time she didn't have parents who could help her with her very tricky emotions. It was suggested that, now she had parents who could help her, she might be able to start lifting the lid; perhaps have a peek, a little bit at a time as she grew older and felt safe enough to do so.

In drawing a treasure chest she was able to celebrate positive memories and things in her life, bringing a sense of balance and acknowledgement that there were also some positive as well as the negative memories associated with her birth parents.

Drawing onion layers or concentric circles can be a helpful way to uncover the child's world and how they see themselves. The concept of the onion is that it has many layers, and they are as delicate to unravel as one's past experiences. It raises many questions to be discussed such as who is in the centre layer with them, who is in the next, and so on. Is there something hidden beneath each layer? What could be underneath the layers that they cannot see? How many layers are there? How many emotions? How many experiences or thoughts could the child identify within their internal or external world? Do the layers represent their family members and those they have not met?

These layers need to be explored with care and caution. Removing a layer takes time and respect as it could fall apart. A child may recognise themselves in this – falling apart and desperately trying to keep it all together, internally and, therefore, externally.

We can support this process by taking care to unravel the layers at the child's pace. The child chooses how the layers are represented from their perspective. There is no right or wrong way.

The work needs to go at the child's pace, and it is important to only go as far as they can. A child will clearly show you in their actions, body language and drawings if they are having difficulty. Some children may not feel safe enough to review their feelings despite all you do to create a sense of security in the sessions. One child included weapons in each of his drawings on the wallpaper. Food and weapons were a feature in his happy, sad and safe places when we did the balloon journey. He added a protective suit to his body outline, including a belt with guns and knives, and jet boots with poison fangs. When we came to consider where feelings might be located in his body, he moved to cower against the wall. The image he drew suggested that he was protecting himself from painful emotions, and his behaviour demonstrated that he was not ready to delve into his feelings at this time. As Wrench and Naylor (2013 p.93-4) suggest 'Sometimes you need to recognise that at this stage in a child's life cognitively and emotionally he has done enough.'

3. Building Self-Confidence

Regular visits from a practitioner, together with the message that they and their views and feelings matter, give the child a sense of greater worth and being valued. The child needs to feel supported and nurtured in the sessions by the parent and worker. Exploring a child's perspective on their life and that of their past can involve a great deal of thought.

The image of three mountains in Figure 18 was drawn by a 17-year-old. The mountains represent how, after learning more about their birth family and their experiences in care, they felt in the middle, between their past and present.

Figure 18: Three Mountains Imagery

The image shows that, from the child's perspective, life can feel insurmountable and the problems they have had to overcome have been enormous. However, when exploring the mountains they have 'climbed successfully', it offers a different perspective on what they have achieved. They are supported by resilient qualities they may not even be aware they possess.

This child examined how they felt after learning about their past and the loss, trauma and rejections they had experienced, including separation of birth siblings and birth parents. They considered how this had affected them in their present life and how they saw themselves when they thought about their future. Learning about who they are and what strengths and achievements they have accomplished can be unsettling for children, especially when they believe they have not achieved anything, are not good enough and cannot do anything right.

Keane (2016) describes resilience as 'a special skill because it is so defined by outlook and response. It is an adaptive mode of thinking which has to be developed gradually, alongside techniques for improving one's initial response to something bad or unwanted.' If we consider this child's initial response to their experience, as illustrated in their drawing, life felt insurmountable. Compare this to their response after completing the exercise and exploring what they had achieved and how they now felt: 'Wow, I have accomplished a lot!' Their internal world and their perspective on life had shifted. Denborough (2014) identifies this as reworking or rewriting storylines of identity.

The child's drawing also gave them a sense of holding and taking time out, while building up more strength to continue their journey of life and face the important decisions ahead of them: decisions about their education, career, meeting birth parents, whether to have a relationship with birth parents and what sort of relationship it would be. This is what we provide in Therapeutic Life Story Work, time out to sit with the child, to hear about their thoughts and feelings, and past and present experiences. To take a breather and not rush through a process which enables and promotes their acceptance that change is a part of growing up and moving forward. To take decisive actions to work towards their goals, and use this as an opportunity to self-discover a more positive view of themselves and nurture a more hopeful view of their life and future.

This process offered a healing and repair of the trauma this child had experienced and provided them with an opportunity to reframe their current internal working model (Bowlby 1969) to that of a healthier and more rewarding one based on their attachment experience with their primary carer.

There are so many exercises that can facilitate the development of resilience, strengths and self-esteem. Which one 'speaks' to their internal working model and will enhance their experience of themselves depends on the individual child.

Hand of Pride is a simple but effective exercise for building self-confidence. It uses the same technique as the hands of interests and safety, where the child and parent draw around each other's hand to create an outline. They are then asked to write into three of the fingers something about themselves that they are good at or proud of, and then to add two qualities to each other's hands. This exercise will tell you a lot. Initially the child and parent may both find it hard to identify things they are good at but having a discussion together for support and encouragement can help. If the child and parent identify more than five things, as is often the case, these can be written in the palm of the hand or a second hand can be added.

The concept of **Zones of Regulation** identified by Kuypers (2011) can be helpful in encouraging the child to notice their emotional state and think about strategies they can use to self-regulate in order to build resilience. The original version by Kuypers (2011) depicted superheroes such as Superman and the Incredible Hulk, but any characters can be used, to suit the child's interests, for example from films such as *Inside Out* and the Harry Potter films, or video games such as *Fortnite*. The Harry Potter characters in the adapted Zones of Regulation chart in Figure 19 were chosen by the child. Blue can be used for sad, green for 'good to go', yellow for anxious and red for angry: similar to traffic lights.

Figure 19: Adapted from Kuypers' (2011) 'Zones of Regulation'

Strategy Cards such as Treisman's (2018b) grounding, soothing, coping and regulating cards can help the child to identify strategies for dealing with powerful feelings. You can create your own using clip art and a laminator. Include in them strategies that the child has identified and leave some blank ones for the child to fill in.

Suzanne: *As sessions progressed, one child told me he no longer felt preoccupied with the thoughts that had been causing his 'off-the-scale' anxiety and repetitive behaviours. He reported recognising the triggers and finding his own helpful strategy for managing his anxiety. He had noticed that he felt terrified when hearing scary music on a film shown to his class at school. In sessions he had also noticed the same feeling of terror during the dramatic opening music at a concert. We considered how the music had triggered his survival response, made him feel that his life was in danger and that he needed to flee at any cost. His strategy was to find and listen repeatedly to the music on his phone as a way of successfully de-sensitising his fear* *response. The school reported that he was showing markedly increased confidence. He transferred this learning into managing his fear of asking questions and standing up in front of the class to present his work, which were things he had felt too terrified to do prior to our sessions.*

4. Exploring a Sense of Self

We develop a sense of self as we grow, starting from when we are born. Children who have experienced the trauma of abuse and neglect can hold a negative sense of themselves. They may view themselves as unlovable, caregivers as not meeting their needs and the world as unsafe (Bowlby 1969).

Supporting children in exploring and developing a sense of their own identity is an important part of the Therapeutic Life Story Work process. This includes identities around gender, race, age, ability, sexual orientation, religion, culture, legal status, position in the family, and so on. There are useful books and videos available to support this area of work with children, such as the YouTube video *Identity Explained for Children* (Pike 2020).

When we set out creating goals for our work together, many children have identified wanting to know themselves better. There are various techniques and exercises you can use to help a child to understand aspects of themselves or the way in which they perceive life, people, communication, and their way of responding or reacting.

Exercises we use to facilitate exploring a sense of self include:

- Finding the Warrior Within
- Fact, Fiction, Fantasy, and Heroism

- Suitcase Exercise
- Word Exploration
- Body Outline
- The Thoughts, Feelings, Actions and Behaviour Tree

Finding the Warrior Within is an exercise that encourages children to connect with qualities they are not aware they have. A warrior may possess strength, courage, control, bravery, resistance and belief in themselves. Finding the warrior within helps the child realise that they too have developed such qualities.

We use this exercise to gain a better understanding of the child's view of their inner self. We look at what they believe and compare it to how they are perceived by others. We write one list of the child's inner qualities from their perspective and another from the perspective of someone who knows them: a parent, friend, family member or member of school staff. We discuss these qualities and if there are any differences make a note of them. We weigh up the differences and how they 'fit' the child. What they believe internally is challenged by how others experience them. If the child is unable to identify any qualities, we take time to sit with how this feels and wonder where and when they might have formed this view. We might suggest they list their negative qualities and then compare this to others' views. We can revisit the exercise in a later session as a means of 'internal check-in'; we then see if their original belief still stands or if there has been a change due to the information they have processed with the parent and practitioner.

Karla: *I remember one 15-year-old who was determined not to accept that not all things are as they seem and there is space for change to occur, however scary that feels. It is life altering when this happens; the warrior within learns from others and becomes more at peace mentally and emotionally.*

I understood at the start of his Therapeutic Life Story Work that this child was worried about turning out to be just like his birth father who was a convicted paedophile. He found himself in trouble at school for lashing out at others and using inappropriate or unacceptable language. Deep down he knew he could not control this behaviour because he did not understand where it was coming from or why.

In our work, we want every child to feel worthy and to know that they hold an important place in our thoughts and feelings. When a child does not experience this they cannot develop a sense of worth. This child based his worth on the behaviour of his birth father. Many times he had been told by his previous foster carers and children at school, 'You will turn out like your birth father, not your dad who is bringing you up, who nurtures you, loves you and knows you are worthy'.

He said there was no space in his head to take these messages in until he did this exercise. When he realised that his parents were the ones listing all the facts about how good a person he was and that he would do wonderful things in his life, he was left feeling quite proud of himself. This caused a massive change in his perception of the truth. It altered his way of being, feeling, thinking and his behaviour towards everyone.

He continued to reflect upon his character and how he felt about himself, as opposed to who he had thought he was, or who others said he was. At the end of the Therapeutic Life Story Work he stated, 'I am not like my birth father at all. How could I have thought that or felt I would turn out like him? I choose my path and I just want to be me and a bit like my dad!'

The child's warrior within him was his 'little self'. Figure 20 shows an image that he related to; he sees himself in the present as guarding his little self with a more 'knowing' hand, his hand. He became aware of how he wanted to live his life, knowing now of the inner strength that he held, and started to become the best version of himself.

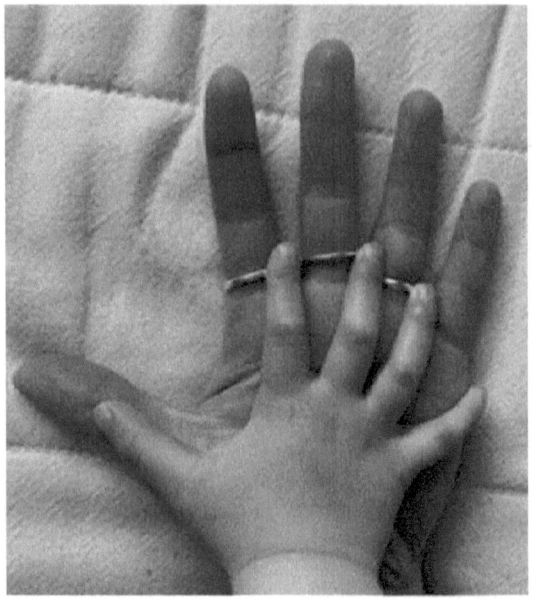

Figure 20: Finding the Warrior Within

Fact, Fiction, Fantasy and Heroism (Rose 2012), also called Magical Circle, is an exercise where a circle or body outline is drawn and divided into four sections which are each considered in turn.

- *Fact*: what do I know about myself that can be proven, such as my date of birth on my birth certificate or DNA proving my paternity?
- *Fiction*: what do people say about me?
- *Fantasy*: what do I imagine or wish for in my ideal world, what are my hopes and dreams?
- *Heroism*: who will help me realise my hopes and dreams?

Karla: *I once worked with a child who was confused by what he had heard about himself and what his records said, and what he felt about himself. I used this exercise to help him gain a better perception of the truth about himself.*

During the session we discussed who were good and bad role models. He identified John Cena, the American professional wrestler, bodybuilder, rapper, actor, and television presenter, as a good role model. He is the host of 'Are You Smarter than a Fifth Grader?' on Nickelodeon and has starred in various films. The child thought a lot of what John Cena did was good.

I invited him to consider the facts, fiction, fantasy, and heroism about himself and he wrote down quite a few things. He discovered that, through everything he had experienced, he had survived a great deal of trauma and felt he had a warrior within him. He was making sense of the truth. He learnt that:

- *His persona as the 'main bad guy at school', was based on wanting attention and hoping to be loved for who he was.*
- *His thoughts about the past – that as he was his birth father's son he must be like him – were fiction; he didn't want to be like him at all.*
- *His present thoughts, around how his dad loved him and treated him with respect, encouraged him to want to be like this in his future, because he knew he wanted to have a family of his own and a home that would be safe for all of them.*

This process increased his self-esteem, resilience, and belief that he was not a bad person. He was able to balance out what felt real and what was fantasy. Working through fact, fiction, fantasy, and heroism enabled him to see things as they are and that he had choices. He realised that he was nothing like his birth father and more like his dad. He also accepted that his past does not define him: he does!

The Suitcase Exercise is a visualisation technique that can help children gain a greater sense of themselves and an understanding of the 'excess baggage' they may be carrying around, such as events from their past and things they have picked up along the way that do not belong to them.

Invite the child to imagine they are going on a trip with their family. Each person has their own bag and has packed the things they want to take. The child (depending on age) can pack their own things or at least say what they would like to be included. Everyone gets in the car (or taxi, bus, or train) and travels to the airport. When they arrive at the airport the baggage is taken inside and put on the plane. Once they arrive at their destination they go and collect their baggage.

Just as when we collect our own baggage, we assume that everything in our bag belongs to us, but this is not always the case. Did Mum, Dad or a sibling add more things in there? Like life events, we collect things along the way unintentionally or unconsciously and that can leave a child feeling left alone to deal with incidents, feelings, or traumatic experiences. When they are picked up from their home to be dropped off to a foster carer or children's home, they have had their bags packed; this may feel like their 'life being packed' and taken to the next stop, without their permission.

When a child is left with everyone else's baggage they are unable to lift it let alone carry it on their own. One child illustrated in the drawing in Figure 21 the positive and negative things they carry in their bag: the loss of siblings, arguments, friends, freedom, fun, lots of love, lack of support, isolation, alcohol and loneliness. The weight can feel enormous and impossible. However, through Therapeutic Life Story Work we can begin to unpack this, making better sense of what belongs to them and what belongs to others, such as their birth parents.

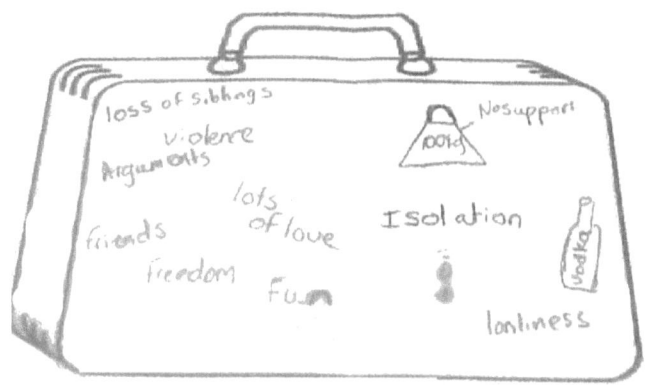

Figure 21: Suitcase Exercise

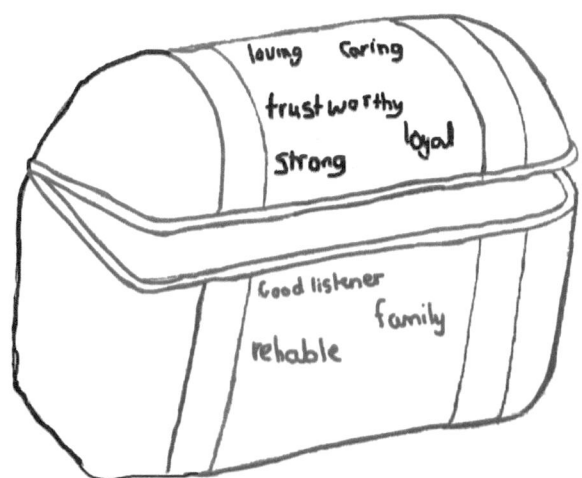

Figure 22: Treasure Chest

In the drawing in Figure 22, the child was able to display the treasures within them. They did this after they had let go of the 'excess baggage' by doing the suitcase exercise. They were able to focus on their qualities, feelings, strengths and the areas of their life that were important to them. 'Shredding' the excess baggage and 'other people's stuff' as the child called it, afforded a sense of relief, understanding and clarity. They realised how much of other people's baggage they had been carrying. No wonder they had felt so depressed, anxious and not good enough; their self-esteem, self-worth and confidence had been deeply affected. During the work they concluded they were a good, worthy person, and they felt they belonged for the first time within their adoptive family. The child's statement, 'It's my family and I belong', was immensely powerful.

Word Exploration: Exploring a word, just one word, is an amazingly simple technique to use to help a child gain clarity around a word that sticks with them. It can be any word that comes up for the child at any time. It could be distress, concern, excitement, boredom, or any other emotion. Whatever the word it can be explored.

Karla: *I used word exploration to help one child who repeatedly said, 'I feel blocked', 'There is this block in me' and 'I can't seem to get away or around this block and I don't know what it is'.*

I love to be playful with words, so I suggested we investigate the word 'block' to see what came up. The child agreed. I asked them to write the word 'block' and then draw a speech bubble around it. I mentioned that there was 'no right or wrong in writing whatever comes up for you. Just allow yourself to write.'

The child took a few minutes and then wrote, 'If whatever I'm doing is wrong or right'. From there, she wrote about: fitting in when she was fostered and then adopted, her concerns about her mum's health, her early years' experiences of her birth mother's deteriorating health, not knowing the truth about her past, her dreams which caused her confusion, and possibly suppressed her thoughts and heightened her fear and uncertainty around her past and her feelings of uncertainty about people's reactions when she did something or disagreed with them.

This child held a great deal of anxiety that impaired her ability to join in with friends or go outside, for fear of people staring at her. She was anxious about leaving her mother at home on her own, in case she needed something. She herself had been left behind by her birth mother when she was two minutes late coming out of school once.

This exercise revealed insights into why she was feeling blocked and what was causing that. She felt relieved to see this on the wallpaper; it was all there, right in front of her and it validated everything she was holding. It allowed movement, healing and repair to her sense of self.

Suzanne: *In exploring identity with a child of dual heritage, creating a body outline of how they saw themself facilitated discussion around how others might perceive them in the community. We considered the unconscious (or implicit) bias others might hold and how this might affect their experiences. The child was also able to consider their own bias in relation to their view of others and gain insight into how this can arise and the impact it can have.*

Body Outline: We have already shown how useful the body outline activity can be in the section on working with emotions. Here we examine it as a means of developing the child's sense of self. With the child's permission the parent draws round them on the wallpaper, taking care around and avoiding any sensitive areas. You can then hold the image up for the child to gain a sense of their physical size, which may appear larger than they imagined themselves to be.

The outline can be used in many ways. Their length at birth, if known, or approximate length can be added inside to illustrate the positive reality of how much they have grown. The child can choose whether they wish to draw in their features and clothes to represent how they see themselves now or how they imagine themselves to be in the future. Talents, interests and qualities can be added to the body outline to create a deeper picture of themselves, with the parent and practitioner suggesting areas and examples of strengths that they have observed. It can help to buy or create a set of strengths cards to facilitate identifying positive qualities, such as Treisman '*A Therapeutic Treasure Deck Strengths and Self-Esteem Cards*' (2018b).

The Thoughts, Feelings, Actions and Behaviour Tree: The behaviour tree is an exercise outlined by Rose (2012), that can be used to explore a child's understanding of themselves and the roots of who they are. The picture in Figure 23, drawn by an 11-year-old child, shows how phenomenally successful this tool can be in symbolically linking past 'roots' to present 'leaves'.

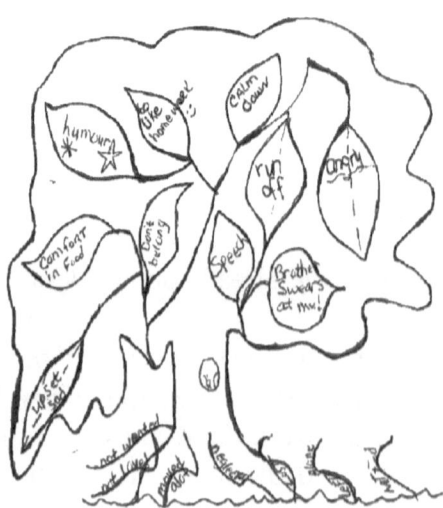

Figure 23: Feelings, Actions and Behaviour Tree

Karla: *I explained the process of the behaviour tree to the parent and child and they drew together, starting with the leaves, which represented the child's feelings, thoughts, worries and present experiences.*

The roots denoted the child's past experiences, which included loss, emotional and physical harm, neglect, trauma, rejection and separation. This child's development and needs had been interrupted by these experiences, along with the lack of security and need for food. The child appeared to have realised this as she drew over the roots making them darker, as if she were making this clearer to herself.

The child placed a little bird in the trunk of the tree and when I asked what this meant for her, she responded, 'That is me in the middle, past and present. I'm here, in the middle. This is all me!' As she drew the branches, symbolically connecting all the parts of her experience together, I realised this provided a narrative and visual story.

However difficult this was for the child, she learnt a lot about herself. She confirmed this when she said, 'I am the way I am because of what I experienced before I came to live with Mum and Dad. This was hard to do but when I look at the roots, which are my past, I understand that the past is connected to me today. Maybe that's why I hide food; I'm afraid I won't get any! That now makes sense.'

After they finished the tree, her parent asked her how she felt and her response was, 'It helped me to share things and I know there is more for me to learn about what happened in my past. I feel pretty pleased with myself that I was able to do this, and that's why I wrote on the scroll... "one small step for man and one giant leap for ... [she wrote her whole name down]".'

This was an amazing experience and reflection of how her past traumas affected her in her present.

The child's parent stared at the tree for a few minutes in silence and said, 'I never put the two together. It's all right there. I can see it. It all makes perfect sense.' This was an 'aha' moment for both child and parent and they hugged each other. For the first time the child said to her parent, 'I belong', owning this moment of what felt like victory and healing. We all had tears in our eyes. It was very moving to witness this treasured moment.

The behaviour tree is a powerful tool which offers insightful reflections and a means of connecting the present and the past, yielding vast learning potential for both child and parent. Here it identified the source of the child's behaviour, the actions of those in her past and the consequences for those in her present and future. It helped her work through her anger, trauma and fears, with her parent beside her to witness the enormity of a new awareness, supporting her child appropriately.

The behaviour tree shows us how our brains can be shaped by our experiences. It provides an insight into the child's internal working model which helps us and them to understand their current feelings, actions, repetitive behaviour and struggles, with the effect of reducing shame and increasing empathy towards these as a response to past trauma. At the same time it enhances the secure base of support and bond between child and parent. It gave this child an opportunity to express herself and to learn how she can begin to self-regulate, with a greater understanding of her internal and external world.

5. Creating a Timeline: witnessing the child's story, sharing the information gathered and making meaning.

So far in this chapter we have equipped you with a set of tools, techniques, and strategies to create 'scaffolding' which will strengthen the child-parent relationship, increase emotional literacy, self-esteem and manage powerful feelings. With this in place, you can progress to working through the birth family and the child's history, at the child's pace, based on the information gathered. The aim is to assist the child in sequencing and reframing (Rose 2012).

We cannot change the past, but we can change our understanding of past events and how we see ourselves in relation to them. A greater understanding can help those who have experienced childhood trauma to feel more positive in their present and see greater possibilities for their future. JK Rowling (2000 p.572) writes 'understanding is the first step to acceptance, and only with acceptance can there be recovery'.

In this section we suggest practice ideas and techniques that we have found helpful in supporting the Therapeutic Life Story Work process. We hope these may be of use to you and that you will experiment with them as well as creating and developing your own set of tools and techniques.

Rose (2012) suggests starting by exploring with the child the things that might be good and not so good about finding out more about their past. You could record these on the wallpaper as a list, a spider map or weighing scales. The good things might include knowing what happened and when and having answers to their questions. It is important to discuss the things that may not be so good; if it feels like too much information the child can ask to stop; if they are feeling sad or upset they can have a hug from their parent. If the child wishes to go ahead, you can identify goals for the timeline as part of the work; they will often be similar to the good things about exploring the past. These can be recorded as a scroll, with a goal post, or as a list. One child drew a golden trophy cup to write their goals on.

Next, using the wallpaper, or other medium, you can create a timeline of what the child knows or understands. By doing so you are witnessing the child's story, and starting here helps to identify not only what is known but also where the gaps are. Care is taken not to correct the child's understanding at this stage, but rather to witness and record it.

Once we have recorded the child's understanding of their timeline on the wallpaper, we start a new timeline to share the information we have gathered (the process of information gathering is detailed in Chapter 3). This is to share the family history and stories of those who have acted in the child's life, fill in the gaps, review information and consider the why, what, where, who, how and when, as well as associated feelings. This is all recorded on the wallpaper, including the thoughts and feelings, with the child or parent writing and drawing as much as they feel able.

To make it playful, we like to give the child a choice of how the timeline looks. It could be a river, road, racetrack, garden path, or whatever sparks the child's imagination. They may wish to choose a means of travelling along their timeline, such as boat, shark, tank or racing car. One child chose a tractor to travel in because they wanted to go slowly and not miss anything! The child can draw these images on the wallpaper, cut and paste from a magazine, or use electronic images if working online.

The information is then shared, a little at a time, usually in chronological order starting with the earliest information, for instance details about birth grandparents' lives, birth parents' childhoods, how birth parents met, the children they had, concerns and events leading to the child's move, details of moves and how the child came to be in their current situation.

Some children find it easier to start with the present or with their birth and work backwards. We give the child a choice about where we start. For example, one 17-year-old with autism needed to start with his birth in order to connect with and make sense of his parents' lives.

There is a wealth of ideas, activities and imagery to assist the child's exploration of their past. We have found the following to be particularly helpful: mind maps, squiggles, explaining why/ The Parent Thing, parenting wall, telling the truth, the Shield of Shame, the Cycle of Change, scaffolding questions and The Tree of Life.

Mind Maps, also known as mind models or spider maps, consist of a circle or other shape drawn on the wallpaper to contain the main idea, with lines that branch out to add information, insights, connected ideas, thoughts and feelings.

You can invite the child to make a representation of their life journey on paper using a mind map. It is an amazing way to support children with thinking, problem-solving, making new discoveries, visualising new ideas and looking at their life as one big puzzle. It helps to unlock their creativity, enhances memory recall and the clarity they gain from the exercise can transform their life.

Karla: *One child of 11 years drew an image of a road map to represent the number of foster carers he had lived with and how many dead-end streets he felt he had been on. Some of the* *streets went round and round, coming back on themselves, illustrating that he felt he had been in the same situation repeatedly, always coming back to being in one place for a short period of time and then being moved on to another. He spent several sessions drawing out his life map, which revealed a great deal of confusion, mixed messages, and a clear message that he did not belong yet! These streets accurately represented his life patterns and this sense of not belonging was, sadly, what he could trust.*

Doing this life mapping enabled him to understand why he felt as he did: sad, unhappy and wanting to feel settled. He accepted that one street can lead to another and that if he came to a dead end he could turn around and try another route. His ability to communicate what he needed improved and in time he was placed with a long-term foster family where he was much happier, feeling a greater sense of security and belonging.

We can use words to write a description of an experience or life event. A mind map, however, allows us to express or represent our understanding of this experience in one picture that captures more than we have originally understood. It invites and enables a child to contemplate more of their internal world, thinking and perspective on their life. You can use words, pictures, spider diagrams or maps, flow charts, drawings, systems maps, or be as creative as you like.

Karla: *We have already demonstrated the value of using **squiggles** to investigate feelings in Chapter 4. Figure 24 illustrates how an amazing seven-year-old child used this simple technique to create a timeline. She started out by using it to explore her emotions and the subsequent questions that she would like to ask her birth mother. It was not her intention to do a timeline. However, the squiggle she drew presented itself in* *such a way that it encouraged her to follow her instincts and develop a timeline in that moment. She began by drawing her safe place, that of her grandparents' garden. She helped to grow beans, potatoes, and strawberries and she felt proud of her gardening skills. This was a place where nothing bad could happen or be allowed to happen. She referred to her Therapeutic Life Story Work as her 'learning journey'. She was learning about herself, her past, her birth parents, why she was in care and how she felt about her life in the present.*

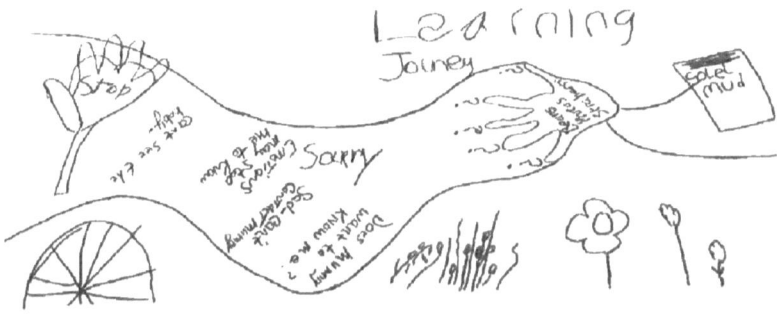

Figure 24: Timeline

There were places in the drawing where a stop sign appeared, meaning there was no entry. This indicated an area she was uncertain about; until she had answers she would not allow her birth mother any information about her and her siblings. Her squiggle drawing demonstrates the emotional growth and development she underwent through exploring the ideas, emotions, safety, and questions she wished to have answered. She was aware she might not get any answers but she felt confident in knowing what she knew about her past. She accepted that in time she might gain further clarity, or not. The hand she drew was her grandmother's and it was made of solid mud. It represented her security; she was safe in her grandmother's care. She wrote the word 'sorry' because she wanted her birth mother to say this to her in relation to all the harm, neglect and lack of thought she had experienced when in her care. The shape that looks like a wheel represented how her thoughts and feelings went round and round in her head. She acknowledged that she would like this wheel to help her move forward in life, for instance, in her dance and gymnastics competitions. This child was able to make use of the symbols in a way that would allow her to shift from one place to another internally and symbolically.

Explaining Why and the Parent Thing

There are many concepts that can help to explain why birth parents may not be able to look after their children. We find it helpful to keep in mind the five reasons that Nicholls (2005) identifies as to why children cannot live with their birth families.

1. Birth parents may have problems or troubles that make it really difficult for them to care for others and do all the parenting tasks.
2. They may never have been taught how to parent or care for others.
3. They may be too ill to be a parent or care for others.
4. They may not be able to learn how to be a parent or care for others.
5. They may have been shown the wrong way to parent or care for others.

We would add that, while it could broadly come under problems or troubles, some children cannot live with their families due to war and/or poverty in their country of origin. Parents may have made the difficult decision to send their children away from danger for their safety. For refugee and migrant children travelling alone there is often little information available to explain why, and they may be too traumatised and frightened to talk about their past.

Nicholls (2005) also proposes **The Parent Thing** exercise, based on Fahlberg's (1994) three parts of being a parent. Looking at parenting in this way can highlight for the child the complexities and many tasks of being a parent, as well as helping to clarify who performed each of these roles for them in the past, and who fulfils them now.

There are 3 parts to being a parent:

| **Birth parents** (birth parents first names) are the people who gave me Life, the way I look like my height, shape and build, colour of my hair and eyes, the size of my hands and feet, some of my character traits and natural talents, what illnesses I could get or might not get. They also gave me my birth names. | **Parenting parents** (name/s child uses) give me all the things I need to grow up strong and healthily. They keep me safe from any hurt or harm, give me hugs and cuddles, keep me warm when it's cold, look after me when I am ill, help me with school work, give me good food, help me learn to do new things, make sure I go to school, show me how to look after myself, take me on holidays and days out, give me clothes toys and books, show me how to enjoy and play games, teach me right from wrong, help me through problems or troubles, make me feel good about myself, show me how to care for others, **love me no matter what I say or do.** | **Legal parents** (Adoptive parent, or SW/ LA name if in foster care) give permission for me to go on holidays abroad, give permission for me to have an operation or medical treatment when needed, give permission for me to join the army, navy or air-force if I want to join before I am aged 18, they can decide on changing my name. |

Figure 25: Adapted from Nicholls 'The Parent Thing'

Nicholls (2005) suggests making a letterbox for each of the three categories shown in Figure 25, to post cards in. An alternative is to use a small box with three boxes which fit inside; this can be used in sessions as a game where the cards are sorted into each of the boxes. It serves to identify that there are things the birth parents have given the child, such as the way they look or their name, there are legal parts which may be separated from the other parts when the child goes into public care, and that there are many things the parenting parent needs to do for the child to be happy and healthy. One child Suzanne played the game with exclaimed, 'Hey, there are more of the parenting things'. The foster carer and I confirmed with a smile that there definitely are!

Parenting Wall
Many writers have identified how being a parent is like building a wall; we find this imagery helpful to use in our information sharing sessions. Suzanne has created the tool shown in Figure 26 for building a parenting wall by attaching the parenting parts of being a parent to wooden blocks and adding an oval shaped piece of wood on top with an image of a happy baby on one side and a distressed baby on the other.

The blocks are built up as a wall, to show how parents need to put all these things in place for their children to be happy and healthy. When exploring the child's or birth parents' early childhood, blocks can be taken away to show the elements that were missing, and the child can predict that the wall will fall down. The exercise provides a powerful visual demonstration of what went wrong; alongside the narrative, it helps to explain why the parents were unable to build a strong wall for their children.

Figure 26: Development of Nicholls 'The Parent Thing'

Please note that when doing this exercise in the context of the child's experiences it is important to rebuild the wall again based on their current situation, checking with them that they are currently receiving all the things children need from their parenting parent. It is also important to prepare the parenting parent for doing this exercise in the session: reassure them that this exercise is not based on what children want, but on what they need to be healthy and happy; this includes things like clear boundaries and guidance for safety.

Telling the Truth
Telling the truth and deciding when and what to share with the child in the sessions is an area that has caused us some concern and one where we have found it prudent to tread gently, due to the impact it may have on the child and family. It is important to consider how much the parents want us to share or how much the child can comprehend emotionally or psychologically. The amount of information that a child can process will vary greatly according to their abilities, learning challenges, age, or level of trauma. You may feel it is imperative that the child hears everything, but this may not always be possible as some children are not ready, able, or in the appropriate place to hear everything. Ask yourself the question, '*Who is this about?*' The answer must always be, '*The child!*'

We may want to come into a session and offer all the information we have gathered. However, that could be construed as our agenda and not that of the child. The child may have specific questions they want answers for, but this does not mean that they are ready to hear all the information gathered. Also, the parents may not want them to hear everything for various reasons. All of this needs to be taken into consideration. We find this can be frustrating as it is our role to share information with the child. However, we need to always keep in mind the request of the parents; they know their child and they trust us to respect their decision. It is about the child: they are the priority.

Not being able to offer the information you have gathered can leave you feeling as if you have not completed the work, but it is important to honour the parent's decision in relation to what we provide and how much. When we finish the work, they are the ones who continue to support the child, and we do not want to cause any further trauma. If we remember to stay alongside the child and do what is best for them, we will not cause any emotional or psychological harm.

With children of all ages, there will be times when they let us know they do not want to hear all the information we have gathered. They may not be aware of the actual information we have gathered, but they may have a sense that there are some things that they really do not want to hear.

We have worked with children who have made their feelings abundantly clear, either through their reluctant or hesitant behaviour, shutting down emotionally, or verbally expressing, 'I don't want to know any more'.

Karla: *In session five, one child of 13 made her preferences noticeably clear. Her older sister was in contact with their birth family and ran away from home constantly, disappearing for days. Observing this, the child made the decision that she did not want to know anything about her past, her birth parents or birth family and indicated this on the wallpaper. After several months her family reached an emotional crisis point, with various professionals becoming involved. The contact with the birth family resulted in so much fear, anxiety and a sense of being at risk even at home that meeting her birth family, at that time, was not something she wanted to engage with. The child* *concluded, 'I do not want to know. It is not safe and I don't like what's happened'.*

Throughout the work I was kept informed of what had been taking place. During session five we did a timeline, and my knowledge of events prompted me to approach it in a different way to that which I had learnt. Reflecting upon the child's needs, my thoughts before the session were to provide her with enough time and space for her voice to be heard. Her mum always attended the sessions and was incredibly supportive, but the child's voice was not always heard. Mum provided us some time at the beginning of the session as she had during the last session. The child let mum know that she could come back later!

I suggested we do a timeline and invited the child to draw a scale or curving line and mark it from the age of zero to five in her own way. The child immediately took her pen and drew out a curved line and marked it accordingly. We agreed that she would choose a coloured pen to mark down what she knew of herself, based on her experience and her memory. She first wrote what she knew and remembered up to the age of three (this was when she was adopted), noting that some of the events she recalled were based on family information. She then added a few things for ages four to five, such as nursery school and moving to a new home.

She chose another coloured pen to mark down the information that she had been told about herself from the ages of zero to five by others, such as her parents, older sister or professionals that she had seen up to the age of 13. She began writing and writing, extremely quickly. It appeared that she could not get the words out fast enough. She did not speak or look up from the wallpaper during the whole process; she just let it flow out of her.

This space was hers and it allowed her the security and freedom to own what belonged to her.

When she had completed that part of the exercise I offered her another coloured pen to attach feelings to what she had written. It became apparent that this part of the exercise needed a little longer to process and complete. She reflected on her experiences and what others had told her about her past. I noticed that she wrote down her feelings only in relation to her own experiences and not in relation to the information that had been given to her by others. There were a few places where she was not sure of her feelings, so we talked about it, and once she had matched the appropriate feeling to her experience she wrote it down with precision.

When she had finished, she sat back and looked at her timeline. We reflected on all that she had experienced, the information she had heard from others, and her feelings at this point. We were beginning to connect the traumas and difficulties that she had been experiencing recently to those that she had experienced early on in her life.

She then decided to add ages 10 to 14 years, as she was going to be 14 that year and wanted that to be a part of her timeline. She repeated the identical process she had carried out for ages zero to five. To observe her body language, the intensity with which she poured out all her experiences, thoughts and emotions, her facial expressions of determination and the tightness with which she held the pen, was an amazing experience and a privilege.

When she had completed this process from ages 10 to 14 we sat back and looked at everything she had written, experienced, remembered and knew of herself and others. She looked over to me and just said, 'I feel better now. And I do not want to know any more about my past or my birth family. I do not want to meet them. I do not want to have them in my life. End of!', all of which she wrote on the wallpaper. She also added *'This is a straightforward decision'* and *'It's MY decision.'* The room was full of a tangible sense of relief, clarity and conclusion.

I was very aware that the child's mother had not been present in the session. I felt for the mum who was very caring, attentive and loving, and was being very patient and respectful of her daughter's wishes; I knew this must have felt difficult for her. But this session was all about the child having the space and time to express herself without having to be concerned about her mum's feelings. It was clear that in this session the child had made her voice fully heard. She felt empowered and at peace with what she had been waiting to safely share.

In this work you never know what is going to occur in the sessions, let alone how your planning of the session is going to be received. On this occasion I trusted my instincts to allow the child to lead it in the way she needed. The sense of release and validation that this child experienced was enormous. Healing, emotional restoration and repair had taken place! It is vital that we listen to the child, parents, ourselves and other professionals so that we can be fully present in the room with the child and all they hold in them.

Van der Kolk (2014 p.47) notes that traditionally in psychology and psychotherapy talking about distressing feelings is advised as a way of resolving them; *'However, as we've seen, the experience of trauma itself gets in the way of being able to do that'*. Children may not always have clear memories of their life experiences that they can recall, but as Van der Kolk (2014) identifies, memories will be stored in the body. Children can sometimes show us what they have experienced with their body, for example one child moved uncomfortably on the floor in a session when we were thinking about his early childhood experiences of abuse and neglect, it was helpful for him to be guided to notice this and connect with how frightened and uncomfortable he felt. His adoptive parent was alongside, comforting him, and this experience seemed to help release the trauma from his body and change where and how the memory was stored so that he could recall and consider the experience without feeling and acting as if it was happening in the moment.

Suzanne: *With one young child, who had a short attention span and had not quite mastered the alphabet or spelling, I found that making stickers with images from birth family photos and clip art proved a helpful way of exploring his story. As we talked about each person in his story, such as great- and great-great-grandparents', he put a sticker on the timeline we were creating on the wallpaper and added symbols and drawings to record our discussion. When we came to inspect the events which led to him and his older brothers moving from his birth parents' care, Lego proved helpful for playing out these events. We built a Lego house and created pipe cleaner figures to represent all the people involved including education, health and social services professionals, and people in his local community. Seeing his home surrounded with the 12 people who had had concerns about him and his brothers, proved a powerful image for him. It served to provide a light bulb moment of what people were concerned about, how he wasn't being kept safe and why he wasn't able to continue living with his birth parents. We started off using the child's Lego, but I realised on reflection after the session that these were his toys and would come to serve as a reminder of his neglect. I now have a set of Lego boards, bricks and minifigures to use and have taken care to ensure they reflect differences in age, ability, and ethnicity.*

It may be necessary to stop the sessions if safety is compromised. Stopping the work can be a difficult decision but it may be best for the child and family. When a family goes into crisis during this work, for various reasons, it is fundamental to prioritise what is necessary for them.

It is imperative that you discuss your concerns with the parents, and supervision can support you in making your decision. One child had started daily contact with her birth family during her Therapeutic Life Story Work. She became confused because what she was learning from her sessions contrasted with what her birth family were telling her. She did not know who or what to believe. It triggered her early traumas and she became violent, repeating what she had experienced in her early years. As this escalated it became apparent that she was not in an emotional state to continue the work while she and her parents were at risk. It was decided to stop the work until the child was more settled and was able to engage in the Therapeutic Life Story Work process while feeling safe and secure. This was not an easy decision, but it was crucial to safeguarding the child.

We have also had to stop work, or to focus more on repair and strengthening of the relationship, where the relationship between a child and parent has been in crisis and their adoption close to disrupting. These experiences indicate to us that Therapeutic Life Story Work does not work as a crisis intervention. The child needs to feel safe in the present before they can explore their past experiences. Other work and support may be needed for parents and/ or the child before undertaking or resuming Therapeutic Life Story Work, as previously discussed in Chapter 2.

Conversely it may be the parents who are reluctant about information being shared with the child. It is important to discuss this at the outset, and to support parents in exploring their feelings and the underlying reasons for them. Keefer and Schooler (2000) provide a helpful guide, *Telling the Truth to Your Adopted or Foster Child,* highlighting important areas for parents to consider and how having information within the safety of the sessions can assist their child in making sense of the past and how not telling children important information about their past can impact negatively on their relationship when they find out in the future.

The Shield of Shame

We use the concept of the shield of shame (Golding and Hughes 2012) when we are sharing information to help understand choices and behaviour. Shame is part of healthy human development. It tells us when we have done something wrong and may need to apologise or change our behaviour. Within safe and secure parent-child relationships children can experience small amounts of shame that are manageable for them when boundaries are set. The parent sees the shame and helps the child to understand that it is their behaviour, not them as a person, that is not okay. There is no threat to the relationship; rather it is part of parenting and learning.

However, in the context of abuse and trauma, shame becomes linked with a core belief, where the person feels shame about themselves as a person rather than appropriate guilt about their actions. The resulting perception that they are inherently bad and not good enough is so overwhelming and terrible that it triggers a fear response which causes them to get defensive or hide. The person can develop a 'shield of shame', consisting of a range of strategies, to help protect themselves against this feeling, as illustrated in Figure 27.

Figure 27: Adapted from Golding and Hughes (2012) Shield of Shame
(Captain America shield drawn by young person)

These strategies are generally unhelpful for the person, but the feeling of shame is so terrible that they can become established patterns of behaviour for those who have experienced trauma and abuse. Brown (2006) considers how people may protect themselves from intense feelings of shame by avoidance, getting angry or trying to please.

The shield of shame can be drawn out on the wallpaper to show the child how people defend themselves against feeling shame by lying, minimising, blaming others and getting angry. The child may recognise themselves in this and it can help them to understand not only why they may behave in this way, but also why their birth parent may have been unable to accept children's services concerns, make changes and make use of support offered.

Suzanne: *With one set of birth parents whose six children had been removed nine years previously due to chronic neglect, it* was clear that they still laid the responsibility for this with others. The birth parents maintained they had been unable to clean the mess in their home because of the social workers' presence and that children's services had conspired with the housing department to get their four-bedroom house back by removing their children. They also blamed the maternal grandparents and the children's behaviour, and claimed that the situation had not been as bad as everyone had said it was. They felt the judge had only listened to what the social workers and police had said and not to what they had to say. After further discussion they were able to accept that there were some things that had needed to change but could not identify what these were, stating that every household has things it could improve on. The 'shield of shame' proved helpful for the child to understand their birth parents view and why they were unable to make the changes needed.

The impact of shame is a useful concept to consider in Therapeutic Life Story Work sessions. Hughes (2007) suggests that 'when shame becomes exposed and expressed and is responded to with empathy, the resulting intersubjective experience is often transforming'. We have witnessed powerful moments of healing where the child has exclaimed, 'Now I get it, so it wasn't all my fault!'

Suzanne: *I remember working with one child who drew his brain as being full of rubbish and commented that was him; he was all rubbish. In a later session, when we discussed his birth maternal grandmother's life, he became disengaged. I decided to try the 'glasses exercise' (Rose 2012 p.57) which consists of two glasses representing the parent and child relationship. Water is added as each person's 'essence' to show how in secure attachment the water is passed freely between the glasses as the baby cries to get her need met and the* *parent meets the child's needs (gives attention and care) and the child gives back to the parent (perhaps through smiling and growing). Insecure attachment can be demonstrated by showing how the parent's essence was being spilt due to adverse experiences causing them to put a lid on their glass to protect their essence and survive, which serves to block them from responding to meet their child's needs. This provided a visual demonstration of attachment namely why his birth grandmother could not give the love and care his birth mother needed. This proved to be a powerful healing moment for the child. He took the glasses and demonstrated secure attachment, as I had done, saying this was him and his (adoptive) mother. He then mirrored my demonstration of insecure attachment, saying that his birth mother had not been able to give him the love and care he needed because she had needed to put a lid on her feelings.*

This caused a significant shift in his understanding; he could now see why his birth mother had not been able to parent him, in the context of her own childhood experiences, and that it had not been his fault or failing. This shift in thinking led him to exclaim 'That's why my birth mum couldn't look after me, because her mum couldn't put the cloak of love around me like you do Mum'. In reviewing the child's drawing of his brain towards the end of our work he said he no longer felt he was rubbish. He appeared to feel more settled and was no longer displaying unrest and resulting challenging behaviour.

The Cycle of Change: It can be difficult for children to understand why their birth parents were not able to make the necessary changes to their parenting that were identified by children's services. The cycle of change can assist them with this and offer insights into their own behaviour. Prochaska and DiClemente (1983) identify that the cycle of change consists of six parts:

1. Pre-contemplation: no intention of changing behaviour
2. Contemplation: aware problem exists but with no commitment to action
3. Preparation: intent on taking action to address the problem
4. Action: active modification of behaviour
5. Maintenance: sustained change where new behaviour replaces old
6. Relapse: fall back to old patterns of behaviour

It explains to the child that you first need to be aware that a problem exists before you can make changes, and it acknowledges how hard it can be to make changes to learnt ways of behaving. It gives hope as it emphasises that from relapse you can start again at the action stage and continue on an upward spiral as you learn from each relapse.

Suzanne: *Following a long period of no incidents of aggression, one young person I worked with hurt his parent and there was subsequent police involvement. He needed help with his feelings of devastation and shame. Working through the cycle of change with him on the wallpaper gave him hope that he was not back at square one as he had thought, but was on an upward spiral of change where relapse can be an inevitable part of this change. We were able to consider what had triggered the relapse and to ensure that he could learn from this.*

Scaffolding Questions are useful when creating a timeline on wallpaper with a child. Vygotsky (1962) suggests scaffolding questions can be used to guide and support exploration of thoughts and feelings, these can be used to assist the child in making sense of the past. You can ask the child a series of incremental questions, such as, 'I'm wondering what that might have been like ... what you are thinking as you hear this? What do we know that might have led to this action?' In this way you generate curiosity, engage the child in meaning making and add new and multi-perspective layers to their understanding. By giving voice to the thoughts that may be raised internally and transferring these onto the wallpaper by writing or drawing, the child's internal world is brought to the outside, so it can be explored and new meaning may be gained. Scaffolding questions can be compared to climbing a set of stairs or constructing a frame alongside a building to ensure safety. You need to start at the ground level and build the layers as you go. Doing this as you create a timeline secures the child the feeling of safety they need to continue the journey of exploring their past, at their pace.

The Tree of Life: Jenny Chigwende, a therapist who undertook the Therapeutic Life Story Work Diploma in 2016 and a valued peer supervisor, has taught us how helpful the tree of life exercise can be in Therapeutic Life Story Work. This model was developed by Ncazelo Ncube, a child psychologist from Zimbabwe, and David Denborough (2014), narrative therapist at the Dulwich Centre in Adelaide. It is designed as a workshop but can be beneficial in Therapeutic Life Story Work when exploring the past, present and future. As we have already shown, the metaphor of a tree is so helpful in therapeutic work; here the message is that trees can face similar experiences to humans, suggesting that if they can survive then so can we.

There are three parts to this exercise: the tree of life, the forest of life and the storms of life.

1. Tree of Life
Participants are asked to draw a tree, its roots, trunk, branches, leaves, fruit, the ground it is in, and imagine that each part of the

tree represents something about their life. What type of tree would it be? What sort of roots would it have?

> *Roots*: the roots of the tree represent where you come from (village, town, country), your family history (origins, family name, ancestry, extended family), names of people who have taught you the most in your life, your favourite place at home, a treasured song or dance.
>
> *Ground*: the ground represents where you live now and activities you are engaged with in your daily life.
>
> *Trunk*: the trunk of the tree is an opportunity to write your skills, qualities and abilities (caring, loving, kindness) and what you are good at.
>
> *Branches*: the branches of the tree are where you can write your hopes, dreams and wishes for the directions of your life.
>
> *Leaves*: the leaves of the tree represent significant people in your life, who may be alive or have passed on. Think about people who have influenced the person that you are now.
>
> *Fruits*: the fruits of the tree are the gifts you have been given, not necessarily material things, but gifts of being cared for, of being loved and acts of kindness.

In a workshop setting, participants have some time to create their trees and then tell the story of their tree to one another in pairs. They then reflect on how it felt to tell their story. The aim is to build and acknowledge 'a second story' about each person's life; this second story consists of the skills, abilities, hopes and dreams of each person and the histories of these. This can help to celebrate the things in their life that have gone well, not just past traumas. It can help the person to recognise their skills, gifts they have been give and things that make them special.

Suzanne: *I used this first part of the activity in a session with a child where the trunk helped to show how many skills and abilities she had. The branches, leaves and fruit showed the richness of her key adults, her memories and the gifts she had received. Her birth family were in the roots, along with many unknowns and unanswered questions, as she had been adopted at birth. Answering these questions and filling in these gaps became the goals for us to achieve during our work together.*

2. Forest of Life

In a workshop the trees are stuck on the wall to create a forest of life. Participants choose one or two trees on which to write words of encouragement, support, and appreciation. The therapist asks each person what they were drawn to, what images came to their minds as they listened, how these expressions resonated with them and how they were moved as a result of hearing these stories. In Therapeutic Life Story Work sessions parents could create their own tree on the wallpaper alongside the child's, to form a 'forest'.

3. Storms of Life

Like us, the trees and forests are still open to the dangers of life. From their new place of strength, ability and hope, participants are invited to consider the challenges they are experiencing, how these difficulties are affecting them, how they have responded and if there are other ways they might respond more successfully. They write their ideas on paper. The aim is to talk about difficulties in ways that are not re-traumatising, using the collective language of storms of life can make it easier for people to talk about less positive stories by creating distance between their experience and the problem. It can enable them to draw on the ability and knowledge they already have to respond and treats them as experts rather than victims of their own life and can offer a sense of hope. Storms are seen as part of life and, if we can see how we have overcome them, we can grow from experience and become stronger.

6. Exploring Hopes and Dreams

After the meaning making sessions, we reserve the penultimate session to look at hopes, dreams, goals and aspirations. Now that they know about their past and can understand their present situation, you can guide the child in thinking about their future. This can include considering what jobs or career they might like, where they see themselves living, or what they imagine their interests and hobbies will be.

It can be helpful to have a worksheet with sentence completion statements such as those listed below:

- In the future I would like to be ...
- I would like to be living ...
- I would like to be feeling ...
- I imagine my hobbies would be ...

One 7-year-old child said they wanted to be an artist, remain living in their current home, and go fishing. Another child, aged 9, wanted to be either working for the government as a spy, or working in Asda, to own a black Lamborghini, to be tall, to be paying bills in their current house and to remain kind, helpful and loving.

Footprints Exercise
Suzanne: Karla suggested this exercise to me, it is one that she developed years ago as a play therapist. I used it in working with

a young adult, as a way of exploring the past, the present and future. The aim is to draw three footprints on the wallpaper, either the person drawing these freehand or the practitioner making an outline from the child's foot, to represent the *past* (where these feet have been), *present* (where they are now) and the *future* (where they are going). The exercise worked well in identifying three powerful words: that his childhood experience had been *tricky*, in the present moment he was feeling *lost*, in the future he wanted to be *stable*. Thinking about the past, present and future in this visual way gave the young adult a sense of clarity, empathy and direction about his next step along with a sense of hope for the future.

7. Ending Session

We have developed a format for the final session, but it is really important that the child and parent are involved in the planning and preparation; it may be the first positive and planned ending the child has had.

The child may wish to consider who they would like to be present. Would they like to invite close family members such as parents, grandparents, brothers or sisters? Consider when and what time this session will take place; an evening session might enable a working parent to attend. A cake is, of course, a good part of any ending so you may need to discuss who will make it and what type it should be.

Our final session, as advocated by The Rose Model of Therapeutic Life Story Work, usually consists of reviewing the work done by 'walking along the wallpaper' with the child narrating the story it tells. This can be an extremely valuable way for the child to let a second parent know about the work undertaken. In turn the reflections from this parent about the information they are hearing can be extremely helpful for the child. Bear in mind that the parent may need preparation for this session if they have not previously been involved.

A 'box of hearts' provides a lovely visual representation of all the people who love and care about the child. You will need around 20–30 hearts (8–12mm red glass heart-shaped beads work well, or wooden ones that they can write names or memories on, with a variety of sizes to provide choice) and a box to put them in. We suggest you have a range of boxes available for the child to choose from, in various sizes, shapes, material and design (heart-shaped, with hearts on, plain, colourful, wooden, tin or metal), from around 5cm in diameter. A small metal treasure chest with velvet lining has proved a particularly popular choice, together with a wooden one that they can decorate themselves.

The exercise starts with the child making a list of all the people who have loved and cared for them in their lives. The child often chooses to include parents, pets, brothers, sisters, friends, and sometimes you as the worker. You can prompt the child to choose whether they would like to include any birth family members. The child counts the number of people on the list, chooses a heart for each one and places it in the box they have chosen. They can look at their box and count the hearts anytime they want to remind themselves just how many people love and care about them.

The ending can then be celebrated with a cake, adding a candle for each of the hearts the child has added to the box. Tell the child that the candles and the light from them represents all the love and care that people have for them. As they blow out the candles, they can imagine all this love and care shining in their heart. Then it is time to eat the cake and welcome in any other family members the child has invited to join the session. Suzanne also presents the Therapeutic Life Story Book, created from and reflecting the work undertaken, at the final session. The life story books are explored further in Chapter 5.

It is such a privilege to witness the process the child goes through as sessions progress, and to be part of the moments of movement where healing takes place – the goal or true purpose of this important work. The Rose Model provides the foundation for this, and we too develop and grow within this process.

Chapter 5
Creating a Record of the Sessions: The Life Story Book

In this chapter we consider how to undertake stage three of The Rose Model of Therapeutic Life Story Work, where we create a life story book for and with the child. Here we provide an outline of the styles and format we use. We acknowledge that while we each have our own styles and approach there is no specific format. Each book will be as unique as each child and as different as each intervention.

The aim is for the life story book to reflect the process of the work you have done together, the meanings made, and to celebrate the child's journey. In this context the resulting life story book differs from the more traditional life story books made for an adopted child at the point of, or shortly after, their adoption. The Rees (2009) Model is generally used as a guide for life story books made for children at the point of adoption, though we have found the quality, accuracy and usability varies greatly. Life story books made for a child at the time of their adoption are designed as a tool to support the child's future journey of understanding their story.

At the outset of Therapeutic Life Story Work, any existing life story books and later life letters that have been compiled for the child can be viewed and kept in mind. A Therapeutic Life Story Work book can complement and build upon an existing life story book if this has been helpful for the child.

We take care and attention in producing a book and ensure that it is well presented and an accurate reflection of the process of the work. The length can vary depending on the needs of the child and how far the work was able to progress, but generally a completed Therapeutic Life Story Work book may consist of around 80 to 150 single-sided A4 pages. We estimate they take around 40 to 80 hours to complete, though generally as independent workers we can only charge for around 30 hours.

We usually create the life story book electronically, using programmes such as PowerPoint or Publisher. We recommend involving the child in creating their book. During the final few sessions, they can be involved in editing and choosing fonts, layout, colours and content. This has often been a valuable learning process for us, especially where the child's knowledge of using PowerPoint has been greater than ours. The children we have worked with teach us so much in so many ways!

The child decides what they wish to have in their life story book. It generally includes photographs of the child, their current family and birth family members as well as images of the wallpaper from the sessions, alongside the narrative created from the information we gathered and the child's reflections, thoughts and feelings that have been explored.

The books are usually printed on A4 100gsm paper and presented in an A4 folder in a colour of the child's choice, with the pages displayed in good quality and thickness (70 micron works well) individual plastic punched pocket top opening sleeves. This presentation style enables the child to remove pages or sections if they wish to when showing their book to someone, or to make future changes if new or conflicting information comes to light. We have also used photo album 12" x 12" size books for older children who like to have something different. We provide a copy of the child's therapeutic life story book in electronic form, usually on a memory stick that can be password protected. This provides a backup copy which can be changed in the future if needed, re-printed if the original is destroyed or damaged. We have used wooden cased memory sticks with an image of a tree and the words 'Life Story Book' printed on them. A ribbon can be added to tie it to the folder the book is presented in or given to the parent for safe keeping. The child and legal parent can decide if a copy should be held by the department responsible for the child. It is helpful to have a discussion with the child and parent about whom they might share their book with.

The aim is for the book to reflect the content and journey of the sessions, including the child's thoughts and feelings. We generally follow the Rees (2009) model by starting with the present, then telling the 'what, why, where, when and how' of past events, including the different perspectives of those involved, returning to the safety of the present and then looking to the future. However, a great deal more is added which reflects the work undertaken.

The following is an outline of the general format we use if we have covered these areas, as the order and content should reflect the sessions, including discussions and conclusions reached:

Front page: drawn or designed and directed by the child. Usually a photo of the child, of their choosing, and a heading containing their name and the words 'Life Story Book'.

All about me pages: the child in their lives now with photos and information of themselves, family, pets, home, and photo of their 'hands of interests' drawing.

Working together: a photo of the child and parent working on the wallpaper, an account of why you were meeting and what the book is about.

Creating safety: examples of the games you played and exercises undertaken to create safety, such as photos of the parts of the wallpaper showing 'Hands of Safety', the working agreement and the balloon journey to explore happy, sad, and safe places.

Self-esteem and identity work: photos of the wallpaper showing 'hands of pride', the body outline, and strengths and qualities exercises.

Exploring feelings and strategies to help manage them, which may include the hand model of the brain (Siegel and Bryson 2011).

The good and not so good aspects of exploring the past, and goals identified for the next part of the work.

Timeline: starting with what the child identified knowing or understanding about their lives.

Outline of the types of child abuse and roles of professionals such as social worker, judge and courts. This can include the different ways children join families, what children need, 'the parent thing' (Nicholls 2005), the parenting wall and attachment exercise (Rose 2012).

Birth family trees: a genogram of the birth father's and mother's family trees can be constructed from information gathered. Geographical location and professions can be included where known, as well as symbols and layout to show adoptive and foster families.

Birth family history in chronological order, starting with birth grandparents' lives (if information is known) and birth parents' childhoods. You could start with maternal birth family up to birth mother's adulthood, and then paternal birth family up to birth father's adulthood.

How parents met, details of the children they had and the events that occurred, such as children's services' concerns before the child's birth.

The child's birth: pages to celebrate the child's birth can include any photos of the child, the hospital they were born in, birth parents account of their birth, how their name was chosen, the meaning of their name, the day of the week they were born and what was happening in their country or the world at that time.

Chronological timeline of events: the child's journey to the present, telling the story of what happened, including the views of the birth family and the professionals involved. The exploration of this information and the child's reflections on it.

Birth parents present lives, including their wishes for the child's future. Some birth parents may wish to be supported in writing a letter to their child, a copy of which can be added here.

The child in the present, including how they tell their story now and any thoughts and feelings about it.

Looking to the future: the child's hopes and dreams for their future.

Ending: page about the ending exercise if you have done one, for example the heart exercise representing all those who have loved and cared for the child.

Letter from the practitioner, perhaps acknowledging how well the child has done, identifying the child's qualities you have noticed, and wishes for their future (an example can be seen in Appendix D).

Additional blank pages and sleeves for the child to add to their book if they wish.

Rose (2012 p.157) identifies that *'the therapist is the writer, the parent is the proof reader and the child is the 'editor-in-chief – and whilst the child does not write her own book, she is the arbiter of what goes in and what stays out. This will include photographs, pictures, family trees, memories, letters, and art work by the child, the carers and the therapist'.*

The child's thoughts and feelings are to be included in the book, we add these as speech and thought bubbles alongside the narrative and/ or in a different colour to help them stand out from the information that has been shared. Different colours can be used in the text for each person, for example, purple for the information birth mother has given, green for the information birth father has given, black for the information from children's services and blue for the narrator/ child's voice.

We follow the advice from Rose (2012 p.157) that *'It should be written to meet the needs and awareness of the child and information should be focused on the child's journey and not on others. The child must be able to recognise her work within the book and the narrative has to be first person and reflect the child's interpretation of the story of her life'.*

It is important to only include things you have discussed or that the child knows about. There should be no surprises for the child in their book. A decision may have been made not to share some details of information, or there may be information that the child did not want to hear; this will be given to the legal parent.

Rose (2012) suggests returning a month or so later to deliver the life story book. However, we generally present the book to the child (wrapped as a gift) on our last session.

We have received lots of positive feedback from children and their families about the books we have created. One child we worked with showed his book to his adoptive grandparent after the final session, which provided a way of telling her his story. The child's parent felt this process had given the grandparent a greater understanding of the trauma the child had experienced. This in turn led to a greater understanding of his behaviour, which strengthened their relationship. Another child, we were told, read and reread their Therapeutic Life Story Work book over and over.

Yet another was so delighted she shared it with her brother. They did not usually get on well, but her book felt so special that she went through it with him page by page, taking time to reflect on the wallpaper work and the photos that she had selected. She was able to tell her brother what had been causing her all the difficulties from their past and it gave them an opportunity to become closer than before. She even shared the chocolate cake we had on the final session with him!

It validated the importance of this work when an adult made contact to say they had shown their Life Story Book to their teenage child as a way of helping them know more about own (the parents) childhood experiences.

Chapter 6
The Importance of Endings

> 'We either own our stories or they own us.
> Only when we have the courage to own our history are we able to write a brave new ending to our story
> THIS IS TRUE IN OUR LIVES, OUR FAMILIES, OUR COMMUNITIES, AND OUR COUNTRY'.
> Brené Brown 2020

There is so much to say about endings. How we approach them can offer a child a very different experience compared to the endings in their past.

It may sound odd, but we believe that endings start at the beginning. When we meet with a family, we have already put some kind of plan together regarding what we are going to cover in the initial session with the parents. Then we consider how we will work with the child and parents. As we start that work, we start to consider our ending. How many sessions are we offering, when will we be finishing and how would the child like us to say good-bye? We need to know when our last session will be. While the date may change for various reasons, it is important to have a timescale in mind in order to have an ending to work towards.

Endings require planning. Therapeutic Life Story Work has a beginning, middle and an end; that end can also feel like the beginning of a new chapter. Many of the children with whom we work have not had the opportunity to say goodbye to their birth families, or to people with whom they were close. Their experiences of endings may have been very abrupt, chaotic and unplanned. Some children still hold the idea in their minds of saying goodbye to their birth family, and so it is imperative that we model a positive and planned ending which will hopefully have a positive effect on their overall wellbeing and future relationships.

We find that it always supports the child to know when we will be ending our work together. At the beginning we let them know how many sessions we are going to have, and at various stages throughout the sessions we remind them how many we have had and how many remain. This ensures the child is fully aware that we are working towards an ending in our work.

We prepare them for how they (and we!) might feel as we end our work together; there is likely to be a feeling of sadness, but we may also have other feelings, such as a sense of achievement at finding their story. For children who have been able to externalise, investigate and internalise their thoughts, feelings and wishes, it can be said that you are ending as you have reached the goals you set and that they have now heard all the information about their past that you know.

The child is very much part of the ending, as it is their journey, but sometimes we need to take time out to work through our own endings or lack of experiencing good endings. Our endings could include bereavement, loss of a job, home, family, pet or separation from those that we love or care for. It may be that we need to have support so that we can support the child appropriately. You need to be aware that coming towards the ending of our work could feel like another loss. It is the ending of a relationship that the child has come to trust and we need to say our goodbyes in a planned and positive way. The aim is for the child to feel heard, valued and respected by the work.

THE IMPORTANCE OF ENDINGS

We believe it is imperative to talk about endings. At one time one of us finished working with her supervisor of many years, at the same time as ending Therapeutic Life Story Work with six children and their parents. We have realised that we need to take not only the child into consideration concerning the endings, but also the parent and ourselves. Everyone is affected and everyone will have their own experience to manage. We plan to give the child and their parent a positive experience which will have a beneficial impact on them as a family unit, and upon us too!

Our work is exciting, challenging and rewarding, and can resonate with us years later. To this day we can become tearful remembering the relationships with children, young people and their parents, the lessons we have learnt and the loss of the phenomenal experiences that we shared, which have now come to an end. The journeys we take with these children are powerful and can be healing and poignant to ourselves as well as for the child and their families.

We know in our work we can have abrupt and unplanned endings due to circumstances beyond our control. Sometimes a parent chooses to discontinue the work, due to fear of the child learning the truth about their past, or funding cuts mean the work has to stop. We have experienced unplanned endings where there have been family difficulties or risk to the family due to the child's anger or heightened behaviour. In all these circumstances it is important to aim to have some form of goodbye and acknowledgement of why the work is ending.

Karla had to stop a Therapeutic Life Story Work intervention because the child was threatening to physically hurt Karla and her parents. This was not an easy decision to make and it took time to process; the experience led her to consider whether she could have done anything different, and whether accepting this referral had been the right decision.

It is imperative for us all to be aware of what is taking place within us and, in light of that, we invite you to consider the following questions: do you make time to work through endings, whether that be with a child, family, colleague, friend, supervisor or someone in your peer group? How do you work with an ending and are you aware of what it brings up for you, perhaps from your past? How are you supported while supporting a child and parents through Therapeutic Life Story Work?

While you support the child and their family, you also need to consider your own needs. Talking to your clinical supervisor and peers about your endings can help you to understand what impacts you and how that might affect you in the next ending you have with a family.

Karla: *It is extremely helpful and supportive to include the child in the planning stages of the ending. The first time I undertook Therapeutic Life Story Work with a child I asked her, during session 12 of 20, if she had any thoughts about how she would like to spend the last session. It may sound premature, but I knew about her history. She had been moved from one foster carer to another, with a total of nine homes before she was four years old, the endings of which had been abrupt and scary.*

I knew I had to prepare her well in advance for the ending of our work so that it did not leave her feeling abandoned. I wanted her to have a different experience of an ending, and especially one where she was involved in the planning. Knowing the child, I knew she would want a chocolate cake: it was her favourite food! So, using the wallpaper we wrote down the things we thought we would like to have and do in that last session. I drew a chocolate cake with a card and the child also drew a chocolate cake alongside a box, which represented a gift she wanted to give me, although she wouldn't say what it was. Her mum also drew a card and a box with 'thank you' in big letters.

The family and I agreed the date of our planned ending: it would be on a Saturday so the whole family could attend. We also considered the amount of time we would need for our ending so that it was not hurried; not like the child's previous years' of experiences, being rushed from one carer to another, with no proper ending and no discussions or warning that she was going to be moved yet again. It was important that I got this right for her and that the time she needed for this ending was in place and available. It turned out to be a positive ending and the child declared it was a 'celebration of her and her life'.

An ending can lead to another beginning and new beginnings can be referred to as a 'new chapter'. For instance, if you move out of your home after many years, you make a new start or a beginning. You live in a different house, in a different environment and area. You are presented with a piece of paper that says 'This is your house', while also knowing that your old home now belongs to someone else. When we complete our Therapeutic Life Story Work we present the child with their book; this is part of acknowledging the ending of this work. We knew at the beginning that their book was part of the ending.

Take a moment and ask yourself: what would you like to be presented with as an acknowledgement of your part of this work? Be aware of these wants and needs. They may also form part of the child's needs to mark this ending. You are very much a part of this ending and it is important to be mindful of yourself, alongside the child and family.

Coming to the end of our work with a child and their parents, we have a review or ending meeting to take stock of what their experience of Therapeutic Life Story Work has been like. This is an opportunity for all of us to share our experiences of this journey and to acknowledge where we were when we started and where we are as we are ending. Like the midway review meeting, we compile a report which is written to the child, in the second person, and invite the child to attend.

Karla: *Children can say the most profound things. Sometimes at the end of our work they ask if they can continue seeing us. I ask them, 'If you had a choice, how long would you like to see me for?' Some responses have been, 'Until I am 100 years old', or 'Until I am 25 so we can go to the movies or get some ice cream'. So, you see, endings are important. They allow us to hear what this work has been like for the child.*

There are so many different activities and ideas you can use to make your last session special, some of which we have outlined in Chapter 4. You will learn, through your own work, experiences and reflections, how best to support each child through their ending of Therapeutic Life Story Work. Clinical and peer supervision can support you to feel as prepared as you can for presenting the child with their Therapeutic Life Story Work book. It all takes time, energy, thought and hours of reflecting and care.

Some children may not want to go through their Therapeutic Life Story Work book during that last session with you, as it is time to focus on saying goodbye, having fun with you and acknowledging what they are feeling, all of which are important parts of the ending of our working relationship.

We write a letter for each child that we include in the back of the book (an example can be seen in Appendix D), together with a final page acknowledging that now is the time to go and live the rest of their lives. We also usually include a few blank pages at the very end for the child to continue writing or adding to their life story.

So much of the importance of the ending of Therapeutic Life Story Work lies in the preparation at the beginning of our work. It is essential that we acknowledge the ending at the very start, not just for the child, but also for the parent, the family as a unit and for you. The power of endings is not to be underestimated!

Chapter 7
Measuring Outcomes

How do we know if a Therapeutic Life Story Work intervention has been helpful, and why do we need to know? Here we consider the outcomes for children taking part in Therapeutic Life Story Work and the importance of measuring these outcomes in order to evidence, be accountable for, develop, reflect and learn from practice, and ensure the quality of the service provided.

It is generally accepted that Therapeutic Life Story Work is a positive intervention which is beneficial to the child's emotional wellbeing. Jones (2017 p.282) suggests that there are broader social advantages of Therapeutic Life Story Work, such as 'improved outcomes for children/young people in care, reduction in intergenerational trauma, improved stability of placements, and increased retention of carers. But how do we measure this?

There are many ways of assessing the extent to which an intervention has achieved its intended results. In our practice desired outcomes are identified at the beginning of the work through discussion at the initial meeting, and are generally along the following lines:

For the child to:

- Explore and process past events and experiences.
- Understand the why, where, when, what, who and how, through sharing information.

- Have a clearer understanding of past concerns, such as why birth parents were not able to parent them safely, and the decisions made.
- Feel listened to and have the opportunity to process their feelings about the past, present and future.
- Gain a greater understanding of their behaviours, thoughts, actions and needs, and identify strategies that help with managing powerful feelings.

Similarly, the Adoption Support Fund (England) provides a list of aims for the child to achieve:

- Improved relationships with friends, family members, teachers, and school staff.
- Improved engagement with learning.
- Improved emotional regulation and behaviour management.
- Improved confidence and ability to enjoy a positive family life and social relationships.

The extent to which the desired outcomes have been achieved can be assessed at the middle and end of the intervention through the structure of midway and ending meetings and reports, informed by views and feedback from the child, parent and any other appropriate people such as the education provider and social worker.

You can also give evaluation forms to the child and parent to complete at the end of the work to elicit feedback, in a similar way to participant evaluation of training. Examples of the evaluation forms we use can be seen in Appendix E.

While qualitative measures such as these, and the examples of practice given in this book, may go some way towards evidencing the positive outcomes of Therapeutic Life Story Work interventions, how do we more quantifiably assess the effectiveness of this work?

In undertaking Therapeutic Life Story Work we aim to achieve improvement in a child's well-being, internal working model and their understanding of themselves, their situation, relationships and the possibilities for their future. These types of subjective or 'soft' outcomes are harder to measure than more concrete things like numbers.

Rossi, Lipsey and Freeman (2004) define an outcomes measurement as a systematic way of assessing the extent to which an intervention has achieved its intended results. Key areas to assess are what has changed and how it has changed as a result of the intervention.

We feel this is a vital process to undertake; measuring outcomes effectively enables us to have a picture of what works well, what can be developed, and what needs to change. In the same way that it is vital to have adequate supervision in our work, it is important to ensure we have an effective means of measuring outcomes.

Therapeutic Life Story Work is a relatively new and constantly developing area of practice. It is generally felt to be of benefit, but Baynes (2008) suggested that while Life Story Work is a complex activity to assess, critical examination and evidence-based practice was needed and Watson et al (2015) identified that there was little rigorous research into the experience or outcomes for the child and parent.

With the need for a robust outcomes measurement in mind, the SHANARRI assessment tool was developed as part of The Rose Model of Therapeutic Life Story Work to assess the impact of traumatic life experiences on the child and measure the outcomes of the Therapeutic Life Story Work intervention. It is based on the domains of wellbeing identified by the Scottish Government policy 'Getting it Right for Every Child' (GIRFEC), introduced in 2006, (https://www.gov.scot/policies/girfec/) which itself is a version of the 'Every Child Matters' agenda, a UK government initiative for England and Wales (Department for Education 2004).

The aims of the approach are to support children and young people to grow up feeling loved, safe and respected, and reach their full potential at home, in school or in the wider community. SHANARRI is an acronym for the desired outcomes for all children in Scotland to be Safe, Healthy, Achieving, Nurtured, Active, Respected, Responsible and Included.

In using the SHANARRI (Rose 2012) assessment tool the parent, teacher and child can complete questionnaires requiring a written account and evaluation on a scale of 1-4 of the level to which the child manages compared to a healthy child of similar age in the community for each of the desired outcomes of SHANARRI. The results of the quantitative measure are calculated on a simple radial grid. A score of one would be where there is acute concern, and a score of four would be where there is no concern. The measurement can help identify areas where the child may need support and strategies for development.

The assessment tool can be completed at the beginning, middle and end of the Therapeutic Life Story Work intervention and the scores plotted onto a graph as a way of measuring any changes. The aim is to see if the child has benefitted from the intervention. For example, through an increased understanding and acceptance of the past they may be able to let go of worries or pre-occupations which have been affecting their development in any of the

SHANARRI areas. It may be that there are greater concerns initially, but hopefully over time some benefits will be seen.

You may see slight differences in each person's evaluation as they are based upon experiences in differing environments. The parent's experience is at home, in the community and with extended family; the schoolteacher's is based on the child's academic learning environment, which includes social skills, physical education, peer participation and much more.

Examples of the SHANARRI (Rose 2012) assessment of outcomes of Therapeutic Life Story Work that we have undertaken are shown in Figures 28 to 33.

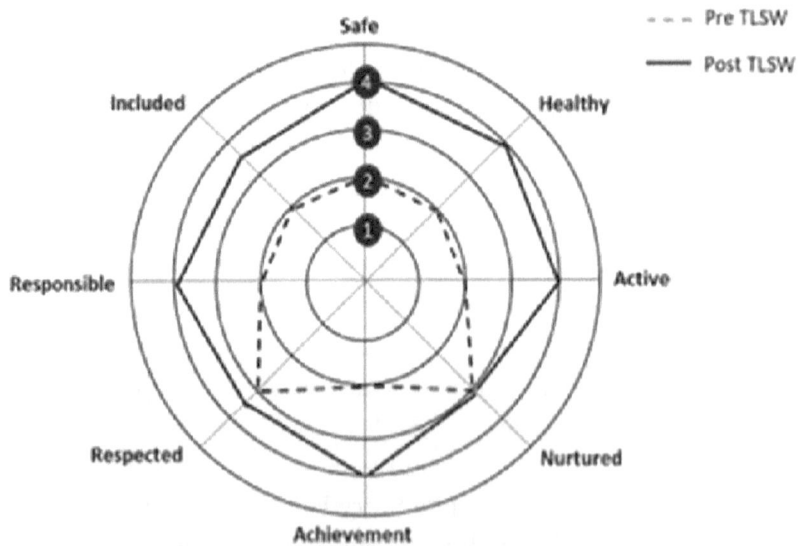

Figure 28: SHANARRI Assessment Chart – Child Age 9 – Parent

The grid in Figure 28 shows the scores from the pre- and post-Therapeutic Life Story Work assessment by the parent. These are similar to those of the child's school, which was something that we were not expecting. We thought there would be more variation due to the difference in environment and those relationships. At the start of the intervention the parent identified concerns around their child not keeping safe when feeling overwhelmed and being uncertain as to what she was feeling or thinking at any given time. It was identified that she was unable to express her emotions safely and would often run from the home or from her parents within the home because she could not process or communicate her past experiences and traumas.

The post-Therapeutic Life Story Work assessment indicated that the parents had seen encouraging changes throughout the nine-month period of the intervention. It was reported that the child was no longer running away from her parents or home and was able to communicate and express her thoughts and feelings safely. She felt closer, was forming a healthier attachment with her parents and was more able to share with them what was going on in her internal world.

During the Therapeutic Life Story Work she realised that she did not feel like she belonged. Towards the completion, however, she made a profound statement to her parents: 'For the first time I feel like I belong'. This was a very emotional moment for the child and parents and one that made a deep impression on their relationship. Her parents were not aware that she had been feeling like this and wondered if this was the reason behind her running from them. The child confirmed this was the reason, while acknowledging that she now runs to them for their support and love.

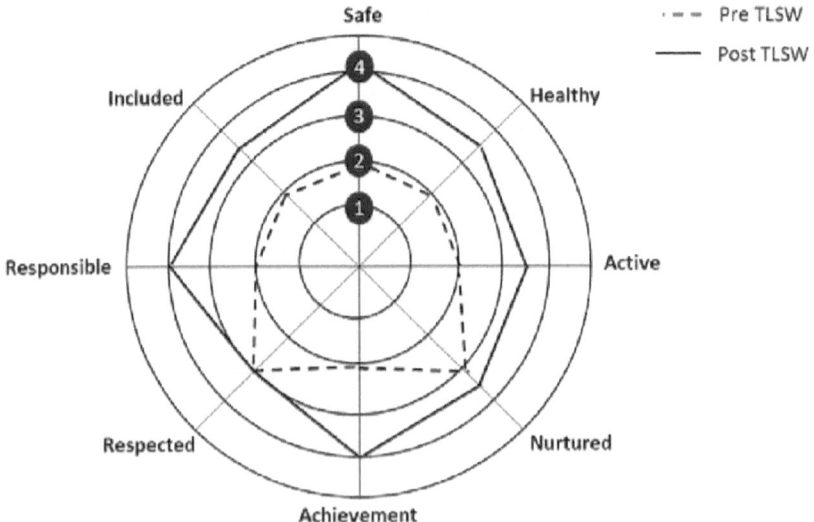

**Figure 29: SHANARRI Assessment Chart –
Child Age 9 – School**

The grid in Figure 29 shows the assessment scores provided by the school of the same nine-year-old child, pre- and post- the nine-month period of the Therapeutic Life Story Work intervention.

The pre-Therapeutic Life Story Work assessment from the school identified the child as worried, anxious and unable to express her thoughts and feelings around her safety. She was finding it difficult to engage with her peers and feeling left out from her friends' group. She was having difficulty managing her relationships and maintaining continuity in participation throughout her school activities, which affected her concentration in class and impacted on her learning.

The post-Therapeutic Life Story Work measurements indicated positive improvements in the child's academic learning, social skills, and concentration. She was now seen as 'thriving and making good progress' which was reflected in improved school exam results, enabling her to enter the school of her and her parents' choice.

During her Therapeutic Life Story Work the child realised that, with seven different foster carers, four different nursery schools and the enormous losses that took place within these life altering events before the age of four, she had always felt unsettled. Through the intervention she was able to unravel that sense of feeling hyper-vigilant and constantly unsettled. She shared that she was always worried that someone would come for her at school and take her away to yet another home. This was a huge moment that shed light on her tendency to run away from her parents and home, and her unsettled feelings at school. The child expressed thinking and feeling that if she hid no one would find her and, therefore, no one could take her away from her family. Once she had accepted that her parents were not going to allow this to happen, she became more relaxed, happier, calmer and more secure within her school environment and relationships, which suggested a more positive future.

The grid in Figure 30 shows the assessment scores provided by the child herself, pre- and post-intervention.

This assessment confirmed she was feeling very anxious, worried, and unable to express her understanding and feelings around keeping herself safe. She would run off when she felt confused and upset. She found it very challenging to feel a part of her peer group and always felt left out and alone. She felt she did not know how to maintain relationships or what she needed to do 'to please others'. This affected her participation in school activities and concentration in class, having a negative impact on her learning.

The post-Therapeutic Life Story Work measurements indicated positive improvements from the child's perspective. Viewing her

**Figure 30: SHANARRI Assessment Chart –
Child Age 9 – Child's View**

academic learning, social skills and concentration as improved. She made new friends, which made her feel included, and she became more responsible, safer and more engaged in school activities. She felt she was making good progress, which was reflected in improved school exam results.

She had learnt, through her experience of Therapeutic Life Story Work, that her parents loved her no matter what and this had a huge effect on her. She felt calmer, happier and more relaxed in different environments, whereas pre-Therapeutic Life Story Work she would not entertain the idea of going into new places. At the end of this work, she felt more secure and felt she had a brighter future ahead.

Further examples show the SHANARRI (Rose 2012) assessment grids completed for a 15-year-old child whom Karla worked with for a ten-month period.

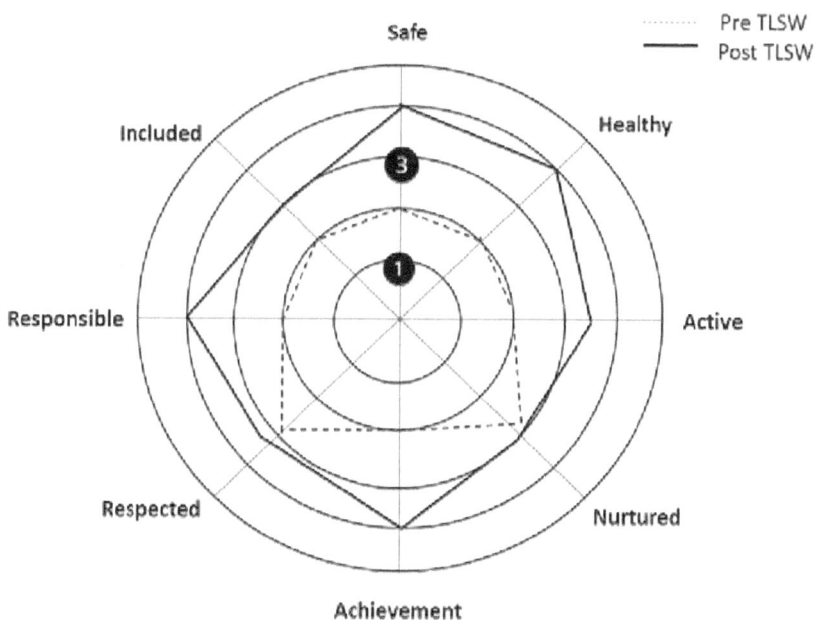

Figure 31: SHANARRI Assessment Chart – Child Age 15 – Parent

The grid in Figure 31 shows the parents' assessment scores for this child. The parents wanted their child to have Therapeutic Life Story Work as she had been self-harming and feeling very anxious. She found it difficult to keep herself safe while out with others, was unable to organise her daily routine and needed constant parental supervision. She was unable to maintain her daily hygiene without supervision and found it challenging to know what to do without being provided with instructions. She would appear confused, as if not knowing for sure what she thought or felt at any given time. The parents could not allow her out on her own as she found crossing the road from her home daunting. It was as if she had regressed to being three years old again; she would stop in the middle of the road and look for someone to tell her what to do or which way to go. The hope was that Therapeutic Life Story Work would allow her to make sense of her past experiences, traumas and loss, and gain a better sense of her identity. The work was undertaken with the child and parents over a ten-month period.

The parents post-Therapeutic Life Story Work measurements identified that positive changes had occurred while acknowledging the child had, at the end of the work, been diagnosed with Foetal Alcohol Spectrum Disorder (FASD). It was also found that she had witnessed severe domestic abuse, of a sexually violent nature, between her birth parents. The dark images that she had been drawing became less frequent during her Therapeutic Life Story Work. This was because the information sharing confirmed some of the situations between her birth parents that she had been forced to witness at the age of three.

Having learnt so much about her past, why she was adopted and that her parents would always keep her safe and support her, the child was able to connect some pieces together that enabled her to have a better sense of identity. It explained why things felt so challenging for her on a daily basis, whether that was at home or school, with friends or extended families. Relationships were problematic for her due to her understanding that if someone showed her attention it meant she could trust them, and this caused a great deal of concern to those at home and school. She learnt to be guided by those who cared for her and began to progress in taking some responsibility for her daily routine while forming a healthier and stronger attachment with her parents.

Figure 32: SHANARRI Assessment Chart – Child Age 15 – School

The grid in Figure 32 was filled in by the child's teacher, who reported pre-therapeutic life story work that she was self-harming, very anxious and found it difficult to express herself emotionally or keep herself safe while in the presence of others outside the family. While in school she was unable to maintain safe and healthy relationships, preferring to seek the attention of her favourite teacher, who could not always be available due to teaching commitments. The child did not feel safe unless an adult was near her or providing her with one-to-one attention.

The school had become aware that she had been seeking out 'dark images' on the internet and were monitoring her computer activities. She would write stories that always portrayed a dark image. The school were perplexed; to their knowledge, they had not shown or studied any material that would have triggered these images. The child could become withdrawn and incredibly quiet, and not engage with anyone. At these times she only wanted to go home and there was a sense that she did not feel safe unless she was with her mum.

The post-Therapeutic Life Story Work measurements illustrated that some positive changes had occurred while taking into account that she had later been diagnosed with FASD. The child had also disclosed during the Therapeutic Life Story Work that she had been touched inappropriately by another student. It became apparent, by looking back at when she started to withdraw and stopped wanting to go to school, that this was the reason she had not felt safe. Changes were seen throughout each area of the assessment. Although the school would have liked to see further development, everyone was pleased that the child was becoming more social, was able to focus a bit more during lessons and was achieving and learning more academically than she had before Therapeutic Life Story Work.

Figure 33 shows the assessment scores provided by the 15-year-old herself, pre- and post- intervention.

Her pre-Therapeutic Life Story Work assessment identified that she was feeling very lonely, worried, unable to express herself emotionally and was aware family and school were having to remind her to keep herself safe. She found this very challenging and felt that everyone was watching her. She was unaware of how to have safe and healthy relationships, and so would go with anyone who gave her attention. This was confusing for her. She felt withdrawn from her school peer group and at times from her family, unless she had her mum beside her. This affected her participation at school and with friends, and her overall wellbeing. She was 'haunted' by dark images throughout the Therapeutic Life Story Work and was keen to make sense of them, as they were causing her so much stress and anxiety.

**Figure 33: SHANARRI Assessment Chart –
Child Age 15 – Child's View**

The post-Therapeutic Life Story Work measurements indicated some positive improvements from the child's perspective. Her academic learning, social skills, and concentration had improved. She had disclosed being touched inappropriately by another student and it was this that she felt stopped her from feeling safe in school. She had become more responsible, safer and more engaged in school and had made new friends. She felt she was making good enough progress, considering her diagnosis of FASD. That enabled her to have a better understanding as to why things felt like such a struggle at times.

Her experience of Therapeutic Life Story Work taught her that she was loved by those around her. She felt happier, more secure and more relaxed accepting help from trusted others to get out more and become more independent. Pre-Therapeutic Life Story Work she would not have left her home without her mum. At the end of this work, she felt confident about her development and future.

The paper based SHANARRI assessment tool has been developed into a mobile phone application called *Therapeutic Needs Assessment* (TNA), which was launched in 2020. TNA was developed by the Australian company Supportive Hands in conjunction with Richard Rose's Child Trauma Intervention Services (now TLSWi). The app provides both the SHANARRI (Rose 2012) assessment and a Therapeutic Life Story Work needs assessment.

The Therapeutic Life Story Work needs assessment is designed to provide an evidence-based assessment together with a holistic understanding of the child, their placements and recommendations for intervention if needed. Seven indicators are used:

- Achieving and learning
- Physical health and development
- Emotional intelligence
- How included the child is
- Identity
- Ability to concentrate and be physically settled
- Attachment to primary carer

A cost per child is charged for using the application. The data inputted can be collated at pre-, midway and final assessment stages and an 18-page report created. Data can be added by voice for up to six people, usually the child, parent and teacher, which makes it accessible and easy to use. An identification number and avatar is assigned to each child to protect identity and ensure confidentiality. Children have said they like being able to use their mobile phone to express their views privately about how they are doing.

When we started writing this book there was no evidence-based research for the Rose Model of Therapeutic Life Story Work, however, this has now been achieved through research undertaken by Deakin University in Melbourne, Australia (Lucas et al., 2022). An evaluation of the Therapeutic Life Story Work programme run by MacKillop Family Services in out of home care was undertaken using a variety of measures including the SHANARRI assessment tool described above.

The outcomes were extremely positive, Lucas et al., (2022, p.39) report "The evaluation process has produced support of the significant advantages and effectiveness of applying the Rose (2012) TLSW Model to support children and young people who have been exposed to family violence, complex childhood trauma or who are in out of home care. Specifically, outcomes such as the increased sense of self-identity, strengthened attachment with caregiver, increased pro-social behaviours, decreased anti-social and negative behaviours and emotions." The report recommends that Therapeutic Life Story Work is offered to all children and young people in out of home care as an initial phase of trauma treatment and recovery-focussed model of out of home care.

The preliminary outcomes were presented at the Therapeutic Life Story Work International Conference in July 2022. Dr James Lucas from Deakin University reported *"The research has shown us that TLSW strengthens the attachment of a child to a primary care giver, which then supports improvement in peer relationships, education outcomes, reduction in trauma symptoms experienced, reduction of high-risk behaviours, improves mental health and wellbeing and overall, a greater sense of identity".*

The research found that participation in the Therapeutic Life Story Work program resulted in reduced trauma symptoms experienced by children and young people in out of home care over time, as well as supporting a reduction in high-risk and conduct behaviours and less peer problems.

The research also indicated that as the children engaged in Therapeutic Life Story Work, there was an initial decline seen in their health and wellbeing, which gradually improved to a significant improvement by the end of the intervention. The practitioners found that children held high levels of shame, anxiety, and concern for how their caregiver and the practitioner would respond to hearing about their story and past behaviours. It seems likely that these feelings of shame, blame and anxiety can be a large contributing factor to the initial decline reported in health and wellbeing.

Only a slight increase in achieving education engagement was found, and it was thought that longitudinal studies would be needed to capture the long-term impact on education of a Therapeutic Life Story Work intervention, as well as on identity, connection, and community inclusion.

Practitioners reported a benefit of the Therapeutic Life Story Work intervention was the flexibility to adapt for children with a wide range of trauma histories, developmental ages, cultural backgrounds, and presenting with a variety of risk factors, in residential and foster care. It was identified that Rose's (2012) Model can be adequately adapted to support cultural safety and inclusivity. It was felt that the activities could be adapted to be inclusive of children who were neurodivergent, for those with learning disabilities and other cognitive challenges. For example, by using Lego, sensory processing toys, play dough, and miniature army sets as well as craft items, to aid understanding of the concepts presented. Further, adaptations were able to be made to the Therapeutic Life Story Work program for it to be inclusive of various cultures including Aboriginal and Torres Strait Islander culture, while maintaining the integrity of the Rose Model of Therapeutic Life Story Work.

The research highlighted the need for practitioners to use their creativity and flexibility to best meet the child's neurodivergent, learning and cultural needs. Further, having the primary carer involved in and supporting the sessions was found to be integral to fully supporting the Therapeutic Life Story Work process in terms of increasing the child's engagement, holistic healing, wellbeing, and progression, as suggested by Rose (2012).

The evaluation found that the intended purpose of the Rose Model of Therapeutic Life Story Work to supporting trauma recovery, healing through connection, building attachment and making sense of their world, was upheld by the Therapeutic Life Story Work intervention.

Thus, the call for research has been answered and, while further longitudinal research is recommended, there is now a clear evidence base for the phenomenal impact that Therapeutic Life Story Work can achieve in relation to attachment, relationships, behaviour, mental health and wellbeing, and identity.

Further research is in progress, Appendix F contains examples of the development of further protocols for critical appraisal that has started in some areas including in relation to the effectiveness of this intervention for children who are adopted which did not form part of the above research.

The research findings by Lucas et al., (2022) fit with our own experiences and it is clear to us from undertaking Therapeutic Life

Story Work that the outcomes are generally extremely positive for the child and family. For children who are adopted, fostered or living with a relative or connected person we frequently see resolution of the emotional issues the child has been struggling with, as they gain a greater understanding of themselves and their trauma.

Parents know their child best. However, a Therapeutic Life Story Work intervention can help deepen their understanding of the impact of trauma on their child as well as validate their experience of parenting a child who has experienced early childhood trauma, and in so doing support them and strengthen their relationship with the child.

We suggest you take time during the penultimate session to review with the child and parent how the experience has been for them. Give them an opportunity to share the difficult times as well as the positives and any changes they may have noticed that have taken place. Their views can be included in the practitioner's ending report for the work. We often observe how similar the parent and child's views become, compared to the beginning of the work where they may be on quite different pages!

Feedback
We have received some wonderful feedback from parents and young people over the years:

From parents
-C's Life Story Work was amazing. He is going off on a 3-day residential with school tomorrow, and he is upstairs sleeping soundly. A year ago, I would never have thought this would be possible – he would have been running around really hyper at the thought of change, unable to sleep, and I would be worrying about how he would inwardly manage when he was there.

Meltdowns would have started a few weeks before and he would have lurched between anger and increased volume, activity etc., to sobbing and being really clingy. He would have held it together mostly at school, but family time would have been spent with me and his younger brother walking on eggshells. I am certainly not painting a perfect picture now, C is a big character and is very emotional, so we still have times that are challenging, but drastically reduced, and I feel better equipped to understand and support him. C understanding his life story has taken a huge pressure from him and continues to do. His jigsaw pieces were put together and hopefully will continue to be. The access Suzanne was able to give us to birth family [details], and manage so well, was and is invaluable. I will be forever grateful we had the opportunity to have this piece of work done, and with such a skilled professional. I hope my younger son will have the same opportunity.

-Thank you doesn't seem enough Karla, you have been a lifeline for me and our children and you have without doubt changed our lives.

-This has been good for me and my 'L'. It has shown me how she feels about her birth family. It has helped 'L' to ask questions and open up a lot more. I think it has been frustrating and upsetting at times, but she has coped very well as she has been honest about her feelings. It has also helped me learn how she feels about things at home and put in some strategies to help her. Before this process she was a very angry little girl but as time has gone on her behaviour has improved. This was the best thing for her. A big thank you to Karla for her patience and putting 'L' at ease so she could explore her past in a fun and safe place.

From children
-You have made clear my life and I cannot thank you enough.

-Now that we have finished with our sessions, Mum had asked me if a 4-year-old was going to be adopted, what would I say to them? I said it's hard and difficult. I would feel happy if the 4-year-old were adopted so they would find someone who would love them and care for them. My sessions with Karla have helped me to know how happy I am being adopted because I now feel I belong!

-This has been hard work with some fun, especially doing the squiggles. I am happier now than I have been, so thank you. P.S. I am not shouting anymore!!

-Thank you, Karla, I will miss you. I love my book. It has everything I wanted to know about my birth family and I can read it whenever I want. Well, Mum and Dad will help me.

The examples shared in this chapter demonstrate the value of measuring the impact of the Therapeutic Life Story Work intervention for the child, parent, family, practitioner and the organisation commissioning or funding it, and how it supports reflection and learning, and informs future interventions. While it is of great benefit and validation to have such positive evidenced-based research undertaken by Lucas et., al. (2022) for children in out of home care, it is important to bear in mind the complexities of measuring qualitative outcomes. We look forward to the outcomes of further critical evaluation being undertaken now and in the future!

Part Three

Considerations for the Practitioner

Chapter 8
Working with Complex Needs, Sensory Processing Needs and Neurodiversity

All children need to understand their past, whatever their ability. This chapter shares some of our experiences of providing Therapeutic Life Story Work for children with a range of complex needs, and highlights areas that are useful to bear in mind.

In taking on a referral which states a child has complex needs, it is always useful to seek a greater understanding of what their needs are and how you can best support them. There are so many resources available and we encourage you to make use of them. We recommend speaking with the social worker about the nature of the child's needs, how they are being supported presently and by whom. Once you have a clearer understanding you can discuss with your supervisor whether you feel you have the ability, knowledge, enthusiasm and skills to accept this referral. After this exploratory process you may feel more confident. There are plenty of books and articles available, many of which we can access online, providing in-depth information, support and the tools to help us deliver Therapeutic Life Story Work for each child according to their needs.

We are not saying you have to be an expert to work with a child with complex needs. What we are saying is be aware of your own knowledge and experience in working with a variety of needs and challenges. Seek support from the resources around you; if you are supported well, the child will feel supported. If in doubt, shout! Ask for assistance, support and information, and be open to adding new tools and materials to the way you work. If you feel you are not equipped to work with neurodiversity, that is okay. You have the self-awareness needed to keep you and the child safe, and at some point you may decide you are ready to accept this type of work. There is no right or wrong: it is about how comfortable you are in doing this work. Also bear in mind that the parent is the expert on their child's needs, bringing the skills from your discipline and a willingness to learn and adapt may be all you need, as you will be working in partnership with the parent and can therefore combine your skills.

We have found working with children with complex needs exciting, challenging and heart-warming. It has enhanced our way of being, our understanding, abilities, skills and techniques, and it has expanded our work in ways that have been totally unexpected. Every child matters and, therefore, every child deserves to be supported according to their needs.

Complex Medical, Physical and Learning Needs

Receiving referrals for Therapeutic Life Story Work in relation to children who have complex medical or physical needs can at times appear daunting. You may question whether you have the experience or ability to support the child according to their specific needs. Each referral requires consideration of the needs of the child and the practitioner, to enable the intervention to be as successful as possible for the child.

Karla: *When a local authority made a request for me to consider working with a 14-year-old who had multiple physical and learning challenges, including a high level of medical* *necessities, minimal speech and mobility, I felt bewildered by all the challenges this seemed to present. I was informed that she needed full-time care, was unable to use her hands to write, was unable to walk and that her speech was hard to understand, although she was understood by her parents and school. The child needed frequent medical testing, operations, hospital stays, equipment and accommodations to support her needs. She was very keen to learn about her birth family and culture; she had been born in Thailand and did not know a great deal about her heritage, cultural belief systems or how people lived. Her parents were incredibly supportive of her wish to know more about these areas and were eager for her to have as much information as possible.*

After reading the assessment of need that had been shared by the referring social worker, I had a lengthy telephone conversation with her parents and the social worker involved. I then took the referral to supervision, which helped me decide to meet the parents and child. I was clear with my supervisor that most of the medical terms in the assessment were beyond my understanding, knowledge and experience. However, my supervisor reminded me of the work I had undertaken throughout my career as a play therapist with children who were diagnosed with selective mutism, global development delay and children with emotional impairment along with those who had experienced extreme trauma. She felt my experience, training and knowledge would inform me and that staying with the child at her pace would help us to work together to overcome whatever challenges arose.

During the first session we looked at where we were all going to sit so that the child could be comfortable, with her parents beside her. We sat around their table where she started off by showing me how she used her communication device. A speech impairment can be caused by physical, sensory, emotional, mental health, intellectual or social reasons, or may remain unexplained. This child used a speech-generating device that has an outstanding battery life which makes communicating fast and easy for individuals with speech impairments. It had a large 14" screen which is the perfect choice for individuals with complex access needs or for those who want larger icons.

She appeared pleased to demonstrate her typing skills, which were particularly good and enabled her to convey her responses, questions and thoughts. I soon realised that we could communicate with one another. The child then pointed out that there was no space for the wallpaper I had brought in with me. We agreed that I would bring in an A2-sized art pad so her parents and I would be able to write things down. She showed her sense of humour when she communicated that she was happy to have offered a solution!

During this first session, the child pulled out the alphabet chart attached to her wheelchair. She used this when she wanted to spell something out to make it clear to me, especially names. It also helped her to convey events that related to age, either her own, or those of her parents or family members. She remarked to her parents, 'I wonder if Karla will keep up with me when I use my alphabet board; I'm pretty quick on it!!☺' I made use of this chart as well, as a means of being playful. She loved that, and her infectious laugh would ring out along with a smile that lit up the room.

At the end of this first session she wrote 'Here are the two things that help me to communicate with others. I am sure Karla will get used to them in our sessions.' I replied, 'Perhaps we won't need these as much once we get to know each other better!' She replied 'I am not sure about that right now! ☺' This session was not only the beginning of the wonderful experience of meeting this child and her parents and gaining an insight into her internal world; it was also an opening for me to a new way of communicating. With the child's eagerness to share and hear more about herself, I felt this was going to be powerful learning for me, the child and the parents, and would inform the Therapeutic Life Story Work model in terms of working with children with additional challenges.

After several sessions, it became apparent to me that, because of this child's attitude towards life and her profound challenges, and her parents' empathy and understanding, this work was not going to be as difficult as I had anticipated. Mauro (2009) states, 'Special needs is an umbrella term for a wide array of diagnoses, from those that resolve quickly to those that will be a challenge for life and those that are relatively mild to those that are profound.' This child's challenges were for life and profound. However, I agreed with her and her parents that the work could be achieved.

This child's amazing personality, endurance, positive attitude towards life and enthusiastic character enabled her to endure medical and physical complexities, and daily challenges. I feel so humbled to have had the privilege of supporting her alongside her parents through her Therapeutic Life Story Work journey. I believe that every child living away from their birth parents has a right to Therapeutic Life Story Work no matter what their challenges are. There is a light within every child that wants to shine and to be seen, along with the need for their voice to be heard.

Suzanne: *I know from our peer supervision discussions that Karla had a significant impact on this young person. By taking time, being committed to learn and having the skills to observe* *her ways of communicating, she demonstrated to her that she wanted to hear her views, thoughts and feelings, and valued them. This experience encouraged and gave the young person the confidence and safety to start using her voice. She was shocked to hear her own voice for the first time, but once over this initial surprise, she went from strength to strength in developing her ability to communicate through speech. Her parents were amazed to hear her speak so clearly for the first time.*

A phenomenal transformation took place. She found her voice and played the lead in her school play, speaking with her own voice in front of the whole audience and her school friends. She came to terms with her sexuality and shared this with her parents with Karla's support. She planned with her parents to go to college and achieve her dreams. Through Therapeutic Life Story Work, she gained a greater depth of understanding of her start in life and why she was adopted, while also learning that she had a brother.

Sensory Processing Needs

Many of the children who are referred for Therapeutic Life Story Work will have experienced sensory deprivation in their early years. This can have a lasting impact on their development and needs, such as not being able to recognise how they are feeling on the inside or self-regulate their behaviour and actions. They may have missed out on loving and caring interactions and all the movement experiences that go alongside. These things are essential to developing sensory integration, where our brain and central nervous system work together to help us make sense of ourselves and our world and equip us with the tools to manage and feel comfortable in our bodies and our environment (Lloyd 2016).

We agree with Lloyd (2016) that it is vital for practitioners to understand the impact of abuse and neglect on a child's sensory processing systems, and these areas may need to be addressed before the child is able to make use of psychological therapies, even play and Theraplay based ones. A child with a history of neglect may have been left alone for long periods in their cot or pushchair with little or no sensory stimulation. They may not have been given opportunities, such as having time on their tummy on a blanket, or encouragement to explore the movement of their bodies and to reach out for objects. When babies are left on their own they may cry for some time, but will eventually give up hope that anyone will come. Lloyd (2016) describes how the baby will go into a state of despair, where they become very still except for small self-soothing movements like moving their head.

Lloyd (2016) suggests that children who have missed out on early movement experience are likely to have underdeveloped sensory processing systems. They can struggle to know how their body is feeling and may find it hard to balance, or feel uneasy when their feet leave the ground, and can display high levels of dysregulation. They do not catch up on the steps they have missed without support and can struggle to notice the messages their body gives them about how they are feeling or reacting. Lloyd (2016) presents a range activities and exercises that can be individually tailored to the child to support their body in learning the early movements they have missed.

Each stage of development builds on the last one, starting with body awareness and control, which is gained when the child has a rich array of movement and sensory experiences. Like building a wall, learning, social and emotional development are built on top of body awareness and control. Where the foundation is weak the wall above will be affected and may fall down.

Sensory integration theory provides a way of understanding how our brains store and process experience on an emotional and physical level, and how neglect and trauma impact on the developing brain. Lloyd (2016) provides invaluable guidance in her book, with practical ideas and activities for parents and practitioners to help develop the sensory processing needs of children who have been removed from home because they have experienced abuse and neglect. Many of these activities can be incorporated into home life and sessions.

Children who present as being highly dysregulated may need assessment and intervention by a specialist before being able to make use of a Therapeutic Life Story Work intervention. This can be carried out by therapeutic occupational therapists or complex needs workers, such as the Just Right State programme (sensoryattachmentintervention.com) providers. This work is aimed at building new pathways in the brain that support self-regulation, which did not form in their early childhood. It is an important area to keep in mind when considering referrals and the timing of Therapeutic Life Story Work. Reading any sensory assessments available and speaking with specialists who may have worked with or know the child can provide invaluable advice in relation to supporting the child's specific needs.

Suzanne: *I worked with one family of three children who had experienced high levels of early years trauma from neglect, physical abuse and possible sexual abuse. The eldest child had a range of complex needs. On a sensory level she had difficulty regulating her emotional and physical states; she found it challenging to focus on activities, learning and noticing if she was cold, hot, hungry, or full. She struggled with balance, touch and things like having both feet off the ground, and when on all fours she made her hands into fists.*

The children were each given an All About Me book, based on Rose (2012), to complete. The eldest child wrote 'no comment' on the page inviting her to give an account of why she couldn't live with her birth family and the same on the page inviting her to identify any questions, thoughts or feelings she had about this. This suggested she might not be feeling ready to look back at her past.

A network meeting was held to discuss the work needed, and it was agreed that a Therapeutic Life Story Work intervention would take place with the younger two children while, in view of her sensory processing needs, the eldest would undertake the Just Right State programme.

When the Just Right State sessions were nearing their end, and the Therapeutic Life Story Work had been completed with the younger two, a further network meeting was held to review the work done and assess whether Therapeutic Life Story Work should commence for the elder child. The Just Right State sessions had proved helpful for her and so we agreed that the Life Story Work should continue on from these.

A handover session with the complex needs worker undertaking the programme was arranged. This session proved invaluable in ensuring that familiar and comfortable activities which helped the child with regulation were carried over into the Therapeutic Life Story Work sessions. (This practitioner has since undertaken the Therapeutic Life Story Work Diploma and can now offer both these interventions without the need for the child to experience a change in worker.)

For this child, each session started with a routine of rolling out a large circle of wool on the floor around the room. The child and worker would walk along the wool, 'balancing' as if it were a tightrope, sometimes switching to walking backwards or doing a 'loop the loop' turn. The foster carer watched due to her own physical health challenges, but gave her helpful praise and encouragement, which set the session off in a positive way.

The time taken for the activity varied depending on the child's state of regulation; often a visible relaxing and calming was seen in the child's body language and verbal responses. As I got to know her and the ways in which she communicated, it became possible to judge how long to do the exercise. The wool was rolled back into a ball to use next time, with the child having the option to roll up the wool as an additional calming activity.

As the sessions progressed it became clear that for this child around 20 minutes of Therapeutic Life Story Work, between beginning and ending activities, worked best for her. Sometimes her 'window of tolerance' (Siegel and Bryson 2011) was less and sometimes a little wider. As with all children, it was important to keep noticing, wondering, and checking with her how she was feeling (Hughes 2011).

The ending activity involved the reassuring pressure of a firm touch, with the child choosing whether to give or receive a hand massage from the parent. This child had previously withdrawn from touch but, as sessions progressed, she began to choose to receive a massage from her foster parent more frequently. She also appeared to be more comfortable in accepting hugs and started to seek cuddles more readily with her parents both within and outside the sessions.

Keeping to the routines established by the complex needs worker and having a clear structure helped this child to be in the 'just right state' needed to engage in and benefit from these sessions.

The handover session with the complex needs worker also highlighted the need for a slower pattern of speech. The session proved valuable learning for me, as I became aware of speaking too fast and saying too much; I keep this in mind now in all my sessions and have incorporated it into my practice.

The Just Right State Programme

The Just Right State programme is aimed at supporting children who have experienced trauma to regulate their emotional states and behaviour when engaged in activities that are normally challenging for them. The sessions give the child opportunities to experience and engage with a range of regulating sensory activities and foods. Parents can begin to learn how to observe their child's ability to self-regulate and how to provide a regulating environment at home. Parents also explore their own abilities and need for self-regulation, as their sensory and attachment patterns have an impact on their child's emotional state, given the co-regulatory nature of attachment.

The programme uses a series of books depicting 'The Scared Gang' cartoon characters (Bhreathnach 2006) who represent the different attachment and survival patterns of behaviour. Each character tells the children how they react to situations and what each of them needs to do to achieve the 'just right state'.

The intention of the programme is to help children become more emotionally aware of themselves and others, provide regulating experiences which calm their autonomic nervous systems, give them simple tools to use in challenging areas of their lives, and enable them to self-regulate and achieve the just right state.

This involves making changes to ways of eating, washing, playing and socialising that are regulating for the child. Perry (2009) suggests that a neurodevelopmentally-informed approach can be more effective in providing these tools than any specific therapeutic technique.

The Just Right State programme is underpinned by theories of sensory integration, attachment and trauma, neuroscience, and psychodynamic theory as it addresses the underlying reasons for behaviours. On referral the parents complete a sensory-attachment profile questionnaire to gain a picture of their child's survival, sensory and attachment behaviours. They learn about these areas and how to create an enriched environment tailored to the parent and child's sensory-attachment needs. Both child and parent work can be done in groups or with individual families.

We all know about the five senses of touch, taste, sight, hearing and tasting, but sensory integration theory identifies two further senses associated with body movement, called the vestibular and proprioceptive systems, which when not working correctly can lead to difficulties with balance.

Our vestibular system helps us balance and allows us to steady ourselves when we start to fall. It sends information to our brain about the position of our body and gives us a sense of security and connection with the world. It has been referred to as our internal global positioning system (GPS). The proprioceptive system needs lots of movement to develop and all the other sensory systems build on this foundation. It enables us to do things like pick up an object and bring it towards us. It gives our brain messages about how much effort we are putting into moving our body and regulates our emotional responses and sensory input. All children need to learn how to use their vestibular and proprioceptive systems, just like the other five senses.

Sensory integration therapy (Ayres 1979) can be helpful for children who have experienced early sensory deprivation, it is embodied in current interventions like the Just Right State programme. Ayres was particularly interested in the interaction between and development of all the senses. She saw these as important in supporting our ability to use our body, concentrate, and develop self-esteem and confidence, as well as having self-control and academic skills.

Dysfunction in the proprioceptive system can lead to a child doing things like:

- Moving too quickly
- Crashing into things
- Walking on tiptoes
- Having poor endurance or posture
- Making flappy or robotic movements
- Having difficulty judging force or distance.

Activities that target the proprioceptive system include weighted blankets, climbing, pushing and pulling, stress balls, and sucking through a straw.

Symptoms of vestibular dysfunction include:

- Difficulty with attention or following instructions
- Delay in speech or language skills
- Poor eye control
- Dysregulation
- Clumsiness
- Poor control of posture
- Poor hand-eye or eye-foot coordination
- Unsteadiness when walking on the ground
- Being unable to be held up in the air, upside down or spun around
- Dislike of tilting head backwards

- Stabilising self by walking with hands on walls
- Lack of fear of heights or moving equipment
- Not getting dizzy even with excessive spinning or getting overly dizzy with hardly any movement at all

Activities to target the vestibular system include rocking, swinging, jumping, sliding and spinning.

Just to further boggle our minds, Bhreathnach and Breen (2017) identify an eighth sense of interoception. Interoception is how our body tells our brain what is going on inside our body, such as when we are hungry or when our heart is beating fast. This sense can also be disrupted for children who have had adverse childhood experiences and can be a common feature of the children who are referred to us for Therapeutic Life Story Work.

As with our other senses, it is essential for us to have healthy and well-functioning vestibular, proprioceptive and interoceptive systems. Without these, life can be unpleasant and confusing. Vestibular, proprioceptive and interoceptive dysfunction need to be diagnosed by a professional occupational therapist with a specialisation in sensory integration.

We are often asked to undertake Therapeutic Life Story Work with children and young people who are highly emotionally dysregulated, to the extent that they mostly operate in highly aroused states of fight, flight or freeze. Van der Kolk (2014), drawing from neuroscience and attachment theories, similarly identifies how trauma affects the brain, body and nervous system. Unprocessed trauma can be held in people's bodies, hence the title of his book *'The Body Keeps the Score.'* Van der Kolk suggests that while we cannot undo what happened, we can change the impact of our traumatic experiences by creating new experiences to counteract them. Positive experiences can include physical exercise programmes such as such as Yoga, Tai Chi and Qigong, these can serve to '*contradict the static feelings of the frozen or panicked self of trauma replacing them with sensations rooted in safety, mastery, delight and connection.*' (Van der Kolk 2014 p.308).

Neurodiversity

As previously discussed, neurodiverse children who are referred for Therapeutic Life Story Work need careful consideration. They may benefit from specialist assessment of their sensory and any additional needs if these have not already been undertaken and supported. It is extremely supportive to the child that we understand their abilities as fully as possible, so that we can tailor the sessions according to their needs.

Karla: *I worked with an eight-year-old child who used play to discover new ways to communicate his internal world and to make meaning of the world he lived in. Using objects, toys and art materials alongside the wallpaper he produced the picture in Figure 34. These tools enhanced his emotional literacy and social and personal development and provided a safe way for him to share his world while learning more about himself, his past and the reason he was in care. He found a safe way to play out his own experiences and tell the story of his fears, fantasies, hurts, traumas, loss, and confusion. In view of his level of anxiety and issues with his proprioception system, I made him a weighted lap pad filled with rice to have on his lap at any time during the session. This helped to reduce his anxiety levels.*

The picture he created shows his world as he experienced it. It is exceedingly busy and cluttered, and involves a great deal of movement. Some areas indicate boundaries and in other places the boundaries are being pushed. The aeroplane, bus and train tell us that he has travelled many times from one foster carer to another. He wanted the animals to be kept safe and so has gathered them with a 'keeper' who watches over them. The alligator represents danger. The tortoise is where the child wanted to be; however, in later sessions he realised that his parents are like his tortoise. They are wise, and they protect him from harm.

Figure 34: Use of Play for Communicating Internal World

He did not worry about coming up against judgements or rejection of what he created. It enabled him to be understood while preparing him to receive information about his past, his birth family and answers as to why he was in care. This delicate therapeutic work facilitated healing for this child, and when we came to the end, he was able to verbalise his thoughts and feelings. His social skills developed to the extent that he was able to join other children in play and not feel so isolated. His parents were able to model a new way of communicating that enhanced their family bond and attachment. There is no right or wrong way to help a child with this process; sometimes, as with this child, they find their own way.

In the two pictures shown in Figure 35, you can see how a child used the squiggle game they referred to as 'chase'. This child was eight years old and liked to use coloured pens to communicate her internal world.

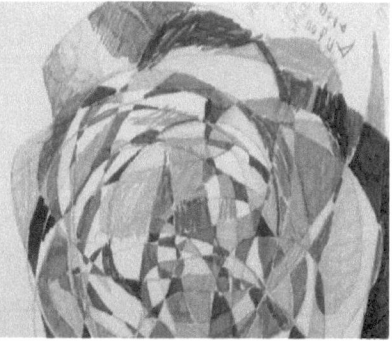

Figure 35: Use of Squiggles for Communicating Internal World

The squiggles were created by the child and parent together. The child would draw a squiggle of swirling lines and her parent would 'chase' her with her pen. The child would then colour the picture in with the support of her parent. Doing so presented her with an opportunity to laugh, relax and share the words she had for what she was feeling.

For the past couple of years, the child had appeared withdrawn and distressed at home and school, and at times displayed challenging behaviours. These concerns had created a barrier to her learning, social skills and participation in lessons and family life. This safe and non-directive activity opened up a means of expressing her internal world and helped her to remain calm and relaxed throughout the sessions. The drawing technique was shared with her school: when she became distressed a staff member would offer her some paper and they would play 'chase'. She would sit and colour it in afterwards.

Addressing these sensory concerns increased the child's engagement with her family, the education curriculum and her peer group, and her learning improved overall. She was able to continue with her school activities and not feel so distressed and withdrawn. This is just one of the fun, creative activities that we used to support this child and bring her and her parent closer together.

We believe that each child will find their own way of communicating if we are open to being creative and thoughtful about what tools we have within us. We need to find inventive and sympathetic ways of inviting the child to examine their feelings and make sense of their past at their pace. Working with neurodiverse children such as those with autism, is no different. Always gather as much information as you can at the point of referral, from the parent, school and assessment reports; building as detailed a picture as possible of how the child's neurodiversity presents and impacts on their lives will enable you to better serve their needs.

Suzanne: *The child may be very literal and keen to please, saying what they think you want them to say. They may find it hard to notice and name what they are feeling. In sessions with the child it is important to be clear about what you mean. Use shorter sentences, slower speed and fewer choices (of course, this can be helpful for everyone!). With the help of their carer, one child asked me not to ask too many questions and to offer only two choices in the sessions for what we would do, what games we would play, and so on. We included this in our working agreement, and creating and keeping to a routine helped this child stay regulated during sessions. For instance,* *we started each session by agreeing a numbered plan on the wallpaper which included a calming or grounding game to start with and ended with a choice of two games such as Beetle (an updated version of hangman) or Dobble.*

Once safety has been created, either in a later session or anytime they raise it, it can be helpful for an autistic child to investigate how they see and understand their autism. Be gently curious: how do they experience social situations, do they notice feeling uncomfortable, not getting jokes, not being sure what to do, and so on? Do they find it hard to have friendships? Do they prefer being on their own?

You can explore and identify what helps them, such as remembering to say hello when answering the phone or focusing on an area in the middle just above people's eyes if direct eye contact feels uncomfortable. It may be better to start the timeline from their birth as they are likely to be more interested in this. It may provide a better starting point for them to make sense of what the past is, and from which to connect to their parents' lives.

It is also important to emphasise the positives there can be for people with autism. They may see things differently and think in different ways which can be good to have on a team. Many celebrated inventors and great thinkers are now believed to have had autism; Marie Curie, who developed a cure for cancer; Bill Gates, who co-founded Microsoft; Albert Einstein, best known for his theory of relativity which phenomenally changed the way scientists look at the world and set the foundation for many inventions including nuclear energy.

Although engaging in Therapeutic Life Story Work with children with complex needs may appear daunting at first, we have generally found it to be extremely rewarding work. Getting to know and understand the child and their needs is pivotal; make sure you draw upon all the expertise and support of specialists available to secure this. Each child is unique, the work is unique to them, and you will be working with each one as an individual, according to their needs.

Remember, however, that it is also okay to say no to referrals where you feel you do not have the relevant understanding and experience to undertake the work. The child's needs are paramount, and you need to make sure you feel informed and prepared. But also bear in mind, as parents have told us, that you have skills others who are specialists in the child's complex needs may not have, and that you will be working in partnership with parents who are experts in relation to their child's needs.

Chapter 9
Creativity

Creativity is vital in undertaking Therapeutic Life Story Work and you need to nurture it to make it part of your practice. It will enable you to respond to chance experiences arising within sessions, which may unlock meaning and understanding for the child.

The word 'creativity' can mean different things to different people, but generally it involves the use of imagination and original ideas to generate something new, drawing on your experience and your ability to make use of what is in front of you. It involves taking risks, ignoring doubt and facing fears, breaking with routine and doing something different, just for the sake of it, and challenging yourself every day.

Creativity requires time, space and thought. With practice, creativity will become something that you can turn on at will, just like a light switch. It is important to concentrate on the four essential elements: focus, tools, people, and time. *Focus* keeps the emphasis on the child and incorporates their interests into the sessions. Make use of a variety of *tools*, such as art materials, the wallpaper, toys and games like Lego and Jenga, or anything that might be at hand. Keep in mind the *people* involved and the *time* you have available.

We suggest taking time to play and explore your own creativity, especially if it is not something that comes to you naturally. Getting in touch with the child within you and re-kindling your creativity will help you connect with the child in sessions. Some adults do not find it easy to be playful; they feel uncomfortable or awkward, or fear they might look silly and, therefore, do their best to avoid playing. Some practitioners find playing with their own children, nephews, nieces or friends' children useful in opening up that playfulness within them. Children enjoy the playfulness of an adult as it gives them permission and allows them freedom in their playfulness, which can enhance their powers of expression.

Being creative can help you become a better problem solver in all areas of your life and work. It promotes thinking outside the box or out of your comfort zone. It helps you see things differently and studies suggest that creative people are better able to live with uncertainty because they can adapt their thinking to allow for the flow of the unknown. We go into this in more detail later in this chapter. The children we support throughout Therapeutic Life Story Work have had to become creative in some way to survive their life experiences and trauma.

Is creativity a skill or trait? A skill requires technique and you do not need any technique to be creative. Quality is assessed by levels, such as bad, fair, good or excellent. Creativity transcends this; it uses the mind and the imagination to see beyond the ordinary to create alternative possibilities, and new and original ideas.

It offers so many benefits; it can allow you to express yourself, have fun and feel happy, reduce anxiety and stress, give you a sense of purpose and lead to feelings of accomplishment and pride.

A creative act such as crafting can help focus the mind and has even been compared to meditation due to its calming effects on the brain and body. Even gardening or sewing releases dopamine, a natural antidepressant. Creativity can reduce depression and help you process trauma according to Stahl (2018). In fact, tapping into that creative energy can actually improve your overall health. Engaging in creative behaviours, such as colouring in books, improves brain function and mental and physical health. Stahl (2018) states, 'The theory of cognition postulates that being creative is a basis for human life. Basically, being creative is important!'

Karla: *I found it tricky to figure out what would help one young boy to relax at the beginning of our sessions. He was 11 years old, with a diagnosis of ADHD, learning challenges and a high level of anxiety. We discovered that he needed to draw what he wanted, without his parents being upset by the colours he chose, namely black and red. They were concerned that these colours meant something was going on inside him and that something dark and sinister would come out. It was agreed in session three to allow him to draw what he wanted, to communicate what was causing his anxieties.*

This proved highly creative for the child. It appeared to relax him and drew out his anxieties, releasing what was causing him to feel unsettled. His first 'illustration' (his word) was a feather floating in blood from his heart. He explained that he felt he had a broken heart, having been separated from his birth siblings. He could not understand why they could not all be together. He drew a cloud around the image to keep his heart safe, but bits of his heart were still floating away at times. His second illustration was all in red; it represented the love that he felt from his parents, while acknowledging his feelings of sadness and worry about his siblings. This was constantly on his mind, causing him anxiety.

Once he had expressed himself the way he needed to, his parents felt more relaxed and could see why the colours he chose were so important. This illustrates how, even with all the activities and exercises we learnt on the Therapeutic Life Story Work Diploma course, we sometimes have to think outside the box and make use of what the child presents to us.

Another child was very confused as to why he was receiving Therapeutic Life Story Work. As he put it, 'I have my mum and dad. I don't need to know about my birth parents, end of!' This was the challenge we faced.

He was passionate about African snails. He shared with us how he looked after them, what they needed to eat, how much physical contact he could have with them and what it felt like to be the one with responsibility for their care. This led us into talking about his past, his birth parents, what he had needed as a young child and if his needs had been met.

He enjoyed drawing, but did not want anyone to judge his drawings, as had happened at school. He drew an image of a 'roller coaster of feelings', showing himself and his parents going up, down and all around; this was what life felt like for him internally. He was not able to verbalise what he was feeling internally, but could express it through drawing. It gave him a way to externalise and allow his parents to see what was happening inside him, helping them to understand how he felt about himself and his life. Through being open to creativity this child managed to relax and feel safe in order to make good use of the Therapeutic Life Story Work.

Creativity can come in the form of an object, a colour or a saying, to name but a few; it is how we make use of it that benefits the child during their Therapeutic Life Story Work. We need to be open to trying new things or thinking of new ways to help the child communicate their internal world on an emotional and psychological level. In this way we can model empathy, curiosity and willingness to meet the child's needs.

In this book we share with you many exercises, activities and outcomes from our own experiences. Every one of these can be creatively adapted to suit your own style and the needs of each child. Each one of us has an inner resource of creativity drawn from own lives: our own reading, research and experiences of play with the children in our families and social groups.

Suzanne: *I worked with one 10-year-old child who had mild learning needs and a passion for Lego. At the beginning and end of each session we played a game of Lego minifigure battles. His window of tolerance was 20 minutes at most, and at the beginning of our work together any reference to the past led to him say, 'My mummy died', followed by a display of huge sobs of anguish. He then rushed towards his adoptive parent and allowed her to comfort him.*

He had said clearly that he did not want to examine the past and the concern was that he might not be ready to do so. However, he enjoyed creating a Lego house to represent his present home, including his parent, brother, grandparents and pets. To our surprise he then agreed to create and hear about the places 'the baby' had lived in before. Using Lego to create a representation of the past, as shown in Figure 36, and talking about 'the story of the baby' - in the third person - enabled him to tolerate hearing the story of how he had been physically hurt and had needed to live with his maternal grandmother. Sadly, she was not in a position to look after him on a long-term basis due in part to a serious health issue.

We needed to move at a very gentle and sensitive pace, with reminders that he could put his hand up if he wanted to stop (which he was very good at doing). When he put his hand up, we played a game of his choice, usually involving his Lego (I brought my own Lego to use for the information sharing part of the sessions, including a rather fabulous judge!). This child benefitted from the creative thinking that enabled him to re-tell his story. He was able to show and tell some of the things he remembered, even at an unconscious level, such as moving the father figure a long way from the baby to keep him safe.

The play supported him in shifting from a position of being stuck in his grief, towards processing that grief and co-creating a new narrative that his birth grandmother had died; she had been like a mummy to him, and it was very sad. We made a special box for his birth grandmother to contain his favourite photos and memories of her. He and his parent were able to look at it when he felt sad about his loss, along with lots of hugs and cuddles.

Figure 36: Use of Lego for Information Sharing

CREATIVITY

Being creative opens up a wide world of fantasy, experiences, storytelling, healing, repairing and bridging between the past, present and future. This takes place according to how creative we allow ourselves to be. We can use our own imagination, alongside that of the child, however little or much we have in front of us in the way of art materials, objects, toys, books, paper and pens or games.

Karla: *Figure 37 shows a picture, entitled The Fish of Anger, that was created by a 10-year-old child. She used colour, imagery and lines to communicate the feeling of anger she carried inside herself most of the time. This was an exercise that, again, just occurred spontaneously in the session and allowed her freedom of expression and further understanding of herself. With no direction or instructions from anyone, she felt safe enough to demonstrate what she was containing internally. She allowed the wallpaper to contain the feeling as she named it. She then explored where the anger came from, what triggered this emotion daily and where in her body she felt it.*

Figure 37: The Fish of Anger

It is interesting that sometimes children do not feel that we have understood them until we have created something together: a squiggle, a story, a drawing to illustrate their timeline, a favourite character that shows how they relate to their environment, or pictures created from their memories by the use of colour or words. Words can also be very expressive and, therefore, creative; it is how we use them and investigate them with the child that makes the difference. Creating and exploring something new can leave us feeling worried, scared or wobbly or, on the flip side, can be exciting and thoroughly enjoyable, as long as we are open to learning new ideas, skills and techniques.

Karla: *Therapeutic Life Story Work is a life journey for a child, and creativity can offer a wonderful, safe and secure way to make that journey, to explore their past, their present and their internal world, and to achieve some sense of stability. We must be able to step out of our comfort zones if we are to expect the child to do the same. Years ago, someone said to me, 'You have to think outside of the box'; it was at that point I realised I no longer had a box! When I became open to using all that was around me, the creativity flowed spontaneously. This is such a wonderful experience to have with a child.*

Chapter 10
Creating Therapeutic Stories

This chapter focuses on the Creating Therapeutic Stories model Suzanne initially developed where an individually tailored narrative is created for the child about their lives using their favourite character or area of interest and employing fact, fiction, fantasy and heroism. The aim is to provide a safer third-person narrative for the child which fits with themes that are relevant to and resonate with them.

All children can benefit from and grow through stories which provide a way of talking about inner experience and learning from the experience of others. Stories give children the experience of feeling understood and not alone in how they feel, and can influence how children think and understand relationships and how they see and understand themselves.

The power of a story to transform and heal is well documented, and Karla has used therapeutic stories in her play therapy work. Writers such as Golding (2014) identify storytelling as a valuable tool for helping children and adults learn about their feelings and their inner world of hopes and dreams. She purports that children do not have the inner resources to be able to fully process and digest their troubled feelings and that stories can support them in this. She reminds us that we are all story creators and suggests ideas for creating 'helping stories' as follows:

> 'Stories can be simple or complex: short or long: anecdotal or more metaphorical: told, acted or written ... to be human is to tell stories.'
>
> (Golding 2014 p.33)

Mellon (2019) suggests that all stories are healing and therapeutic; they touch us in some way or give a different perspective. Further, those stories can trigger our imagination and take us to a different world. Creating a therapeutic story for a child requires that we ignite our imagination, creativity, and story-telling powers. Mellon (2019 p.1) describes stories as maps to learning and healing and, to encourage us, she writes that 'a treasure-trove of imagination powers lives within us all'.

Mellon (2019) believes stories have the power to help us through our difficulties and can feed our souls like good food. Similarly, Sunderland (2000) likens stories to being an important part of a child's healthy, emotional digestive system. Like food, feelings need to be properly digested; if not they can affect our ability to function.

In her forward to Mellon's (2019 p.ix) book Perrow suggests the world is made of stories, and that stories are a way of connecting with others and can 'soothe our soul and touch our hearts ... Stories can change our perspectives, motivate and strengthen us on many levels as they bridge unseen and visible worlds and connect us to all life'. Perrow further suggests that through storytelling and the art of imagination, fears can be faced, and hurdles overcome; stories are, in her view, healing imagination.

Indigenous communities worldwide hold a deep respect for the sacred healing capacity of stories. For thousands of years, story making and storytelling have been integral to our humanity – teaching moral and history lessons and keeping complex traditions alive. Many cultures have rich storytelling traditions, dating back many thousands of years, that are unique to them as a way of protecting their heritage and culture. For example, the Maori culture in New Zealand uses oral storytelling practices as a way of preserving and passing down knowledge through generations. The Australian Aboriginal 'dreamtime' is a way of describing spiritual beliefs and existence and is embodied in Aboriginal artwork.

Each culture has its own stories or narratives, which are shared as a means of entertainment, education, cultural preservation or instilling moral values. Within those cultures each family has its stories and belief systems. We were writing this book at the time of a worldwide pandemic in 2020, and we have created stories and narratives about this event as a world community, within countries, friendships, relationships and family groups. There is not just one story but many and these change over time as we look back and reflect on events.

Therapeutic stories have the potential to help a child with their difficult and painful feelings, which may manifest themselves in behavioural or emotional issues. To process painful and difficult feelings means to fully feel them and think about them. Through images which resonate with the child, the therapeutic story aims to speak with accuracy and empathy about the emotional issue or problem with which they are struggling. That might be a sense of abandonment by a birth parent, a loss or longing, or a deep hurt which causes them to feel the world is unsafe.

In the Creating Therapeutic Stories model, the therapeutic story is usually created from information gathering and through sessions with the parent, rather than the child and parent. It takes the form of a narrative account of the child's life, in the guise of a story book about a favourite character. It can be created with the child, adult or even with a birth parent for their child, but here we are mainly referring to co-creating the story with the parent and network around the child. For families living in England who meet the criteria, this work has been funded by the Adoption Support Fund. There has been great interest shown by both commissioners and practitioners in this developing area of practice.

The story serves as a tool for parents and we run preparation sessions to support them in using it. The story will guide them to be empathic and offer their child quality listening and understanding, which will help them process painful and difficult feelings, contemplate their own narrative and make sense of their world. With some slight differences, Creating Therapeutic Stories draws from the principles of The Rose Model of Therapeutic Life Story Work in having three stages: information gathering, sessions and creating a book. The book created is aimed at enabling the child, with the parents support, to make meaning, externalise thoughts, ask questions and internalise a more helpful narrative, rather than a Therapeutic Life Story Work Book which reflects the process, thoughts and feelings of therapeutic life story work sessions.

This way of working stemmed from receiving referrals where children were not cognitively, emotionally or psychologically ready to access Therapeutic Life Story Work, and we found that it was a useful model to use during the 2020 worldwide pandemic when in-person work was not possible. The work can be undertaken online and does not require the child to be seen. However, we would like to make it clear that therapeutic stories are not intended to be done in place of Therapeutic Life Story Work; they are different processes. As we have outlined in this book, Therapeutic Life Story Work is an extensive intervention with a child, aimed at helping them make sense of and process feelings about the past over the process of sessions between the child, parent and worker.

A therapeutic story can be created for a child at an earlier development stage who may not be cognitively ready for extensive Therapeutic Life Story Work. It might be suitable for a child who is showing unrest about their past but is not perhaps at the level of reading, writing and way of understanding the world that would be a prerequisite for a Therapeutic Life Story Work intervention. This would not preclude Therapeutic Life Story Work, which could follow at a later stage, with the narrative from the therapeutic story perhaps informing and being incorporated into the extensive Therapeutic Life Story Work if it has been helpful for the child. A therapeutic story can also form part of the extensive therapeutic life story work, for example, where you find that a child is struggling with hearing directly about themselves.

Therapeutic stories can also be used where there is a need for a child to understand information being shared with other brothers or sisters who are having extensive Therapeutic Life Story Work, or where a child cannot be given identifying details of their birth family for safety reasons.

For one six-year-old child who was referred for Therapeutic Life Story Work, having details such as names of birth family members could potentially have revealed his identity to them; relatives from the wider birth and adoptive family had recently formed a partner relationship and the child could potentially have met with birth family members such as cousins at wider family gatherings. His identity was unknown to the wider birth family members at that time and, given his age and the safety issues, a therapeutic story was felt to be the most appropriate way of helping him to have an understanding of his story in an anonymous and, therefore, safe way.

The Creating Therapeutic Stories model draws from narrative theory, founded by Michael White, an Australian social worker and family therapist. Narrative therapy (White and Epston 1990) is based on the premise that we make meaning of life events using the stories that are available to us. These stories shape our lives, and problems occur when the wider stories and expectations in society do not fit with our lived experiences.

The process of narrative therapy is to separate the person from the problem, thereby externalising the problem so it can be reflected on and reframed to help the person identify alternative ways to view, act and interact in daily life. A narrative approach respects the person by viewing the problem as external rather than being within the person. Similarly, in Creating Therapeutic Stories we are externalising the problem by using a character with whom the child identifies: one who has had the same experiences and emotional issues or feelings as them. By doing so we aim to transform the child's way of thinking about themselves, as well as their past, present and future.

White and Epston (1990) suggest that where people hold a 'thin' story, such as one narrative line, or a one-sided view, they can benefit from interventions which develop a richer, more multi-layered story containing a sense of greater possibilities in their life, as we aim to do in therapeutic life story work. This process can be cathartic and provide healing from trauma.

Externalising the child's story assists the parent in supporting their child to reflect on their thinking and understanding; in this way the parent and child co-create the child's own story. The narrative can help in understanding current and past behaviours, both their own and those of people who have been significant in their lives. Repetition through re-reading the story book can support understanding and processing; it can be re-read many times, perhaps each time with different questions and deeper meaning and insights being revealed.

Therapeutic stories have what Perrow (2012) refers to as a helping intention, namely to provide an opportunity for the child to make sense of their past, present and associated feelings. The aim is to give the child information in a way that will open up a different understanding of their life that is more helpful to them and that strengthens, adds new layers and re-shapes their identity.

The therapeutic stories we create are based on the child's favourite characters, themes or interests, whatever these may be. Characters and themes for our therapeutic stories have included Dave the Minion, Captain America, Bakugo Katsuki, Tiana, and Elsa from Frozen, to name but a few.

Many of these characters lend themselves to the child's story, and most superheroes have experienced some form of adversity and trauma in their lives, with many having been separated from their birth parents. For example, Spiderman lived with his aunt and uncle after his parents died in a plane crash; Superman was adopted; Batman's parents died when he was eight, and as an adult he took in Robin whose parents had also died. Many Disney characters have also experienced some form of trauma or adversity, such as loss and rejection, which they struggle with until finding resolution through learning new strategies, usually with the introduction of a helper.

These characters can be a gift to transfer into the child's story, but even where there is not an existing history of childhood adversity or trauma, storytelling provides the creative licence to write one in. For instance, you can start a story with, 'Now I imagine you know Dave the Minion from his films as he is an actor, but what you might not know is that in real life he was adopted when he was younger. This book tells the story of how that came to be ...' A story about a dinosaur can be started with, 'In this story you have to hold on tightly because we are going to travel back in time! Back 60–80 million years ago to a time called the Cretaceous Period ...'

Attention is paid to ensuring images and language are chosen which reflect diversity, such as using an image of a black female judge. Furthermore, if explaining the ways in which children come to live in their families we would identify that a family may consist of two dads, two mums, one dad, one mum or a mum and dad, and so on. Consider the characters you can use. For example, in one child's therapeutic story, 'The Story of Captain America', the helper chosen was 'The Falcon', who is a Marvel superhero of African-American heritage.

Therapeutic story books are created for a child with input from their parents and from reading key documents such as, in the UK, the child permanence report (CPR) or a chronology compiled by the organisation who were responsible for safeguarding the child. Birth parents may be contacted where agreed and with permission from the child's legal parent; this is done where information is needed that only they can provide.

A birth parent's feelings and views may not have been recorded and finding out about those views or their present situation can be helpful for the child. This is particularly important in situations where a child displays anxiety and unrest about a birth parent who became homeless or was a teenager estranged from their family at the time the child was removed from their care. Including information such as the parent being in a better situation, or expressing their wish (in other words, permission) for the child to be happy in their lives, may allow the child to feel more settled as a result. The books can be professionally printed as they do not contain any identifying information about the child.

The model of Creating Therapeutic Stories also draws from writers such as Judith Foxton who wrote *Nutmeg Gets Adopted* (2001) which tells the story of three squirrels who come into foster care due to domestic violence, alcohol misuse, parental depression and neglect, and are then adopted. The story of Nutmeg is one that fits with the reasons why many children come into care. These sorts of stories provide an opportunity for the child to ask important questions about why they could not live with a birth parent. They can also lead the child to an understanding of how they feel about the trauma of separation and loss, even for those who may be too young to frame their own questions.

Sunderland (2000) created a range of therapeutic stories to help children who have experienced trauma with feelings they may have, such as anxiety, anger, loss, and low self-esteem. The stories are designed to help children make sense of feelings which are too painful or difficult and may be leaking out in challenging or worrying behaviours. These books can be of enormous support for children, and we agree with her view that children need help in making sense of their troubled feelings as they do not have the inner resources to do so on their own.

Children do not talk easily about their feelings, as we have experienced in our work! Sunderland (2000, p10) suggests that a therapeutic story, as with other methods such as play and drama, '*can work as an admission ticket into a child's inner world, enabling you to enter their emotional world with care and understanding*'.

Wrench and Naylor (2013) suggest preparing metaphorical stories as a powerful tool to help children explore difficult issues, with optional use of toys or figures in telling the story. Metaphors can be extremely useful within stories. Drawing from an attachment perspective, Golding (2014) highlights how they can help us understand our inner experience by likening it to processes in the physical world. One example of this is the children's book *Have you Filled a Bucket Today?* (McCloud 2006). The bucket here represents being filled up and filling up others through kind and loving thoughts, words and deeds.

Siegel and Bryson (2011) propose that in making sense of our childhood experiences by creating a coherent narrative we can 'rewire' our brain, transforming our attachment models towards security, enhancing our relationships, and making us feel better about ourselves. Further to that, understanding our story can heal the deep wounds, behaviours and beliefs about ourselves that we carry from our earliest attachments, which unconsciously direct our lives. Making sense of our past can help us resolve old traumas so that they no longer haunt us in our present, as well as support us to cultivate security within ourselves and our relationships. This makes identity narratives an important tool in working towards recovery from trauma.

Similarly, narrative therapist Denborough (2014) discusses how our lives are shaped by the stories we tell about ourselves, especially in relation to our identity. If we hold negative stories, they make us weaker and are likely to lead to poorer outcomes: 'If we tell stories that emphasise only desolation, then we become weaker. Alternatively, we can tell our stories in ways that make us stronger, in ways that soothe our losses, in ways that ease sorrow' (Denborough 2014 p.vii) we have the potential to have more positive outcomes in our lives.

The therapeutic stories we create for children have the power to re-story or reframe the narrative of their lives in a way that is helpful for them. They do not sanitise or deny experience but provide meaning, understanding and hope. The stories can show the events before the character's birth that got in the way of their birth parents being able to provide the parenting things that children (or mice, snails or robots, and so on!) need. This can challenge the child's perception that the outcomes, such as birth parents not being able to look after them, were the child's fault.

When co-creating the story with parents as a tool for them to use with their child we suggest that around four to six sessions are undertaken with the parents for the purpose of gathering information, co-creating the story, and preparing them for reading the story and any questions the child may have.

The first session serves as an introduction to therapeutic stories, agreeing with the intention to support a greater and more helpful understanding of the past, and creating safety within the relationship between the parent/s and practitioner.

It is important to learn about the current family culture and belief systems, as well as those of the family of origin. It is vital to learn this from the families themselves, where possible, or from information that they may have given in the past, rather than general or at worst stereotypical views of a particular culture or religion. We have worked with children from diverse cultures, such as travelling families, Russian, Vietnamese, Indian, Filipino and Ethiopian, and while there may be shared values and practices, each family will have their unique ideas, views and beliefs. Curiosity around cultural diversity can assist us to respect and accept ways of being that may not be automatically our own and it can help us to learn the value of our differences.

We use later sessions with parents to review the information gathered, agree if and what further information may be needed, share the story so far and co-create the story with the parents' feedback and input, incorporating their ideas and additions.

We share the final draft towards the end of sessions and prepare the parent for sharing the story with their child using role play including questions the child may ask and exploring their emotions. We then present the professionally printed book in the final session. The first and final sessions may include the child (this will be required if funded by the Adoption Support Fund in England). The therapeutic story writer may undertake sessions with the child and parent to help identify the characters or themes, but it can also work well for the book to be done without the child's input to create the magical and anonymous elements.

The story can consist of one or many books, which may be very short or very long and may contain chapters, all depending on the child's needs and level of understanding. Generally, the areas we cover are:

- Introduce the character and what the book is about
- Setting the scene: show the character in the child's situation now/ how they are safe
- Different ways children come to live in families
- What children need (parenting wall)
- Feelings and themes the child may be struggling with
- Getting help and finding solutions
- The past in terms of the child's story and their birth parent's lives
- The present situation, the characters thoughts and feelings
- Hopes for the future.

Depending on the age of the child another book may be made with greater detail for when they are older. For one child Suzanne made four story books: Dora Explores Adoption, Dora Explores

Feelings, The Story of Dora Part One and The Story of Dora the Explorer Part Two. For another child we created a two-part story book: Brittany the Chipmunk and Brittany the Chipmunk's Life Adventures.

A therapeutic story book based on the child's own experiences provides them with an opportunity to reflect upon and understand their story but may also link them with painful and traumatic memories of their early life. Talking about the characters in the story can help children process their own sad, angry and frightened feelings. The books can guide the adults in talking with the child about areas such as adoption. This does not affect Therapeutic Life Story Work being done at a later stage and is, in fact, likely to benefit it. Being aware of the child's history and moves can support and inform the child and those in their network. The aim is for these books to be read to or with children by their parents or social workers. The child, where appropriate and with parental guidance and support may choose to share their book with other key people in their lives as a way of providing a greater understanding of the child and their thoughts, feelings and actions.

Suzanne: *Afshan Ahmad, co-author of My Life Story CD-ROM (Betts and Ahmad 2003) and a chapter on 'Digital Life Story Work' in Ryan and Walker (2007), with whom I was very fortunate to work as a life story work coordinator, wrote a therapeutic story from the perspective of a birth parent. The theme was a mama bear telling her story to her bear cubs who were not able to live with her. The story proved to be extremely powerful and healing for not only the children but for the birth parent as well.*

The families we have provided this work for have reported finding the books an extremely helpful tool for answering their child's growing questions. We have received lots of enthusiastic feedback from parents about their therapeutic stories, including these positive comments:

-The book was beautifully written and offered our child everything about their past in a way she could understand. Having a story about a third person has been really helpful for us. I think we will need to revisit the book in the near future for a second reading.

-We have found the book really useful. We approached using the book in a relaxed way as that was what [our child] needed. She dips in and out of it. We felt very relaxed with your approach and with you. You really listened to us and incorporated our ideas. You guided us through the more complex parts of her life story and encouraged us to be brave with the terminology that was needed but age appropriate. The quality of the book was good. There really isn't anything that we would change.

-The girls enjoyed their books which were full of answered questions and they loved how their favourite character knew how they felt.

Children need their parents to go there with them into the tricky bits with all the feelings, to be able to hear and re-hear, to adapt, retell and own their story. A therapeutic story book can give parents the confidence to do this.

As this model evolves we, and the people we have trained on our Creating Therapeutic Stories programme, are co-creating more therapeutic stories directly with children and adults. We have found the story books created for a child work well for younger children, while the stories co-created with the child can work well for older children and adults.

Who better to talk with precision about the emotions the character has than the child or adult themselves, it can be hugely therapeutic and transforming for the child or adult to write about and explore, make sense of their feelings and experiences through the safety provided by separating these from themselves and externalising them into the character in the story.

Chapter 11
When Things Go Wrong – and What to Do!

We did not feel we could write this book without a chapter on our learning from when things have gone wrong. While we aim to reduce errors, mistakes happen and the best we can do is to admit them, work through them and be open to the learning they afford, however painful that may be, to ensure they are not made again. Below are some of these occasions we have experienced, and you will see we have each owned our mistakes and how we managed them.

Challenges During Sessions

When You are Unprepared for a 'Freeze Response' in a Session
Suzanne: I was not prepared for the experience of a 17-year-old who froze in a session while exploring a traumatic incident from her past where she had been left alone to sleep overnight in a car as a very young child. The young person went into an unresponsive state with glazed eyes for the remaining forty-five minutes of the session. I had not experienced this before and realised I did not know how to explore ways of seeing if the young person could gently be brought back from her survival response. It was helpful for me that the parent was present and able to tell me that they had tried many things over the years to try and help her out of her freeze response, that she needed time

to come out of it while they stayed with her physically and emotionally with empathy.

I learnt a lot from the experience, it helped me to remain calm in subsequent situations that were similar. I have since learnt about grounding exercises that you can try to see if they help bring a person back into the present. You can assess this by asking if the person can hear you and seeing if they can respond either with words or with a gesture such as nodding or blinking. You can then try to get them in touch with their sensory experiences by encouraging them to notice what they can see around them, what sounds they can hear, what they can feel beneath their feet; can they feel the ground beneath them and how the chair they are sitting on is supporting them, and anything they can taste or smell; you could have an essential oil such as lavender in your toolkit to use, or suggest they have something to drink or eat.

Lack of Privacy
Karla: When working with one child, another family member repeatedly disturbed the session. The interruptions would play out in this way: the family member would sit down to talk about their own feelings and how their needs were not being met. This would disrupt the child's process; they would feel overlooked, dismissed and ignored, and declare 'Not again!' The child would become frustrated and begin to argue with the family member. The parent who was supporting the child in the session got involved with the argument and the family member then became distressed.

It was important to acknowledge the change that had taken place, but it was also important to choose the right time and place to discuss such changes. It did not seem appropriate to address what had just happened with the child present; it felt more supportive to remind the family member that we could discuss this later so as not to take focus away from the child.

We have found it helpful to know what support is available for each family so that when situations like this occur we can contain them and maintain the safety within the session for the family by suggesting 'It might be helpful to consider talking about this at a later time so that we can continue with this session'.

When this incident occurred, it would also have been helpful to revisit the agreement made at the start of the work. We could have re-established the boundaries, maintained the child's privacy and safety and continued with the session.

Chaotic Household
We consider where sessions are to be held at the initial meeting. However, you may not be aware until your first session that the room lacks privacy and calm. Depending on the issue, you may need to consider meeting outside the home, such as in a room at the child's school, or a community centre or library room.

Karla: With one family, it became clear that meeting at home was not appropriate due to the number of family members, the available space and the level of music that came through the walls within the home from other family members. One child in the family who felt left out kept interrupting and wanting to join in.

In this case my actions were to acknowledge what was taking place so that the child receiving the session could feel held, safe and confident that I could contain what was occurring, speak to the parent and social worker after the session and agree it was best to hold further sessions in the child's school and highlight that the child who felt left out was in need of support. We do not always know what the environment is going to be like in a family's home, so it helps to consider all aspects beforehand so that the work can remain safe and contained for the child.

Child and Parent Have Just Had an Argument
Suzanne: As I arrived for one session, the parent greeted me in a distressed state and warned me that the child was also distressed and threatening to jump out of her bedroom window, following an argument. My previous experience of being on call as a supervising social worker for foster carers, helped me to remain calm and focused on calming the parent, which in turn helped to calm the child. I modelled giving the child space while keeping her in sight. She sat for some time in the garden and eventually came in. I suggested a gentle game which served to help the two reconnect. However, the argument started again once the game was finished and resulted in the child, in her distress, drinking some washing up liquid.

These were familiar dynamics for the parent and child, and I felt that my presence might have been providing an audience for the child and so heightening the situation. My response was to tell her I could see how upset she was and that I knew how much her mother cared for her, suggest I leave as it was past the time for the end of the session and later get in touch with the parent, who told me that the situation had calmed.

It would also have been helpful to explore the child's feelings after repairing and reconnecting through the game, use story boxes to consider what happened before, during and after the argument and go on to examine what each one was thinking, feeling, and doing at each time.

Child Disengaging from the Sessions

Suzanne: One young person found it hard to come into the sessions, choosing mostly to remain in their bedroom instead. In fact, they had disengaged from school, community and home life, spending most of their time in their bedroom. It was hard not knowing if they would feel able to take part in the session.

I tried a variety of strategies, for example, the session time was observed by staying for an hour with the parent and leaving a note to let the young person know I had missed seeing them but understood and accepted that they had not felt up to meeting that day. I continued to visit, with the hope of gaining trust through the consistency and persistence of fortnightly visits, and it was helpful to know that this had happened with previous practitioners. Sometimes on arrival it worked to speak in a loud voice about the plan for the session. On one occasion I asked if the young person could help with a new iPad and show me how to play a game on it. That drew them into the room and engaged them in conversation. I always left at the appointed time. Sometimes they would come into the session for the last 20 minutes and this was accepted; we agreed it was important to stick to the session time as the shorter time may have felt safer and more manageable for them.

Occasionally they were in the room and ready for the session on my arrival; on these occasions they were so engaged and insightful that the session felt powerful and magical. When the next session was not attended it was hard not to feel disappointed and a sense of personal failure. Supervision helped me examine these feelings.

Therapeutic Life Story Work has been kept on offer to this young person over a number of years and there have been periods of engagement and disengagement. They recently commented to their parent that they valued the fact that I had never given up on them and identified the issue as not feeling able to trust anyone. The periods of engagement have been helpful for them, and my learning has been that the engagement can only go at the young person's pace and in relation to their feelings.

Unplanned End of Sessions
Karla: One young boy I worked with was excited to learn more about his birth family. He had been born in a different country and he had all sorts of ideas and images in his head about why he was adopted. He was curious about who his birth family were and was keen for his sessions to start. During the first three sessions one of his parents kept wanting to direct the child, steering him away from sharing his thoughts, ideas and feelings in relation to his birth family.

When I arrived for the fourth session the parent announced, 'I don't think this is working. I don't feel he is ready for this work. I want it to stop.' I wondered what had gone wrong; the child had been engaged, excited and had wanted to learn more about his past. Having seen his enthusiasm in the sessions so far, I found this quite difficult to accept. However, it became clear that one of the parents did not feel able to continue this work.

At the start, both parents confirmed that they wanted their son to have the Therapeutic Life Story Work intervention. It was not until weeks after the sessions had stopped that we learnt the reasons behind the change of heart; one of the parents told the social worker that she had become highly anxious and she realised that although her son was ready to hear about his past, she was not. The parent felt a need to control what was to be shared, but knew she could not control the truth, and her own fears and childhood experiences of trauma had also been triggered in the sessions, causing high levels of anxiety.

It was agreed that this was not the appropriate time for this therapeutic work to take place, as the parent needed emotional support first. We considered whether we could have done anything differently with this family, but the issue had not been raised in any of the meetings that took place. In the end we felt that no one could have known that the parent would be triggered in this way, not even the parent herself.

Sessions do sometimes need to be put on hold for parents to obtain support with issues arising for them. Therapeutic parenting or individual therapy sessions can help explore, process, and contain the issues and feelings. A parent can also have this support alongside the sessions.

Working with a child over time can provide an opportunity for mistakes, if recognised, to be addressed and corrected. Children can be very forgiving, and it can be a learning process for us all to know that we can make mistakes and own up to them. For instance, when you have missed something important that the child said in a session you can revisit this and discuss it in the next session. Sometimes the moment has gone, or the child's focus is elsewhere, but if you acknowledge that your intention is to listen the child will feel valued.

Challenges with Parents and Birth Families

When You Upset and Get it Wrong with a Parent

Suzanne: It can sometimes seem that a parent wants the intervention to change their child's behaviour, and they may be less open to considering how they might change their response to the child, for example the child's outbursts of anger. Suggesting that the parent's response may have escalated the situation, however, can lead to the parent feeling unheard, unsupported and blamed for the child's challenging behaviour.

This happened in one situation with the result that the parent's shame is likely to have been triggered. Their shield of protection may have led them to end the work rather than feeling able to discuss what had happened and whether the situation could be resolved. The parent would not allow any form of ending with the child, though an ending session was requested, and a card was sent.

I am now more mindful of and sensitive to triggering this response. This parent had experienced their own trauma and I believe found it difficult to connect with their own emotions and needs. My gut feeling after the initial meeting was that the family would benefit from an intervention prior to the Therapeutic Life Story Work that could support therapeutic parenting. However, the parent had not continued with other interventions and had perhaps thought Therapeutic Life Story Work would be more focused on their child rather than the child parent relationship.

When a Parent Does Not Give You Their Permission to Speak with the Birth Family and the Information is Not in the File or Records

If the legal parents are unhappy with us contacting the birth family we try to discuss this with them to understand their concerns. Sometimes they change their mind, but if not we need to respect their decision. It can be recorded in the child's Therapeutic Life Story Work book that there has been no contact with their birth family, together with the parents' reasons for making this decision.

There are valid reasons for not wishing to make contact and these can be explored with the parent. For example, contact could endanger the safety of the child; if the birth family learns where the child lives they could make direct contact and cause the child further emotional or psychological harm or confusion.

It could cause emotional or psychological distress to the birth parents who may be suffering from mental health issues, or feel it is too painful to talk about their child not being in their care. Contact could be distressing for the legal parent, they might find it too upsetting to hear what the birth family has shared with us. A great number of our parents feel for the birth family's loss of the child, and contact could trigger emotions in them that they do not want to revisit.

The legal parent may be concerned the contact may re-ignite birth parents' or child's curiosity about their child/ birth parent and wish to communicate with, search for or live with them. All of these areas need to be considered to ascertain a clear understanding of the legal parents' decision, and to help them make informed decisions. The practitioner needs to respect this and support accordingly.

In our experience birth parents have rarely forgotten about their child/ren and meeting with the worker can help reduce feelings of shame and anger, lead to greater understanding, acceptance, giving permission for the child to be happy in their current family, and sometimes apologise to the child. The information gathered can also help inform decisions around future contact.

If a parent provides you with their permission at the start of the Therapeutic Life Story Work and then withdraws it when you are about to make that contact, this can leave you and the child in an uncomfortable position, especially if the child knows the communication was due to happen. Therapeutic Life Story Work is based on the child's needs, while also respecting the parent's decision. Again, when this occurs, you have an opportunity to discuss why and what might be the reasons underneath the change of decision.

Karla: I worked with a child who was struggling emotionally at home, school and with her friends at the beginning of the work. However, during the work the child shifted into a 'good place', according to the parent. The parent decided she did not want her child's good place to be disrupted in any way and, therefore, no contact with the birth family was to be made. The parent believed that if the child received the answers she was seeking it might leave her in a 'bad place' emotionally and psychologically and might affect her academically. The parent did not want to take this risk, so the contact was not to be made.

This left me considering a number of things, namely what should I say in this situation to the child? What should I write in their life story book when we concluded our work? How did I feel towards the parent after I had put time into contacting and setting up a meeting with the birth family member? Did it feel fair?

You may feel disappointed, and it may not be easy, but the legal parent's decision is to be respected and honoured accordingly. What I did was acknowledge the change of decision; the parent and I discussed what to write in the child's book about not providing answers for them and how this might feel for them in the future. A great deal of thought and care had to go into this, as it is not our intention to upset the child or parent. I wrote that the information had been requested on the child's behalf, but permission was not granted. This not only kept my integrity and trust with the child and parent intact, but also provided the parent with the opportunity for discussion if in the future the child read their records and saw that permission had been given by the parent but subsequently withdrawn.

However uneasy we feel when a legal parent decides we cannot contact birth family members we need to trust them to make the appropriate decision in their child's best interests. They are the legal parent and they know their child better than anyone. In this situation we needed to be honest with the child about why this decision had been made. It is imperative to always support the child accordingly, even if we do not agree with the decision. We want to support the child, and that entails supporting the parents.

When You Turn Up Unannounced on a Birth Family Member's Doorstep

Suzanne: As I have already mentioned in Chapter 3, I learnt the hard way why this is not recommended when I arrived unannounced at the home of a maternal grandmother whose grandchildren had been removed from her daughter's care. I had been in the area after a failed attempt at re-visiting the birth mother with the aim of answering some of the child's questions. The grandmother's address had been located through an online telephone directory, and she was understandably extremely angry and upset to have been visited without agreement.

We recommend you always give the birth family member notice so they have the opportunity to consent or prepare for a visit to speak about what is likely to be a very sensitive and painful area for them. This can best be done by sending a letter first, either from a professional the birth relative knows or from yourself. In the letter introduce yourself and outline the nature of your contact, and follow the letter up with a visit even if you have not received a response. Birth relatives often tell us that they did not know how to respond to the letter. However, after seeing us face-to-face they have then agreed to meet.

Not every birth relative may react in this way but it is not something I would repeat. I sent a letter of apology, but any possibility of interviewing the grandparent had been lost along with her trust.

When a Parent Gives You Permission to Contact Family Members and then Wishes They Hadn't

Karla: The parents of a 10-year-old I worked with gave permission for me to contact the birth family, but when I shared the information I had gathered they began to regret their decision. The birth mother had shared her experience of the court decision for her child to be adopted; she felt she had done everything possible to have her child come back into her care. It was painful for the parents to hear her words, causing them distress and tears.

We need to understand that some parents may not be aware of the triggers that can occur, such as fear, doubt or uncertainty. They may became distressed while listening to the information that has been gathered, and it may trigger emotions and memories of the adoption process that they went through years before. New thoughts, emotions and concerns that have never occurred to them before can suddenly emerge. They may not be aware of how this process might affect them and their relationship with their child.

In this instance I postponed a session so the parents could have time to process what they had heard, as they did not feel emotionally ready to continue or to share the information with their child. This is understandable. We need to have the utmost respect for parents and what they are going through and it is vital that we support them throughout this process to stay strong enough to support their children. On reflection it would have been more helpful to have shared the information in advance of the session. Like children, parents need time to process.

We must never underestimate the effects this process has on parents. For another family, the parents of a young man of 18 experienced an emotional rollercoaster of fear, anxiety and stress after giving me permission to contact his birth mother. They felt as if they were going through the adoption process all over again, but on a heightened level, not knowing what was going to happen and fearing they might lose their son in the process. One parent wanted the whole process of contacting the birth mother to be stopped, but it was too late. Contact had already been made.

With support they were able to understand that their son needed to resolve his concerns and this process was helping him, communicate their fears, anxiety and stresses, and work through all aspects of the information gathering. Despite regretting agreeing to the search or contact they were able to agree it was likely that they would feel better once their son received all the information he was seeking.

It is paramount that we take great care in this area of our work as it can unintentionally cause such emotional and psychological harm, negatively affecting the relationship between the parents and child if not supported accordingly.

Contacting birth family members needs to be discussed not only with the parents, but also with your supervisor. This will provide you with clarity as to how you manage the meeting with the birth family and subsequently share the information with the parents and child in the sessions. It is crucial that we are mindful of how tricky and complex this is for each person involved; that includes you and what you may need to process.

When Meeting with a Birth Family Member Poses a Risk to the Worker

Suzanne: Meeting with birth parents has generally been a positive experience for me, as well as being helpful for the birth parent and child, and most legal parents have been in support of it. There have, however, been birth family interviews where I have not felt safe.

On one such occasion the birth parent was adamant that she was not willing to give me any information which would help answer her child's primary question; she wanted to be the one to tell her child about his parentage herself. I could see she was getting very angry. Earlier that day I had read how as a teenager she had terrified members of staff in the many private secure accommodation establishments she had been moved to. She had needed to be the only resident and there were reports that due to her extremely violent behaviour, the staff groups had resorted to locking themselves in their office and calling out the police, for fear of their lives.

I really wanted to answer the child's question about his paternity but I knew I was taking a risk going into the parent's home, and I agreed with the parent that I would leave the interview as I could see our conversation was distressing them.

I had travelled a long distance to view the casework files and see the birth parent, so the information gathering and interview were done during the same visit. Where possible it is helpful to read the files first and arrange any interviews for a later time.

We recommend always letting someone (in my case Karla) know the address you are visiting and arrange for them to call you twenty minutes into the visit. In this instance I left before the time arranged for the safety call, so I let Karla know I was safe once I had left the birth parents home. Our conversation helped me process what had happened as well as my feelings and disappointment at failing to obtain information which would help answer the child's question about his paternity.

Keep in mind that reading files can have a big emotional impact and you need time to process information and assess the safety of a face-to-face visit. It is advisable to consider this with your supervisor.

Challenges with Organisations Holding Records for the Child

Significant Delay in Gaining Access to Records

Karla: While there are worldwide variations in practice and regulations, in the UK it is generally accepted that a worker undertaking therapeutic work with a child will be given access to the child's casework records. Not being allowed to view records on behalf of a child can be a great source of frustration. I once made three appointments with a local authority to view records for a child before beginning the Therapeutic Life Story Work. All three were cancelled with no explanation as to why. This delayed the start of the sessions for months and left the child and family upset, having felt prepared to begin but then disappointed.

After the third cancellation I contacted the social worker and the team manager to discuss this. They were extremely supportive and were able to get clarity as to why I was not being permitted to view these records, but this information was not shared with me. Eventually the records were made available, and it became apparent that the local authority was concerned about the questions that were being asked, and uncomfortable for some information to be shared with the parents. This was worked through in time and, after a delay of six months, I was able to start the work and provide the information accordingly.

The child and parents were furious that this information had been withheld and that the local authority had put them all through such delay and stress.

In Therapeutic Life Story Work we are taught to complete the information gathering before meeting the child; this experience bears this out. If I had started before reading the records, the work would have been put on hold, perhaps causing even further distress. Having to wait for six months was not easy, but during that time the family needed a great deal of support, which meant we did get to know each other. The parents were tremendously pleased with the outcome of the Therapeutic Life Story Work but were left holding some considerable anger about how they and their child had been treated.

During the Covid-19 pandemic in 2020, due to restriction in place on face-to-face visits we were able to access casework records electronically via a secure platform. This enabled the information gathering process to take place, and in some cases gaining access to records became quicker and easier than previously. Some departments continued to allow this while others reverted to only allowing in person visits to view files.

When an Organisation Does Not Respond to Your Request to Contact a Birth Family Member

Karla: This situation can occur quite often and several months can pass by with a child left waiting. You are unable to provide invaluable information to the child, complete the Therapeutic Life Story Work or produce the book. At times we need to stay proactive when making these requests.

Having said that, as proactive as I was on behalf of one child, it made no difference. This family experienced a catalogue of disappointments, namely that at first the local authority would not respond. When a meeting was arranged and although everyone confirmed they were available not everyone attended. Throughout the meeting we all agreed that the contact was necessary, but the previous local authority would not commit to making the contact and kept saying, 'It may be difficult', without further explanation. Four months later, after telling us they had the contact details, the previous local authority stated that they could not locate the birth family member.

It was then clear that the family would not receive the information requested. This left them, especially the child, devastated. The Therapeutic Life Story Work was concluded and in the child's book we all agreed to include the child's experience and the attempts that had been made to access the information. We also added that in the future, on reaching adulthood, they would do their own research about their birth family to enable them to find the answers they so desperately sought.

When the Referring Social Worker or Parent has Their Own Perspective on What Goes in the Child's Life Story Book

This situation can be extremely difficult especially when it goes against the Therapeutic Life Story Work model. It is so important that the book, as the third stage of Therapeutic Life Story Work, reflects the work the child has done on their wallpaper. 'The life story book itself is the third stage, and this is typically presented as the evidence of the work being achieved.' (Rose 2012 p.32).

The important points to be aware of are that the life story book represents the child's journey through this process and it is up to them to decide what they have in their book. If a social worker or parent insists on this being altered according to their agenda, it can leave a child feeling their experience has been devalued, potentially causing emotional or psychological harm. If they insist on the changes you may have to accept that the child may not see their book as it was experienced and meant to be. When this occurs it is useful to investigate the social worker or parent's need to make alterations. There may be a misunderstanding on their part that the Therapeutic Life Story Work book is similar to the life story book the child receives at the time of adoption.

It is important, therefore, to be very clear at the start how we write up our books for the child and that it will not be like that of a pre-adoption life story book. We want what is best for the child. The book aims to be a celebration of the work undertaken. Due to the nature of the book and the experience you have had with the child it can feel devastating if you are told the book will not be presented until all changes have been made. Alterations may involve many more hours of rewriting and changing the book. If you are working independently, funding for your time needs to be considered (if available) and it is possible that you may not be paid for this extra work.

Sharing and exploring your thoughts and feelings in supervision can help you consider how best to move forward. What can be considered in such a situation is to maintain a copy of the original life story book to be kept with the child's records. This way, if the child does review their records in the future, it will be clear to them that you have presented their experience accurately in the original book, compared to the altered version. As difficult as this experience sounds, supervision enables such decisions to be discussed and resolved, keeping the child as the main focus while respecting the needs of the social worker or parent.

Mistakes are not made intentionally, but they are a part of life and learning and we can always make the effort to rectify things. When things go wrong we have the tools of reflection and supervision to support us and to help us consider solutions. It is important that we are open to recognising and learning from the mistakes we make as only in this way can we grow alongside the child.

Part Four

Practicalities for the Practitioner

Chapter 12
Self-Care and Supervision

Self-Care

In undertaking this work, it is vital that we consider self-care. Self-care is the act of caring for ourselves, being determined to enjoy activities that benefit us in order to improve mental, emotional and physical wellbeing.

Bond (2015 p.7) writes 'The care of ourselves as practitioners matters to our clients. They need to know that we are sufficiently resilient to be able to work with them and to withstand the challenges of that work'.

There are many ways in which we can look after ourselves. These will differ for each person, and it is widely recommended that we put them in place on a regular basis. Strategies and activities for taking care of ourselves and unwinding from the stresses of our work can include exercising, reading, relaxing and socialising, as well as seeing a counsellor or therapist to support us on a personal level. All of these are great ways to release anxiety, stress and concerns, and address any other emotions we are carrying that originate from our work or personal life.

We work therapeutically with children who are carrying many powerful emotions related to trauma, loss, abandonment, fear, anger and anxiety. Those undertaking training in Therapeutic Life Story Work are now required to ensure that they have considered their own therapeutic needs and received support with working through and processing any personal issues that are likely to arise and have an impact on their work.

Collier (2019) identifies the importance of protecting yourself while working alongside pain and trauma, using the five pillars of protection shown in Figure 38:

- Being aware of the risks of vicarious trauma
- Ensuring we receive good quality supportive supervision
- Seeking peer support
- Recognising the impact of trauma
- Looking after ourselves

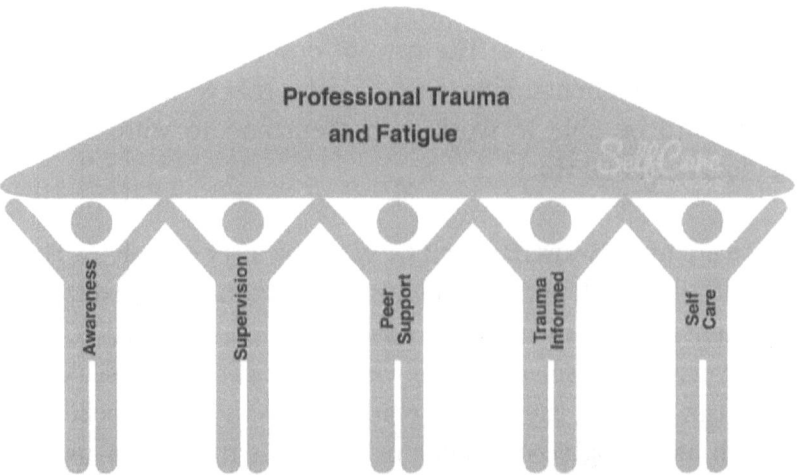

Figure 38: Collier's Five Pillars of Protection

It is beneficial for us to be open about our own health, noticing our own needs and putting structures in place to keep us healthy and safe. An act of self-care can be saying no to taking on new referrals if doing so is likely to result in overload. You may also consider the balance and level of work you take on.

In one Therapeutic Life Story Work session a child said to their parents, 'You're so busy earning a living you're forgetting to live your life!' This serves as a reminder of how we can neglect caring for ourselves and how this can be detrimental to our work, our health, our families, our relationships and our lives.

Suzanne: I suggest this acronym for self-care which we can use on ourselves and suggest to the families we work with:

NAIL it!

- **Notice** what you are feeling,
- **Accept** that your feelings and needs are valid,
- **Instigate** the self-care strategies that work for you,
- **Look** after yourself to enable you to live your best life!

Wrench and Naylor (2013 p.20) highlight the importance of having emotional support for yourself, suggesting that 'without this you will struggle to convince the child that you can bear his pain and share his story emphatically and truthfully'.

It is vital, therefore, that we protect and preserve our physical and mental health in the face of our challenging work and pay attention to needs that may arise in our personal lives, no matter how busy we are. If we do not look after ourselves, we cannot look after others. It is paramount that activities that support our self-care are in our diaries and schedules.

Supervision is a key element of self-care, and our wellbeing needs to be on our supervision agenda. This is where we can begin to act on looking after ourselves, to ensure our overall wellbeing and that of those around us and those who we support through our work.

Peer Supervision and Clinical Supervision

Supervision is a requirement for practising Therapeutic Life Story Work, as identified by Rose (2012) and endorsed by

Therapeutic Life Story Work International. We believe it is an invaluable part of our personal growth and professional development and an essential arrangement for discussing and exploring our work on a regular basis. It needs a great deal of attention due to the role it plays within our work. To be without it would be unethical and even unsafe for everyone involved.

We attended the Diploma in Therapeutic Life Story Work a year apart and were introduced to one another as a potential supervisor and supervisee. We decided, given our different experiences and disciplines, to create a peer relationship rather than a formal supervisory one. By 'peer' we mean with someone at your own level.

In this chapter we focus on our peer supervision, aiming to examine and provide an insight into our experiences and learning. We acknowledge that there are many forms of supervision, such as clinical supervision and group supervision, which we also offer to others, and that many of the principles we consider in this chapter are relevant in all supervision.

In reflecting on our peer supervision we have seen to an even greater extent how beneficial it has been to our practice. We strongly encourage the reader to consider engaging in peer supervision to support their practice, if this is not already in place.

It is important to state that our peer-to-peer supervision is complementary to our clinical supervision and does not replace it. Clinical supervision is a formal arrangement where the focus is on the supervisee's work, experiences and learning. In peer supervision the emphasis is on each of us sharing our experiences and supporting one another's learning, and as such there is no cost other than our time and commitment. We still require clinical supervision, which we each receive regularly and would recommend is undertaken monthly.

In our peer supervision we use telephone calls and live video due to the geographical distance between us. In comparison with face-to-face supervision these online forms of communication have advantages and disadvantages, which we explore later.

In therapeutic work supervision is generally seen as a process of reflection and learning for practitioners working with clients. Leddick and Bernard (1980) identified three primary models of supervision:

- Developmental models view learning as being lifelong and the aim of supervision to identify areas for development and maximise growth
- Integrated models encourage a broader focus by adopting a multiple therapeutic approach
- Orientation-specific models are based on a specific theoretical orientation aimed at ensuring practice keeps to a specific theory; a benefit of shared orientation can be that modelling is maximised.

There appears to be common ground across these three models in terms of valuing a safe supervisory relationship, having a task-directed structure, a variety of learning styles and a range of supervisory roles.

As we have reflected on our experiences of supervision and learning, while writing this book, we have been able to see the differences in our disciplines of therapist and social worker and how these bring in a welcome diversity.

Embracing diversity between you and your supervisor or peer supervisor will enhance your ways of thinking and working in relation to a variety of factors including age, gender, sexual orientation, race and religious or spiritual beliefs, learning and physical challenges, family relationships and dynamics, training background and theory.

We can learn so much from each other's cultural perspective and experiences that can enhance our ways of communicating and understanding the differences between us. Every one of us is a unique individual, with experiences that are unique to us. We share these experiences, belief systems and life events according to our encounters with others and, when we are open to hearing the differences between us, this will allow change to occur in the way we interact with others.

Within supervision it is important to acknowledge and address the differences between you and reflect on how you can effectively communicate in order to work collaboratively and creatively. Such discussions within a relationship of trust and empathy will reduce any fear or hesitation around discussing multicultural issues and increase your own multicultural understanding or competence. You can then model this within your Therapeutic Life Story Work. This awareness can help you to adapt to cultural differences within your relationship with the child and family you are supporting, where the differences can influence the child's own experience of self and perception of others.

Appreciating cultural diversity is important to our professional and personal development. Supervision provides a space to challenge and be challenged with sensitivity and empathy. We value the differences, cultural and otherwise, between one another and between us and the children we support, as well as the learning we acquire from being supervised and supervising.

Karla: As a therapist I learnt about orientation-specific models of supervision such as Carl Rogers' person-centred approach (1957, cited in Leddick and Bernard 1980). The approach advocates a partnership process which creates a respectful and supportive setting, enabling people to understand and support each other well. This is achieved by stepping into the experience of the supervisee who chooses to be influenced by the supervisory relationship.

Building on this, Orlans and Edwards (2001) identified the optimal 'core conditions' that are needed to support the development of a collaborative and creative supervisory relationship. They refer to writers such as Shohet and Wilmot (1991) who identified that there needs to be a degree of warmth, trust, genuineness and respect between the supervisee and supervisor, in order to create a safe enough environment for supervision to take place.

In our peer supervision, as in our clinical supervision, these conditions of acceptance, congruence and transparency facilitate our continued growth and development, while acknowledging these conditions can be extremely challenging.

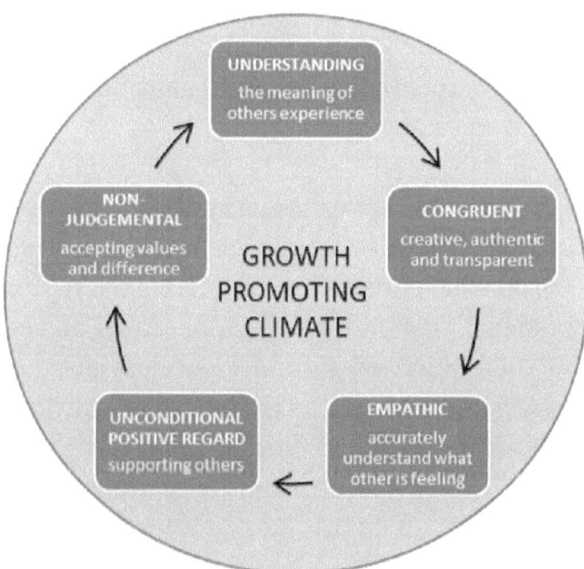

Figure 39: Adapted from Rogers Person-Centred Core Conditions

As seen in Figure 39, in order to be an effective practitioner from a person-centred approach, you need the core qualities of being:

- Understanding, i.e. the meaning of others experience (reflective)
- Congruent, genuine, authentic and transparent
- Empathic, and accurately understand what the other is feeling (attuned)
- Able to offer unconditional positive regard in supporting others
- Non-judgemental, accepting others values and differences.

These core qualities are very much a part of me and how I work with children and adults; they enable me to sit with difficult emotions in the moment, as well as before and after sessions, and promote development of a deeper intuition which uncovers new meaning of the emotions experienced. My focus is on facilitating a process wherein the supervisee can contemplate themselves and their experiences so they can enter the therapeutic relationship more fully and congruently, leading to an enhanced understanding of their internal and external world.

Suzanne: As a social worker, I learnt about integrated models of supervision such as Kadushin's (1976) model of supervision in social work which identifies the three main functions of supervision as being administrative, educational and supportive. Building on this, Morrison (2005) identified four functions of supervision (which can be integrated into his reflective supervision cycle considered later in this chapter and shown in Figure 42):

- Management function to ensure competent, accountable practice
- Development function to ensure continuing professional development

- Mediation function to ensure engagement with the organisation and developing professional relationship
- Support to ensure personal support.

While there may be elements of all four functions in our peer supervision it is not accountable in terms of decision making and safeguarding which need to be shared with the team around the child.

In setting up peer supervision we have made a less formal supervision arrangement focused on the supportive function of supervision. Our aim has been to support one another in our work by providing an opportunity for regular discussion and reflection on our practice. As we both work independently, this was extremely important to us and has proved to be a great source of support in terms of safety, containment, creativity and learning. We have identified four key areas of peer supervision – safety, containment, connection and relationship, and reflection – which we represent as an umbrella protecting our practice, as shown in in Figure 40.

Safety and Containment

Safety

In our view, the purpose of supervision is to provide a safe, supportive and accepting space where we can engage in critical reflection, raise issues, explore problems and discover new ways of handling both situations and ourselves. We require emotional safety in supervision (in a similar way to the children with whom we work) so that reflection, understanding, containment and exploration of doubt, anxiety and uncertainty can take place in our therapeutic work (Vetere and Sheehan 2017).

Figure 40: Umbrella of Support

Therapeutic Life Story Work requires us to be imaginative, perseverant and to fully engage with children on profound levels. This takes commitment, no matter how difficult it may feel at times. A trusting supervisory relationship provides a safe platform where you can be challenged and supported, enabling you to become more aware, informed, skilled and encouraged, both personally and professionally.

Safety in supervision can enable us to be open about our fears, successes and concerns. We have learnt acceptance and can share moments that may have touched us deeply in a session, without fear of being judged or feeling that we got it wrong; it is okay to make mistakes and think about what we can do to address this in the next session.

Suzanne: At the beginning of my Therapeutic Life Story Work practice, I noticed a tendency not to 'hear' what the child had said until reflecting on the session afterwards. I would often truly hear the child's words on my journey home. Examining this in supervision, I was able to identify when it was more likely to happen and recognise the impact of my own anxiety in relation to some areas of the work. By 'noticing and naming' the feelings (Siegel and Bryson 2011) in supervision I acquired acceptance of and insight into my anxiety, and by continuing to notice and name this in sessions (sometimes out loud) the anxiety reduced.

I can still fall into the trap of not listening when feelings of anxiety are triggered. I have learnt to notice this privately at first and then openly during sessions and rectify it. I have also learnt to forgive myself for being human and for making mistakes. It helps that children can be very forgiving; there is always the opportunity to bring what you heard or felt last time to the next session and discuss it with the child, as well as examining what feelings they may be carrying. Demonstrating to the child that you are not perfect and can accept and even use your mistakes can be powerful role modelling.

We have noticed that our peer supervision supports us with self-regulation, as it is a place where we can share our anxieties, perhaps immediately prior to a first session or tricky visit to a birth parent. Similarly, we have learnt how helpful it can be to debrief with a peer supervisor as soon as possible after a powerful or concerning session. This is something we feel even the most experienced and skilled practitioners need to do. It can be especially powerful and validating for the child to let them know when a session has had a big impact on you; for example, when sitting with their pain, traumatic memories, rage, silence or dissociation, you can let them know that you have experienced a little of what they were feeling, have felt exhausted by it and can only imagine how they must be feeling.

It is imperative to have a system for creating physical and emotional safety for yourself, and we find our peer supervision helpful in this respect. When you are visiting a birth parent in person in their home there can be many unknowns. Who else may be in the home? Will talking about the past trigger powerful and possibly angry emotions which could place you at risk of harm? We use peer supervision as a safeguard when carrying out in-person visits. We let each other know the details of who, when and where we are visiting and what time we expect to finish. We may even arrange a check-in call 20 minutes into the interview to give us a pretext to leave if needed, with agreement as to what action to take if the call is not answered, such as contacting the police to request assistance.

Having an agreed safeguarding arrangement is particularly important when working independently, and without the support and safety of a team around you. This has been an invaluable part of peer supervision for us as self-employed lone workers, particularly when visiting a birth family member whose emotions have triggered anger in the past. Having this support provides physical safety, and de-briefing following the visit creates emotional safety and support that is extremely helpful and valued.

It is important to add that we do not always visit the birth parent in their home or on our own, especially where there are known concerns. We may arrange to meet in a social work office or similar public place where there is someone to monitor our safety. We had favoured in person visits to birth family members, but as a result of the restrictions imposed in England during the worldwide pandemic in 2020/21, we have found that online or phone video interviews can work really well, and are more appropriate in terms of safety in some situations.

In our view it is essential to pay attention to how you are feeling after an emotionally intense session, either one that has had great healing moments or has been incredibly challenging in some way. If you are driving it is important to consider your safety when travelling after such a session, and to use the support of your peer supervisor, or other support if needed, to debrief. We have both experienced the need to stop during our drive home upon realising that our focus was on the session rather than our driving. We have needed to stop and take some time to reflect on and process those powerful emotions before continuing our journey. We use this time to make notes on the session, phone a supportive person or just to take deep breaths and notice how we are feeling. We recommend doing a quick emotional check-in after sessions before making your journey to ensure that you are calm and able to fully concentrate on the task to ensure your physical safety.

Containment
Supervision can offer a place of containment where you can learn about yourself as well as the child and the family's journey, and how best to support them through the Therapeutic Life Story Work process.

We speak together as peer supervisors on a weekly basis for up to two hours. While this works well for us, it is not a prescription and may be different for others. Having this length of time gives us an opportunity to consider in detail a session which may have taken place that day or week and may be forgotten by the time of our clinical supervision. We find this time is useful for sharing what we have each been doing in our work and reflecting on the thoughts and feelings that have come up for us. We also occasionally undertake three-way peer supervision with another colleague which works well and brings in a greater diversity of knowledge and experience.

Therapeutic Life Story Work sessions can be full of surprises, shocks and a range of emotions, such as love, anger, frustration and confusion. In one session we can be working with all of these, from one end of the spectrum to the other, and need to support and contain these for the child and their parents. We in turn benefit from support by containing the powerful emotions that we have held for the child and parent in a session and may have come away with, to help us process the feelings and prepare for future sessions.

While supervision is not a place for private therapy, in our peer supervision we may share something from our personal lives that has been triggered or is affecting us. It is important to be aware of anything that might resonate with us and remind us of something from our own experience in connection with the work we are carrying out with the families. Ulleberg and Jensen (2017) suggest that this resonance can affect what we choose to emphasise and do in the session. Our experience can be a resource that we draw upon in our therapeutic work, but we need to be mindful of the danger that it can contribute to non-therapeutic moves or an unseen area in our practice.

It is important to examine and challenge any links between private and personal experiences and our professional practice. This can allow us to understand our own mental and emotional state, and how relevant that may or may not be to our work. We realise that in supervision we offer one another emotional containment which helps us maintain separation between our work and our personal lives. We achieve clarity in relation to which feelings belong to us and which are those of the child or parent, allowing us to sustain a professional relationship with them. Again, we are not offering one another personal therapy, but at times it is crucial to take a moment to examine a life event so that we can understand our position on a personal level.

When our own life events and past traumas have been triggered through our work it can have a detrimental effect on our wellbeing. The danger is that if not addressed it may affect our work. It is important not to allow these personal events to extend beyond our private life into our professional work. We are human and we too need to look after ourselves. Therefore, it is good practice to consider taking these experiences to a counsellor or therapist in order to work through them safely. This will ensure we keep clear boundaries for ourselves and in turn the family we are working with.

It is imperative that in our clinical supervision we are guided and encouraged not to carry too heavy a caseload, and for this to be monitored in terms of the work we take on. While it is not a responsibility to consider our workload in peer supervision, we do find it is something we discuss and about which we support one another.

Karla: With my therapist's background I am able to offer the child and family emotional therapeutic containment, which is invaluable to this work. I also find it helpful to draw from Suzanne's experience and background in social work. Having a peer supervisor with many years of experience in working with children and families in child protection has provided me with a different perspective, especially concerning contact with birth family members and how to resolve issues that may arise. It has increased my knowledge of local authority processes and procedures, enhanced my understanding of care proceedings and the court process, been extremely supportive to my personal and professional growth. It has challenged me to consider all aspects of the working relationship that are not in my awareness. This challenge is what keeps us all safe, ethical and ensures that we are maintaining healthy boundaries for all concerned.

Suzanne: When I became a Therapeutic Life Story Work practitioner, I chose to have clinical supervision with a dyadic developmental psychotherapy practitioner, recognising that the therapeutic element of the sessions was the greatest area for development in my practice. A therapeutic input in both clinical and peer supervision has been invaluable in assisting me with containing emotions held by and triggered for children and their parents in sessions and in working through these. In peer supervision it has proved of great benefit to have Karla's therapeutic insights into the processes taking place in sessions as well as affording vicarious learning from her descriptions of her sessions.

We can become good reflective practitioners when we are able to take responsibility and the initiative to create a network of people and resources who can provide us with support while preserving confidentiality. It is an amazing and validating experience to share with a peer what happened in a session, how it felt, what your thoughts were before, during and after a session, and to discuss things that may be weighing heavily on your mind. We have each experienced how our mind can be put at rest through discussion with someone who has had the Therapeutic Life Story Work training and is aware of its process. It offers the chance to scrutinise things and see if there is anything we may have missed.

Sharing our thoughts and experiences openly and honestly can support us in modelling this to the child and parent. If we are not able to do this, how can we expect the child to do the same with us? Learning from one another in this way can be extremely validating, especially when something one of us has said or done creates a moment of clarity for the other.

Karla: My work with one child can be used to illustrate containment. I had been recommended by a post-adoption team to work with a child aged 17 who had multiple physical and learning needs. These included a high level of medical necessities, minimal speech and mobility, and the referral felt challenging. I was aware that she was unable to write and yet she was keen to learn about her birth family and culture.

I used peer supervision prior to meeting the child and parents to address my multiple questions around how I could effectively plan the sessions given this child's high level of complex needs. How could the Therapeutic Life Story Work take place on the wallpaper? How would I communicate with a child who had minimal speech? How did the child feel about embarking on this journey? Was she too feeling apprehensive? How could I work at her pace while still being directive and achieve a good enough result for her? These questions left me feeling nervous, anxious and lacking confidence in my ability to undertake this work.

Exploring all of my concerns and feelings in peer supervision and naming the anxiety prior to my first session restored my trust in my skills and ability. I was able to contain my anxiety and be more relaxed in the first session. I recalled my experience of working with children with selective mutism and employed some of the techniques I had discovered during this research. The pre-session discussion offered reassurance and grounding. It reminded me to remain alongside the child, 'name the elephant in the room' (something I am always saying) and trust that it would be okay. I had found the space to take a deep breath, remember my way of working and trust my ability to contain these emotions.

The discussion also brought up the likelihood that the child and parents shared similar emotions. Consequently, when discussing the session plan with the parents I was able to help them contain their anxiety surrounding this work. Having sought understanding of my own concerns, I was able to go into the family's home and be transparent and approachable.

Suzanne: Peer supervision provided containment for me and in turn the family I was working with when an issue arose in reviewing and planning sessions with parents of a 14-year-old. The parent had experienced dysregulated and threatening behaviour from the child following the previous session. The child expressed a wish to continue the timeline, but their behaviour suggested they were not emotionally ready. The shared intention was to help them make sense of the past, but it caused a dilemma about how to proceed; the parent could be physically hurt by the child during trauma triggers and rages, and the other parent, who could usually help regulate his behaviour, was not feeling emotionally strong due to a recent bereavement.

Being able to discuss this with Karla prior to the session helped me focus on the importance of staying with the here and now. I experienced an immediate feeling of relief, and an 'aha' moment when I saw how simply and well that would work. This correlates with what Grosvenor (2017) identifies as intense emotional moments of learning that a supervisee can experience in supervision, perhaps of relief, insight, or something falling into place that has been promoted by the supervisor.

In the session we explored together what had been happening for the family and concluded that none of the family members were presently able to continue looking back at the past. Reflecting on the child's thoughts, feelings, actions, and intentions following the previous session and staying in the here and now enabled containment for the family members. The child agreed that they were not feeling emotionally safe enough to carry on with the timeline while family members were feeling vulnerable due to their recent bereavement.

The sessions were extremely powerful in terms of the child being able to show some deep feelings and anxieties without turning the sadness, fear and anxiety into anger as so often happened for them. This was enabled through the safety we had created over time in the sessions, the parent staying emotionally and physically close, and my increased confidence from supervision discussion about how I would address the issue. The child was also able to hear and accept what a positive step it was for them to be able to tolerate us talking about some of these feelings.

Connection and Relationship

We start, as we do in providing Therapeutic Life Story Work, with the importance of making a connection and building a relationship. A good supervisory relationship is based on mutual trust, warmth, respect, authenticity, collaboration and transparency. The relationship must be established before reflection takes place, in a similar way that Golding's (2015) concept proposes connection before correction in relation to parenting traumatised children.

As with Therapeutic Life Story Work, the supervisory relationship is enhanced by creating a working agreement at the outset, which in turn increases safety within the relationship. It constitutes a mutual agreement about how to work together and commit to becoming a team. Creating it enables you to consider your expectations and what you are each offering and require from each other. Doing this together establishes a collaborative and creative relationship. It also provides an opportunity to discuss questions of ethics, legal issues, safeguarding, professional conduct and your ability to maintain the standard that is required by your professional body.

Agree at the start to review the agreement over time. It is important to check with each other to see how each feels the relationship is working. When a supervisor monitors and reflects on the working relationship, it creates a safe and accepting environment of congruence, openness and potential growth and development that is then recreated within your work with the child and their family.

For clinical supervision the agreement may include the following:

- Safeguarding
- Support
- Confidentiality
- Frequency and duration
- Contact between supervision sessions
- Development of your practice and work
- Keeping notes or a journal of your experiences
- Monitoring number and level of work
- Reviewing the supervisory relationship and process
- Continuous professional development (CPD) training

For peer supervision it is equally important to discuss and agree on most of these, though it can be done in a less formal way. For instance, we agreed at the outset that we would maintain confidentiality in our peer supervision by not using the child and parent's names and similarly that things that were said in our supervision were not shared with others unless agreed.

We have developed our own formula that works for us. It has not been formally agreed but developed through reflection and consulting with each other. At the beginning of the supervision, we ask each other how things have been, informally ascertaining who may have the greatest need to talk about their work first. We aim to listen to one another, before reflecting our thoughts and possibly sharing what we have done in a similar situation.

We have based our peer supervision on mutuality, agreeing together how we check in, support and challenge one another. We feel this has enhanced the quality of our learning and development and helped build our supervisory relationship.

It is this mutual sharing which makes peer supervision different to clinical supervision. There are also similarities such as exploring and processing our thoughts and feelings from a session, coming to realisations and making connections, noticing what is not being said or what we did not name in a session and generating 'light bulb moments' of clarity: insight into what we were doing, what the child was communicating, or ideas for the next session.

In addition to the benefits our peer supervision shares with clinical supervision, we have the advantage of both having undertaken the Therapeutic Life Story Work Diploma course. This means we can remind each other of course learning, such as the techniques we use; we can compare how we use them and share ideas or strategies we have found successful. This consolidates the collaborative nature of our peer supervisory relationship.

Having built a sound supervisory relationship, we can replicate this in our working relationship with the child, parent and their network.

Karla: When I started out in Therapeutic Life Story Work the biggest challenges for me were having to plan my sessions, discussing them with the parent and having the parent in the sessions. I felt as if I was going against all my training as a play therapist and, therefore, my 'way of being'. I was used to going into my sessions without any agenda, no matter what others may have wanted me to achieve with the child. I worked from a non-directive perspective, staying with the child at their pace while keeping in mind funding restrictions and the number of sessions that were available for the child.

I used peer and clinical supervision to reflect upon my concerns about this; I felt that by being directive I was in danger of not staying at the child's pace which seemed an impossibility for me. Suzanne's trauma and attachment-led approach, informed by her dyadic developmental psychotherapy and social work training provided me with a balanced alternative and I began to see the value of having the parent in the room to strengthen attachment and support recovery from trauma and loss.

Suzanne: In social work I was used to having a clear agenda when meeting with a child. My challenge in becoming a Therapeutic Life Story Work practitioner was learning to be less directive and more child-led, developing therapeutic skills of noticing, naming, and sitting with feelings. I needed to learn how to be alert to what was happening in the session for the child, the parent, and myself, how to wonder out loud and be curious. Having clinical supervision from a dyadic developmental psychotherapy practitioner and peer supervision with Karla as a play therapist has been invaluable in enabling me to develop a more therapeutic approach in my work. Therapeutic Life Story Work is powerful work to do with a child and parent; supervision has helped me to reflect more on the feelings I might hold following a session, and to understand how these are likely to mirror those of the child or parent.

Ulleberg and Jensen (2017 p.121) identify how the culture of supervision transfers into the supervisee's professional work; the relationship and climate it creates serve as a model of what can happen in the supervisee's own work. They suggest that the concept of dialogue is central. Verbal and non-verbal levels of human communication, conscious and unconscious may have a profound affect both personally and professionally: 'The intention is to create a culture where movements, complexity, diversity, and surprises are dealt with as invitations to be flexible and improvised, in a benevolently open manner.'

It has, understandably, taken time to build mutual trust, respect, openness and transparency, all of which is underpinned by our integrity: being clear what we could offer one another and having a 'joint intention' (Hughes 2007). Our working relationship continues to develop and deepen due to our joint motivation and commitment to maximise learning with one another. This goes on to have a positive impact on the children and parents we support, as well as birth families and the professional network around the child. It is an on-going process in which we continue to learn and transform our practice, never quite knowing where the journey will take us. For us, the exciting parts of supervision are the insights and co-creative learning, in the same way that the exciting part of our work is the child's journey and insights.

When we learn new skills, we can experience a range of different emotions, and understanding. Burch's (1969) conscious competence ladder can help us make sense of this. At the beginning we may be unconsciously incompetent, not realising how much we need to learn. When we realise what we don't know we become 'consciously incompetent' and may get disheartened and give up. We believe that good supervision can help us manage the emotional process of learning and provide an opportunity to move to the further stages of conscious competence and towards unconscious competence, and in turn we can model this in our work with the child and parent.

Supervision requires commitment, dedication a proactive approach to the development of our own creativity, willingness to step outside our comfort zone to become more reflective practitioners, and openness to new experiences and to changing our awareness.

In return it enhances the effectiveness of Therapeutic Life Story Work by offering us new insights into our work and what may be happening for the child and parent.

The diagram in Figure 41 shows our interpretation of the value of supervision:

1. We take our experience, observations and feelings from our work with the child to explore in our supervision.
2. Through the key elements of safety, support, containment and reflection in this relationship we can gain new awareness, clarity, focus and meaning.
3. We take these key elements back into our sessions, ensuring that they are in place in our work with the child.

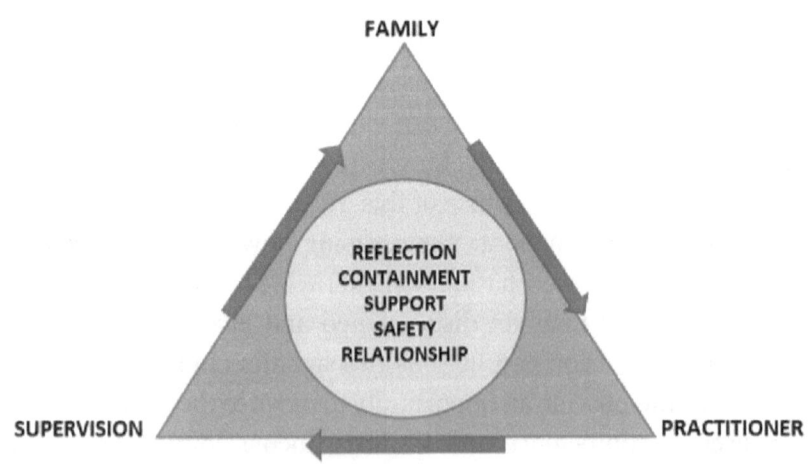

Figure 41: The Supervision Triangle

Suzanne: The value of our peer supervision was demonstrated when I noticed barriers building between a 16-year-old young person and her parents. In discussing the sessions in supervision, I noticed speaking with stronger emotion than I had previously been aware of and realised that meeting with the parents separately would be of value. I expressed my reluctance to add this session to my workload, but Karla validated the benefit and importance of taking this step. In meeting with parents, they reported finding it useful in reminding them of the things they knew about behaviour such as communication and the impact of early attachment trauma. They seemed visibly relieved by a reminder of the simplicity of what their daughter needed, namely time with them to reassure her of their unconditional love, rather than time away.

I had attempted to present Karpman's (1968) model of interpersonal relationships which identifies how the 'drama triangle' of victim, persecutor and rescuer can play out. However, I noticed that this was not resonating with the parents. Focusing instead on hearing and exploring what they were feeling, and then considering what their daughter might have been feeling, proved successful in reinstating their therapeutic parenting. The parents were able to re-focus on the importance of connecting with the feelings underneath their child's behaviour rather than reacting to the behaviour.

Reflection in Supervision

We recognise and agree that reflection is an integral part of any supervision. Reflection has been a key part of our supervisory relationship, being so much richer when combined with each other's insights. Morrison's supervision cycle (2005), shown in Figure 42, is adapted from Kolb's (1984) learning styles model and highlights the importance of learning through reflection on and analysis of our experiences.

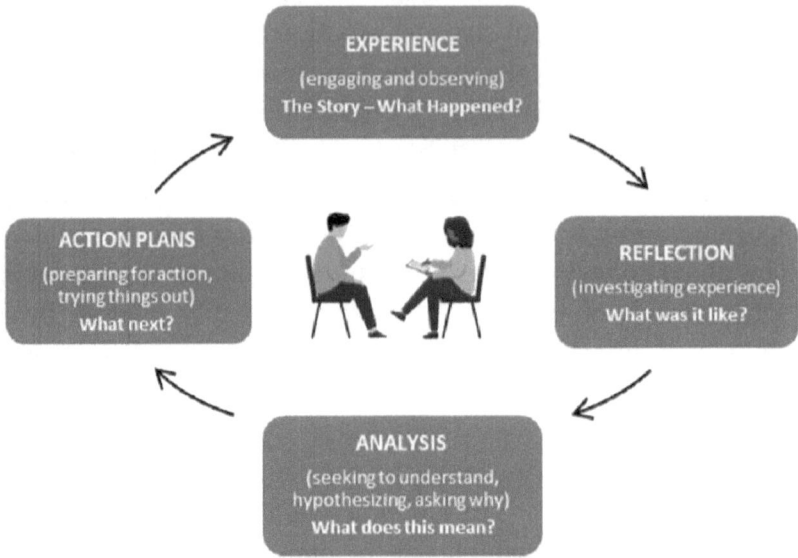

Figure 42: Re-drawing of Morrison's Supervision Cycle

We believe that good supervision enables learning through reflecting on observations and feelings we may have had during the work we have undertaken. We agree with Kolb (1984 p.38) that 'learning is the process whereby knowledge is created through the transformation of experience'; this has certainly been our experience.

There are many different learning styles. We both identify as active learners: one of us through doing and observing rather than theorising and the other through active listening and feeling, observing body language and what is not being said, while being supported mentally by theory. Peer supervision facilitates reflection which assists our learning.

The diagram shown in Figure 43 is taken from Jane Hill's model of non-managerial clinical supervision which she developed as a training course for National Health Service staff in 2010–2020. It identifies reflection as being central for the practitioner to examine their practice in a supportive and safe way: enabling personal growth, professional development and empowerment, which we feel are key components in providing and maintaining a high level of practice.

© Jane Hill, Project Manager for Clinical Supervision

Figure 43: Hill's Model of Non-Managerial Clinical Supervision

Suzanne: Reflection helped me to see how I was often only really hearing what the child said after the session. I became mindful of not being led by my session plan or by my own or the parent's agenda, which can happen too frequently when adults attempt to communicate with children. Through this I learnt to slow down, listen more, and allow and make space for the child's voice, thoughts, feelings and creativity in sessions, all of which are noticed and celebrated. This learning was validated when a child commented in surprise during our first session 'Hey, you're listening to me!'

Similarly, hearing Karla talk about and reflect on her sessions provides me with vicarious learning, especially in relation to her play and psychotherapy experience, skills and techniques. I listen and learn when she describes how she sits with and holds a child's feelings and models to the parent how to do the same, or how she 'names the elephant in the room' to highlight for a parent what their child is communicating to them. She has talked about the techniques she uses, such as the squiggle game, which I have then incorporated into my own practice. I find it a valuable tool that can be used to create safety in early sessions and to help regulate and calm a child.

Karla: I found it helpful to reflect in peer supervision on an assessment of need that had been received for a child who had complex physical and learning needs. In discussing my concerns, I was reminded of my skills and knowledge in this area and willingness to adapt my way of working to meet the child's needs.

Peer supervision offers space to reflect on what happens perhaps before, during and after a session. As previously discussed, it is vital to our wellbeing, that of the child, their family and of the Therapeutic Life Story Work process that we regularly discuss how we are feeling with a suitable other.

The process of reflection helped me to work things through with another child aged 14 who had made it clear at the start of her Therapeutic Life Story Work that she did not want to talk about her past or her birth family. Her parents wanted her to be able to explore her past trauma and loss which they felt impacted on her present behaviours, such as mood swings. In discussing the issue of how best to offer this child a sense of security and structure to safely investigate her sense of self Suzanne suggested creating a 'magazine self-portrait' (Wrench and Naylor 2013 p.53). I thought this would be fun and might provide a window into the child's internal world, being gentle enough to contain the block the child was holding deeply within herself in relation to her past.

However, during the session this exercise was forgotten and left out of mind. Instead, I used the behaviour tree technique (Rose 2012), which was not easy for the child to do, especially hearing her parents talk about the neglect she experienced from her birth parents. Coming away from the session I felt that something was missing but was not quite sure what. During peer supervision I pondered why I had not offered the magazine exercise, and after several minutes of considering the options an 'aha' moment occurred. I had been holding and experiencing the child's 'block' and, just like the child, I did not want to go there. I had gained a powerful and useful insight into how I experienced the child's block on an unconscious level, affording me a glimpse and understanding of the child's internal world.

Due to circumstances, we were not able to use the magazine exercise in the next session. I decided instead that we would explore the child's sense of self through words and colours. She was able to describe herself first in words followed by colours, seeming open to this and very keen to share her thoughts. This resulted in an incredible session which unlocked a door that allowed her to uncover what she had been holding internally most of her life. The child reported feeling relieved at the end of the session and very happy she had let go of some powerful emotions.

The parents commented afterwards that this was the first time their daughter had been able to share her feelings regarding her past. I felt honoured and humbled by the trust the child had placed in herself, her parents and me. I have learnt, through my many years of working with children, to trust the process, believing we always end up right where we are meant to be right when we are meant to be there.

Being a reflective practitioner offers us an opportunity to model transparency by naming the most difficult emotions, trauma and loss with the utmost respect and sensitivity and to consider how we can best support the family, something they too can begin to practice. This support may present itself through psychological projection – projecting undesirable feelings or emotions onto someone else. We can explore this through supervision and become aware of it, as I did.

We have considered whether there can be a danger in validating each other and becoming insular. To avoid this, it is paramount to create the safety within the relationship to challenge one another. This is also why maintaining clinical supervision is vital, as well as our three-way peer supervision.

What Makes a Good Supervisor?

We feel the qualities that make a good supervisor are being creative, collaborative and encouraging. Supporting and guiding the supervisee towards realisation, suggesting options rather than being directive, rigid and prescriptive. This encompasses taking time to understand the supervisee, how they work and having the ability to challenge them with sensitivity. Grosvenor (2017) considers how the supervisor should be aware of their power and mindful of using language that supports learning. Supervisors should maintain clear boundaries, timekeeping, be part of a professional governing body that upholds an ethical framework and have a clear understanding of safeguarding.

We feel that it is useful for the supervisor to understand the Therapeutic Life Story Work process, in order to ensure that the principles of the model are adhered to. In our experience it has not been productive to have a supervisor who does not accept our way of working based on our training. Nor is it helpful to have to spend a lot of time teaching them about our training instead of working with the case material we have prepared for supervision.

Supervision is rich in opportunities for learning, expressing and exploring all aspects of ourselves and the child, and the progress of each. We believe good supervision models the dyadic developmental psychotherapy qualities of playfulness, acceptance, curiosity and empathy, identified as PACE (Hughes 2007). With the addition of sound guidance and insight supervision can be enlightening and inspirational. In turn, good practice aims to model these qualities for the parent, enabling them to provide this form of therapeutic parenting for their child.

Supervision is a place to present and discuss beliefs and theory as well as developing your own skills and competencies within your work. Safeguarding issues can be discussed in peer and clinical supervision, but responsibility lies with the child's social worker and any concerns must be reported to them.

Good supervision provides the safety to discover your own way of working and how best to improve or enhance your way of interacting with the child and family so that you both can have the best experience and outcomes during the Therapeutic Life Story Work process. The process will be enhanced where supervision models good practice.

Good supervisors provide insights for the supervisee, things they have not seen for themselves as 'we cannot see the ocean when we are swimming in it' (Cairns 2002 p.69). For example, when we experience powerful feelings following a session we may believe they are our own, but our supervisor can enable us to see that they may belong to the child or parent. Having the space to reflect safely and openly in supervision can help provide clarity and determine how best to work with this the next time we see the child and parent.

Becoming a Supervisor

We both provide individual and group clinical supervision and are responsible and accountable in preserving and maintaining The Rose Model of Therapeutic Life Story Work which protects and serves the child whilst safeguarding the integrity of Therapeutic Life Story Work and that of the practitioner. We are both members of the Therapeutic Life Story Work International Board which provides an opportunity for greater learning about and input in development of The Rose Model of the Therapeutic Life Story Work, in terms of our own practice and areas for development as well as enhancing our supervisory skills.

We both arrived at our supervisory roles through very different paths, however.

Suzanne: My first experience of supervising others was in my role as a senior social worker in an inner London child protection team. I supervised social workers with a range of ages, experiences, ethnicity and sexual orientation, but received no supervision training. I was able to support my supervisees and enhance their professional development, skills, knowledge and trust in their own abilities because of my experience as a social worker; I knew how to manage time and caseload priorities and work with diversity and differences within the community. My experience in instigating court proceedings and presenting at court provided me with a working knowledge of child protection legislation and procedures. My experience had helped me in developing my ability to communicate, plan and take responsibility within my supervisory role. I combined creativity with a positive attitude, to become a supportive and effective supervisor. I drew from the guidance and modelling of supervision I had received and from my amazing team manager in the London Borough of Wandsworth, Paul Angeli.

On reflection I can see that initially I lacked confidence in this role and would have benefitted from supervision training. However, my own experiences of both good and unsatisfactory supervision supported my development, especially the positive support I received at the time. This past experience, together with my Therapeutic Life Story Work experience and training, has equipped me to take on Therapeutic Life Story Work supervision.

Karla: When I was training as a counsellor I received clinical supervision from a psychoanalytically trained psychotherapist who had years of experience working within a therapeutic framework. Upon qualifying, my supervisor recommended I train as a clinical supervisor to continue my professional development. I attended a training course based on Carl Rogers' core conditions (Rogers 1957) and was required to supervise trainee counsellors. The experience of being clinically supervised provided modelling of supervision that gave me grounding and encouragement. I seek to maintain a level of authenticity and believe that if you offer a safe and accepting environment a supervisee can and will meet their full potential.

Certification in Therapeutic Life Story Work Supervision was launched in 2023 and is available through TLSWi.com.

Practicalities of Supervisory Contact

In our peer supervision we use telephone calls and video due to the geographical distance between us. Our first face-to-face meeting was some time after establishing our online partnership and it added a new dimension to meet in person.

Both telephone and video communications have their advantages and disadvantages. While speaking on the phone the concentration is on what the person is saying, the tone of voice or silences, and so on. However, it is also possible to get distracted in doing other tasks, like preparing and eating food or checking emails! Video calls can create greater focus on the person and the conversation, though you may get distracted from what is said by what you are seeing. Online supervision can save time and cost and can be invaluable if there are few options for supervisors in a local area.

The worldwide Covid-19 pandemic in 2020 placed sharper scrutiny on the use of online video for supervision. In specific therapeutic settings it raises practical, ethical and legal issues, especially concerning the safety of the supervision and the safety of the families we support. Stokes (2018) explores the practice of online supervision and identifies that professionals are having to develop new ways of working. Presently there is little that has been published about online supervision and even less research and documented examples of practice. New models are being developed specifically for supervising online; it is an ongoing learning process.

Stokes (2018) has considered the differences between face-to-face and online supervision in terms of relationship and process, and identified that online supervision requires the technological skills and abilities to manage the communication in a safe way.

In online supervision using live video you usually see only the person's face. This does not provide all the visual clues you have when sitting in the same room and it can be hard to see details like tears or clenched fists. Therefore, more 'checking out' may be required in relation to what you feel you are picking up from the other person, and there is no direct eye contact as the tendency is to look at the screen rather than the camera.

Bond (2015) suggests it is desirable to have supervision using the same method of communication in which your work is taking place, to have a mutual appreciation of the strengths and constraints.

It is helpful for each of us to know the supervision guidelines that apply to our work and whether we are abiding by a governing body. In the UK, the British Association for Counselling and Psychotherapy Guidelines for Online Counselling and Psychotherapy (Anthony and Goss 2009) are useful for those providing online counselling, who in turn will need online supervision for their clinical work. The British Association for Counselling and Psychotherapy accepts online supervision for those working in this way.

Security issues are greater in relation to online supervision and a recommended platform should be used. In the USA, for example, Skype is viewed as unethical and is not compliant with the Health Insurance Portability and Accountability (USA) Act 1996. At the time of writing, Zoom video conferencing was accepted in the UK by the Adoption Support Fund for online therapeutic work. It is important to make sure that the platform you use complies with the security and professional ethical requirements for your practice. Stokes (2018) advocates the need for training in online supervision, and this is an area that has been incorporated into the Certificate in Therapeutic Life Story Work Supervision course available via TLSWi.com.

Summary

Peer supervision has been an irreplaceable part of our work, enabling us to fully support the child and their family. It allows us the time, space and a platform to openly share our concerns, excitement and disappointments, to discover new resources and ideas, and to discuss what has worked well and what has not. We each continue to gain something valuable from supervision, which is why it works on a peer-to-peer level.

Supervision with a peer offers an opportunity to share openly, with no judgement and with the utmost respect, in the knowledge that the concept of the work is mutually understood. It is where we talk through and bounce ideas between us in preparing for a session, and where we reflect and find clarity after an extremely powerful session, either in a favourable or unfavourable sense. This is especially beneficial where it would be hard to hold our feelings and thoughts until a formal supervision session. Even the most experienced and skilled practitioners need to do this.

Therapeutic Life Story Work is intensive yet extremely rewarding work, and it is important to acknowledge the validity of receiving good supervision to support us in working alongside trauma. It is vital to commit to a space that allows the themes of trauma that thread their way throughout sessions to be connected, to reveal their deeper meaning.

Supervision is also a place where we can consider and assess the outcomes of our work, identifying changes, improvement and progress in the child. Good supervision allows us to remain alongside the child in their journey towards recovery. In doing so it helps us and the child to gain a greater understanding of who they are, where they have come from and what the possibilities are for them in their future, once they have put the pieces of their puzzle together. As one child stated, 'It's like putting me back together again.'

In Therapeutic Life Story Work we engage with issues of attachment, separation, loss, anxiety, fear and trauma, aiming to work towards restoration and healing. To be alongside the child and their parent in this way can be very painful. However, it is also a privilege. The rewards are to encourage and facilitate the child's transformation and journey towards healing and enable them to gain a clearer picture of who they are.

Our supervisory relationship offers us safety, containment and opportunities for reflection, and supports us in achieving and celebrating the moments of healing and recovery that continue to occur in our work. The families we work with teach us so much and we need to continually challenge ourselves about what we do with them. Supervision in its many forms provides the platform for this and can maximise the benefit of our continual learning.

Chapter 13
Authenticity and Working Online

Authenticity is totally dependent on your ability to be honest, aware of your own emotional responses and willing to share these with others. It springs from our integrity, models good practice, encourages others to be true to themselves and continues to shape our work. It is not always easy to share what is really on our minds or express the feelings that we are having at any given moment, but it is important and may validate what is transpiring between you and another person.

Karla: I have found that the more I am myself in any situation, the more authentic the experiences are – something I would like everyone I work with or support to experience. My truth is supported by the intentions of what I say. I always speak with sensitivity, thoughtfulness, consideration and acceptance. I may not always get it right, but I will always authentically be present with the other person. Modelling this can encourage the children and families I work with to practise the same within the sessions and to become more real with each other in their daily lives.

Suzanne: Good supervision and mentoring has provided me with a sound model for developing authenticity. Through reflecting on sessions in supervision I have learnt the value of trusting my intuition and noticing and naming out loud with the child. If we incorporate this approach into our practice, we can ensure getting the best out of the session, the child and parent relationship and ourselves as practitioners.

Karla: Before the lockdown measures during the Covid-19 pandemic in 2020, Therapeutic Life Story Work sessions were held face to face. Overnight, for me and many others, the sessions switched to online using platforms such as WhatsApp Video, FaceTime, Zoom or Whereby.

At the outset this raised quite a few concerns for me. It felt impersonal and being authentic under such circumstances seemed challenging. I was unsure I would be able to work in this way and was reluctant to try, due to my level of computer competence. However, I have learnt so much and now feel so much more positive about this mode of working.

Anticipating a lockdown announcement, we had to consider how best to continue with the sessions, if we were to continue with them at all. All the families I was working with wanted to continue no matter what. I discussed with them all the differences that would take place and the implications. This was crucial not just for the children, but for their parents who would have to contain what might occur in a session without my physical presence to support them. This raised a few eyebrows but did not deter them.

Parents suggested that, as they were all going to be at home, having the sessions on a weekly basis compared to fortnightly would be beneficial. This would increase my workload and the task ahead began to feel intense.

My concerns were all about containing the child emotionally. Being able to read and observe the child's body language, distress, sadness and facial expressions are all especially important to me; that is what enables me to secure a safe and accepting environment in which the child can reflect, express themselves, communicate and begin the healing process. Would the child feel comfortable enough to engage as they had when face-to-face? How could I maintain the boundaries of safety and confidentiality when I was not in the room with the child? How would I support the parents if they became uncomfortable with what was taking place, for example, if the child became distressed or angry? Did the family have the technology to do the online sessions?

These and many other questions made my head spin, yet I heard myself telling the children and parents, 'Don't worry, it will be okay. We will find our way together.' Inside I was not so sure. I knew that taking this to supervision for clarity, reassurance and acceptance would support me and give me the confidence to step into a world that was quite foreign to my way of working. I have a friend in California who reminded me around this time, 'Perhaps having had our online video chats since last October has provided you some underlying confidence to work in this way'. I believe she was correct.

So, why has working online worked for my families? I believe remaining authentic has been the key. Some of the children I work with need someone to state what is really happening in any given moment, giving them permission 'to be'. If I express what I am aware of, be it a thought that has popped into my head or a feeling, this could resonate with something the child or parent feels or thinks too. We do this in peer supervision when we listen to one another sharing something from a session that may appear obvious, therefore encouraging one another to address avoided issues.

Working face-to-face we can sense the child's emotions clearly. Online it is not so easy. I have noticed that my senses have become heightened due to this new way of working, but the work still presents challenges.

I needed to help one child have the courage to share their feelings and thoughts around the loss of their birth mother due to bereavement. Having experienced loss myself, I assured them that because we are all unique individuals our journeys are unique to us. The child told me that they had no words for how they felt. I replied, 'Sometimes there are no words. We feel what we feel and by sitting with that it can help us to understand ourselves better or accept that this is how it is for us, right here and right now'. The child's response was, 'That's exactly what I do because that's all I can do: sit with these feelings. I don't think there is anything else I can do with them.' I believe that in that moment that was true for the child; what they felt was enough. They will explore more when they are ready.

In Therapeutic Life Story Work we share with children that even as adults we do not always have the words and that is okay. This is why art materials, games and stories are so important; they permit us to express ourselves while remaining true to ourselves and real with others. They allow and invite us to authentically share what we are feeling and thinking without being judged or rejected. I often hear myself saying, 'In here there is no right or wrong. It is what it is.'

When we are being honest, authentic and trusting of ourselves, it grants the child the opportunity to become more open, authentic, and trusting. The more real we are in ourselves, the more inviting it is for them to be real. It validates that it is okay to be 'in the moment'; it is okay to be oneself.

Overall, the differences in working online have been incredibly challenging, but not insurmountable. I would never have thought I would be happy working online. Without the opportunity to offer a gentle touch on the arm, for example, to express 'I understand' or 'I am with you', it felt impersonal. I am a tactile person, and sometimes find myself reaching out to the screen saying, 'I want to touch your arm gently to acknowledge your tears'.

Working online requires a different way of communicating, where you need to name everything you see, sense and hear. Let the family know you are with them as much as you can be. We have moments of laughter when things feel awkward. If I hear a pet bird adding their two cents worth in the background we all have a chuckle together. Sometimes a dog comes bouncing in wanting to join us or someone comes to the door to drop off a parcel. All of these scenarios are dealt with by naming them and acknowledging the interruptions and how they felt.

I am surprised to say that if I had the choice of working face-to-face or online I would choose both. I have learnt a great deal and if I can contain the differences, challenges, boundaries and all the other elements involved in a session, the child can do what they need to do at any given moment. The parent can be alongside them, knowing that I have my finger on their pulse too.

During the worldwide pandemic I was seeing five young people with their parents each week. I asked them to have paper, coloured pens and any other art materials they wished to use ready for each session. Without fail, they had everything at hand. I might email them something they could use in a session as well; the choice is theirs. Games are still played, such as noughts and crosses, squiggle, or others of their choosing. I have noticed myself becoming more creative in my way of offering different activities or exercises, which has proved to be an enjoyable learning curve. I have found using a digital whiteboard such as the free online programme called Mural has been popular with children as it provides a creative space that is so interactive and engaging.

If I see a child lower their head, I will comment on my observation, and say something such as, 'I have noticed that you have lowered your head and I'm wondering what you may be feeling or thinking.' I may notice a parent turning away as if they are looking at something, in which case I will note, 'I can see you're looking away; I'm wondering if you'd like to share what's on your mind.' If I see a child not wanting to look at me, I might be reflective with, 'I've noticed I can't see your face. I'm wondering if you can see mine.' My intention is to let the child know I am aware and engaging with what is happening with and around them throughout the session.

Being a reflective practitioner lets the child and parents know that you are noticing them, sensing their feelings, seeing what is taking place or observing what is going on for them and are aware of the things you cannot see.

Working in this way online has its restrictions and some people will not feel comfortable offering this way of working. I feel that it is an individual choice, based on one's own circumstances, such as having a confidential space to work in. From an uncertain beginning, I now enjoy the work far more than I had anticipated. In fact, I can imagine myself continuing to use this way of working alongside face-to-face in the future.

It has been amazing to accomplish exercises that were not thought possible in an online session, such as the worry tree adapted from Butler and Hope's (1995) approach to worry and anxiety. These sessions have felt simultaneously overwhelming and powerful and every one of the families I have worked with has continued to progress. I am not saying that it has been easy; far from it. Nevertheless, it has been rewarding, challenging and inspiring.

There are so many variables between face-to-face and online sessions, but I believe it is the way in which we approach either type that can make them effective or ineffective. There is no right or wrong way! As Therapeutic Life Story Work practitioners we too have a choice in the way we prefer to work and what is most appropriate for us. Families can be very forgiving and accommodating when we acknowledge that whatever approach we take involves them; it is their part in it that can make this work beautifully.

Chapter 14
Therapeutic Life Story Work and Beyond

This is an exciting time in the field of Therapeutic Life Story Work as it grows and emerges as an evidence-based effective intervention for helping children towards recovery from childhood trauma. At the time of writing, there are many exciting ways for you to continue your professional development in this area.

It is important that we maintain a level of learning, equivalent to most professions. It promotes our growth and development, and the enhancement of our abilities. Continual Professional Development (CPD) ensures that we and our knowledge stay relevant and current in line with any changes that are going on that may have an impact on our work.

Reflective Journal
As part of the Therapeutic Life Story Work Diploma course we are required to write a journal as a way of reflecting on and recording the process of our learning: like our own wallpaper work! This has proved to be a useful tool to carry into our practice when writing up our Therapeutic Life Story Work sessions. For example, we might note in a different colour, 'On reflection I could have sat with this feeling longer ... wondered out loud about this', and so on.

These reflections can identify and bring together themes for your supervision, as a way of further developing thinking and practice. We realise that writing this book has also been part of our reflection and learning, and is drawn from this practice: a reflective journal of our Therapeutic Life Story Work practice and thinking post Therapeutic Life Story Work Diploma!

The following are not forms of supervision, but opportunities for enhancing continuing professional development, peer support and networking. CPD is a process that helps us to manage our own development on an ongoing basis. It enables us to reflect, review and record what we have learnt. It can remind us of our achievements, how far we have progressed and identify areas that we may wish to progress further. It can highlight goals and objectives we may want to set and discuss further with our supervisor, peer group or networking group. It also offers opportunities to increase our awareness and the possibility of new ways of working.

Therapeutic Life Sory Work Conferences and Symposiums
Like layers of an onion, attending and presenting at workshops and conferences provides further levels of reflection and learning for us which we see as a valuable, continual and lifelong process.

We have been involved in facilitating Therapeutic Life Story Work alumnae events, for example the Therapeutic Life Story Work Symposium in the UK. These provide opportunities for updating practice, sharing experiences and ideas, considering issues and themes to further contribute to the development of Therapeutic Life Story Work practice, and represent reflective learning as a live group.

Therapeutic Life Story Work International Website: www.tlswi.com.
The Therapeutic Life Story Work International website has been purposefully designed by Professor Richard Rose, founder of The

Rose Model of Therapeutic Life Story Work. It has a directory to assist those looking for an accredited and trained Therapeutic Life Story practitioner. The website contains a wealth of resources, including research, templates, training materials and information on courses available for practitioners. TLSWi.com offers a forum for discussion of issues arising and a place to share information and ideas. It provides membership of a global community of Therapeutic Life Story Work practitioners and access to the latest research and blogs, training and support documents and future events. There are different levels of membership and a useful ID card for members.

Life Story Work Forum
Suzanne: I have been attending and helping run the Life Story Work Forum since 2004, alongside Life Story Work author Afshan Ahmad (*My Life Story* CD Rom 2003, 'Digital Life Story Work' chapter in Ryan and Walker 2007) and Andrea Bassi from Birmingham Children Services, UK 'Breaking the Cycle' team who are leading development of therapeutic life story work with adults.

The Life Story Work Forum holds quarterly meetings aimed at providing an opportunity for those with an interest in Life Story Work to create a network of support, share ideas, practice, experiences, and enthusiasm.

The Life Story Work Forum is open to all and is attended by a diverse range of people, including adults who are care experienced, adopters, foster carers, students, social workers, support workers and therapists. The forum provides an opportunity for those attending to present their work, ask questions and suggest topics. Guest presenters have included authors and leaders in the field of Life Story Work such as Katie Wrench and Lesley Naylor, Joy Rees and Richard Rose.

The Life Story Work Forum started in the West Midlands in the UK and, until the 2020 worldwide pandemic, was held mainly in person in this area. Growing numbers of those attending have undertaken the diploma in Therapeutic Life Story Work, and attendance has also been facilitated by online meetings. The Life Story Work Forum is free to join and there is no cost for attending online meetings. If you would like to join the forum's mailing list to be informed of future Life Story Work Forum dates and events, please email LSWForum@outlook.com or visit the page that has kindly been made available to us by Richard Rose on www.TLSWi.com.

Additional Training Courses

We offer training in a range of Therapeutic Life Story Work related areas such as Creating Therapeutic Stories (detailed below), Writing Therapeutic Life Story Work Books and Becoming An Independent TLSW Practitioner. These are endorsed by Professor Richard Rose as helpful additions to the Therapeutic Life Story Work Diploma and CPD for Therapeutic Life Story Work practitioners. They are advertised on TLSWi.com, or for further information visit our websites:

Karla: https://theopentoybox.co.uk
Suzanne: https://therapeuticlifestoryworksupport.com

Creating Therapeutic Stories Programme

We offer a three-day worldwide online training programme which aims to prepare and equip participants with the tools for creating therapeutic stories and incorporating this way of working into practice. The objectives are to provide participants with a framework for creating therapeutic stories, gaining an understanding of the creating therapeutic stories process, what this means for the child, and how to apply it. A therapeutic story can also be created for a child anywhere in the world: the pandemic has opened up such possibilities and we are happy to be contacted to provide training or services. For examples of Therapeutic Stories we have created please see:

https://theopentoybox.co.uk/creating-therapeutic-stories
https://therapeuticlifestoryworksupport.com/creating-therapeutic-stories

TLSWi Support and Study Hubs
Karla: Hubs are offered via Therapeutic Life Story Work International to provide support to Therapeutic Life Story Work practitioners within their regional area. The hubs are designed to offer a place for practitioners to meet others in their area, learn and share new ideas and experiences, have fun trying out new techniques, and have an opportunity to enhance their learning and improve their practice. The hub coordinators are all experienced Therapeutic Life Story Work practitioners who invite you to join them when you can. Hub sessions are held approximately twice a year in each area. You can always join another hub session if you are unable to join the one in your area. Hub members have found these sessions extremely supportive, enjoyable, informal, relaxed and informative. Members are updated about what is going on within therapeutic life story work in their region, country and internationally, alongside new training opportunities, conferences or other related events. Alongside Richard Rose and TLSWi administration, I continue to set up new area hubs in the UK so that everyone has one near to them. If there is not one in your area, I will ensure there is one you can join until one is set up! You can find the list of hubs at www.TLSWi.com.

TLSWi Monthly Community Drop-In
Monthly sessions have been set up for TLSWi members to attend from any region or country. These sessions are online and TLSWi

committee members are your hosts. There is no set agenda; individuals attending drop-in sessions can ask questions, receive support, gain resources or share experiences. (Please keep in mind this is not a forum for supervision; nor does it replace clinical supervision). The community drop-ins are a great place for networking and meeting other TLSWi practitioners and students, as well as providing an opportunity to learn from others and their experiences and add new techniques to your tool kit. Those who have attended these sessions have reported finding them invaluable and insightful, giving a feeling of being supported and less isolated. We encourage you to check them out; they will enhance your learning and provide the opportunity to form peer relationships. You can find more information at www.TLSWi.com.

Here are a few statements from those who have attended the monthly TLSWi Community Drop-In's:

I have come away feeling more confident and it was lovely seeing others and learning new ideas.

I don't feel so isolated now knowing others are finding things a bit tricky at times and I feel so supported.

The drop-in was great. It was good to revisit exercises I was feeling uncertain about. I now also feel more confident about completing the child's Therapeutic Life Story Book.

Thank you so much, this was just what I needed. It was great to connect with others.

Professor Richard Rose
Richard offers a host of Therapeutic Life Story Work training courses. For further information about these training opportunities please visit www.TLSWi.com.

Appendices

Appendix A: Initial Meeting Outline

Please note that this is a guide only. Some of this information may not be relevant for every family but can be adapted or added to as needed.

Introduction
The aim is to hear a bit more about the child/ren, what led to the referral and what are you as parents expecting or wanting. I'm here to tell you a bit about the process of Therapeutic Life Story Work, how I work, and so on to check that we are all on the same page, that this is the right thing and now is the right time.

Any questions?
What do you want to know? Is there anything you are worried about hearing or don't want to know? What story does the child already have? Do they talk much about the past or ask questions? Is anyone else working with the child? We don't want to overload them.

Outline of Sessions, How I Work and Questions to Ask
Stage 1: Information Gathering
The starting point is to gather information about the events leading to the child being in their situation now. Explore and agree who will provide access to a chronology and relevant background information; usually the legal parents/ department

responsible for the child: are there any gaps in the information? Who has what information? Does the parent have paperwork as well as later life letter or life story book?

Who should I contact to request access to casework files, does the legal parent need to give consent? (The legal parent, such as an adoptive parent, or young person if over 16, may need to write a letter consenting to you as the worker having access to the organisations casework files).

Who should be seen? Discuss views about contact with birth family members, previous carers, and so on. Has anyone ever looked on social media to see if birth parents have profiles, photos, or other information?

Stage 2: Direct work Sessions
Sessions are usually fortnightly for 1 hour, ideally at same time and day, with the primary parent/ carer and child. Generally, approximately 16–22 sessions. Sessions will be geared towards and led by the child's individual needs, wishes and feelings. I will review and plan with the parent between each session. We will agree who is to be in the sessions (primary parent?), when to start and what days would work for the child and parent.

At first focus will be on **creating safety** through regular routine and creating a working agreement. We may use relaxation exercises – breathing, identifying a safe place and people the child feels safe with. We will be getting to know one another, for example by creating hands of interests.

We will then assess and work on **emotional literacy**, noticing and naming feelings – using feelings cards, playing feelings charades and demonstrating the hand model of brain to show the impact of trauma.

We will aim to assess and support development of **identity**, **resilience** and **self-esteem** – through exercises like the hands of pride and body outline, adding strengths and talents.

This first scaffolding stage can take up to the first half of sessions. If and when the child is ready we will start **information sharing:**

We will co-create a narrative through a timeline, giving information at the child's pace and level of understanding with repetition and checking. We will start with exploring what they know. We can start from the earliest information, or from the present (where it is safe) and work backwards through time. We will explore reasons why the birth parents couldn't parent – their childhoods and possibly those of their parents – exploring the issues that arose and the choices made. Our penultimate session will be **looking to the future**, by exploring hopes and dreams. In our final session we will review our work by walking along the wallpaper.

Stage 3: Life Story Book

A book will be created at the end which includes sections of the wallpaper work and a narrative reflecting the process of the work done, thoughts, feelings, discussion and any conclusions reached. As the editor in chief the child will have the ultimate say about the content.

Desired outcomes

If we all agree to go ahead we need to consider and agree the aims of the intervention. These may be for the child to:

- Have an opportunity to explore and process past events and experiences
- Understand the why, where, when, what, who and how, through sharing information

- Have a clearer understanding of the past concerns and the decisions made, for example, why birth parents could not safely parent them
- Feel listened to and have the opportunity to process feelings about the past
- Gain a greater understanding of behaviours, thoughts, actions and needs
- Consider and practice strategies for managing powerful feelings.

Support for the child and carers
Sessions are likely to bring up lots of powerful feelings and possibly memories for you and your child. Going through the process of Therapeutic Life Story Work can trigger deep emotions for your child. You may see an increase in challenging behaviours, regression, anxiety and so on, as they process the information. They may ask more questions, but you, the parent, will be in the room and will know what we have talked about and are due to talk about. The child will need greater support and understanding at this time. I recommend letting the school know as well as any carers or parents of siblings, if they have contact. It can also trigger emotions for you. We will speak between sessions to review, plan and see what is coming up for you and your child. Do you know what other support is available to you and what do you feel you may need? I want to make sure you have adequate support during this time.

Confidentiality
I will talk about my work with my supervisor, but I will not use family members' names. As parents you can contact the social worker at any time if you are concerned about the work. Ideally, I would hope we can talk about any concerns together when reviewing and planning sessions, as we will have up to an hour of discussion between sessions. We will discuss confidentiality with

your child when creating the working agreement in the sessions. Undertaking Therapeutic Life Story Work is not a secret, but it is private; they can choose who they tell but they need to be someone trusted and it is a good idea to check with you, the parent, first.

Safeguarding

If safeguarding issues arise, I would need to let the social worker know and would ideally discuss it with you first.

Review

We will have midway and final meetings to review progress and check work is going as planned and agreed. For example, are more sessions are needed? Does work need to be focused on feelings or does the child need a different intervention?

Appendix B:
Outline for Birth Parent Interview

Please note, this is a guide only and can be adapted as needed. Some of the questions may not be relevant to the birth parent you are interviewing, and you may have other questions and areas that you wish to cover.

Allow time for the interview: you may need as long as four hours if the parent is able to talk in depth about their life and their child's life. You may wish to build in some breaks, or return at a later date, but be aware that this is likely to be painful for them and you may only have one opportunity to speak to them.

Thank you for seeing me. It is really important for me to hear your view of things. I'm guessing that it may be hard to look back on the past and it may bring up some tricky feelings and memories. I want to make sure you have someone to support you.

I'm not here to judge, but to hear how you see things, about your life, your views and feelings. The aim is to get a whole picture – not just one view. There are likely to be things that only you will know. I want to understand what happened from each person, to help your child to make sense of what happened.

Would you like me to ask you questions or do you just want to tell me your story first? We can start with what you know about your family – parents, names, ages, heritage, area you were born, where you grew up and so on.

- How would you describe your childhood?
- Earliest memory of your mother or father? (Sometimes we remember events that frightened us or when we were hurt, but can you remember a time when you were comforted?)
- Did you feel loved?
- How would you describe your feelings as a child? Generally happy, worried, anxious or sad?
- Any significant incidents or issues when you were growing up?
- Did you feel popular at school. Did you like school? How did you get on with lessons and learning? Did you feel supported by your parents? Did you have favourite subjects?
- Were you able to tell your parents or carers about your feelings or, for example, being bullied? Why do you think that was?
- What were your relationships with your mum, dad, brother, sister or friends like?
- Any significant partner relationships – first to last?
- How and when did you meet your child's other birth parent? Were there things that attracted you or that you liked?
- How would you describe your relationship? Do you feel it was loving or abusive? Were there changes over time?
- How did you feel when you found out you were pregnant with your child? Was the pregnancy planned? Were you in a relationship together or married?
- What was the pregnancy like? How did you feel and were there any significant incidents? What was happening for you?
- Any details of the birth that you remember – how long the labour was, date and time of birth, who was there, what it

felt like when you first saw or held your baby? Who did they look like? Who chose the names and why? Do you have any photos*
- What were your child's early years like and what was going on for you at the time?
- Are there other children? Any living with you? Do they know about/ ask about this child?
- Looking back, how do you see things now?
- Social worker concerns were ... What's your view of this, what was happening for you? What went so wrong? It seems like things went very wrong. What sense do you make of that now?
- Is there anything you would change if you could go back in time?
- Have you said anything to your child – sorry for what happened? Would you like to say that now?
- Do you have any future wishes or hopes and dreams for your child that you would like me to pass on to them? (They may wish to write a letter or make a short audio or video recording). It can be helpful if the birth parent can say they are sorry and feel sad they couldn't look after their child and are pleased they have a family who can).

Thank you for talking with me today. It will be really helpful for your child. I get that it's hard to admit things weren't right, that it was so difficult for you to be a parent. It is likely that this will have brought up feelings for you. You might feel it more later. It is important to look after yourself. Do you have someone you can talk to if you are feeling low?

* If the relative agrees you can take a copy of any photos they have. Taking a photo with a smart phone usually gives a good image and ensures that the birth parent/ relative can keep their

original copies intact. Make it clear that you will delete the photos from your phone once transferred to your computer and they will be securely held as part of the child's life story book and will only be used for the purposes of the child's life story work.

Appendix C:
Example Letter to Birth Parent

If you are unsure that you have the correct contact details for the birth parent/ relative it is best to send only a very brief letter advising that you would like to speak to them in relation to some work you are doing and would be grateful if they could contact you in order for you to explain more.

If you know that the birth parent or relative lives at the address the following letter can serve as a guide for what you may wish to include and can be adapted as needed.

Careful thought will need to be given by the network regarding if and how to contact a birth parent where there are security concerns, with care taken to ensure the child's whereabouts are not revealed if this is unknown by the birth parent or relative.

Dear ...,

I am [an independent worker] undertaking some life story work with your [child/ daughter/ son].

I would like to talk with you about the work I am doing and see if you would be willing to meet with me, as I feel it is important to hear and include your views. There may be some things that only you will know.

I would be grateful if you could ring or text me as soon as possible so I can explain a bit more. I can ring you back to save your phone bill.

I appreciate that this may not be easy for you, but I feel it would be of great benefit to your child and the work I am doing with [him/her/them].

Kind regards

Appendix D:
Ending Letter to Child

Feel free to write whatever you feel is appropriate and relevant for the child you have worked with. The following is a guide only. You may wish to add a photo of yourself and a speech bubble to say something such as, 'Something I will never forget about you is ...

Dear [Child's Name],

When we first met, we were both filled with uncertainty and anticipation regarding the journey through your life story.

I want you to know that it has been such a pleasure getting to know you and your family. I have been very impressed with your perseverance, even when it felt a bit scary or difficult. You were able to trust the process of our work and gain a better understanding of yourself and your past, with the support of your mum and dad who love you no matter what!

You were very brave in facing some difficult thoughts and emotions, and I hope this book will be a reminder of the time we spent getting to know about your life, the thinking we did together and some of the feelings and memories you had.

I wish you all the best for your future and hope you continue to make good use of your [artistic] talent; I know you will do well in whatever you put your mind to.

Take care and continue being YOU!

Appendix E:
Sample Evaluation Forms for Child and Parent

Child Evaluation of Therapeutic Life Story Work Intervention

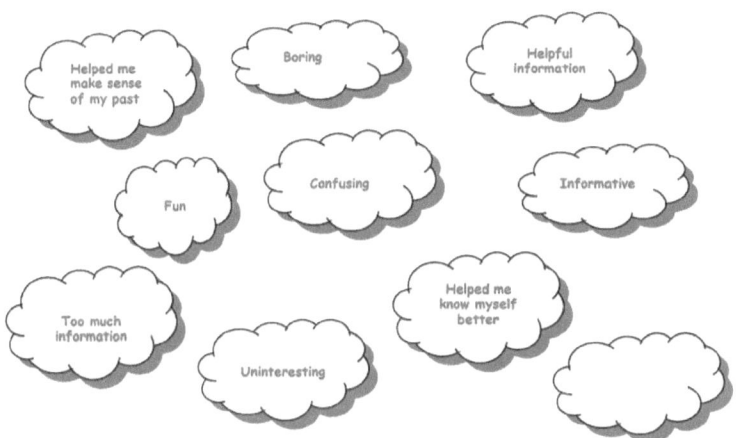

Please tick any of the above that apply and feel free to add some words of your own.

You can use the space below to let me know about anything that was particularly helpful or not helpful, anything you think could be done differently or included, or anything else you want to say:

What would you say to a friend who was going to do some Therapeutic Life Story Work?

Thank you for your feedback

Name: Date:

Parent Evaluation of Therapeutic Life Story Work Intervention

Name of child:

Local authority:

Dates provided:

I would be grateful for your feedback on the Therapeutic Life Story Work intervention that I have provided.

1. How helpful do you feel this intervention was for your child and why? Please include any areas of concern.
2. Was there enough communication with you before, during and following the sessions?
3. Did you feel consulted with and involved in planning sessions?
4. Did you feel that you and your child were listened to?
5. What do you think about how the intervention was delivered? Were the sessions delivered at a suitable pace for your child? Was the content of the sessions age appropriate and geared towards your child's needs and level of understanding?
6. Were the identified outcomes achieved?
7. Would you recommend Therapeutic Life Story Work to other parents, and why?
8. Anything else you would like to say?

Signed:

Date:

Please return the completed Therapeutic Life Story Work feedback form to:

Appendix F: Development of Protocol for Critical Appraisal

The Lucas et al., (2022) Final Report, Deakin University in Melbourne, Australia, provides a clear evidence base for the effectiveness of The Rose Model of Therapeutic Life Story Work interventions. A variety of measures were used, including the SHANARRI Assessment Tool (Rose 2012). The results are extremely positive as detailed in chapter seven.

An inductive thematic analysis (Braun and Clarke 2019) was also undertaken of 'stakeholder narratives' (interview responses from parents or carers, teachers and social or care workers) which revealed five key themes:

- Enhanced working relationships
- Sense and meaning-making to understand their experiences and reconstruct their narrative
- Increased emotional, social and behavioural skills and resilience
- Positive identity development
- Healing and recovery

Further outcomes research and findings from Australia were due for publication at the time of writing. Joint research was being undertaken in Australia by the Victoria Police Department and Deakin University Building a Community around the Child

Project (https://www.deakin.edu.au/psychology/our-research/deakin-child-study-centre) which started in 2018 (Watkins and Kontomichalos-Eyre 2018). The research was looking into the impact of reframing how youth behaviour can be a symptom of complex trauma, requiring therapeutic intervention rather than punishment. The aim was to see if there was a correlation between Therapeutic Life Story Work interventions and reduced involvement with the criminal justice system, and early indicators were promising.

In the UK two outcomes research projects were studying Therapeutic Life Story Work interventions: one by Coram, a leading adoption charity, and the other by Ipsos MORI, a market research company.

References

Ayres, J. (1979), *Sensory Integration and the Child*, Portland: Western Psychological Services.

Anthony, K. & Goss, S. (2009), *Guidelines for Online Counselling and Psychotherapy*, 3rd Edition, Rugby: BACP.

Baynes, P. (2008), 'Untold stories: A discussion of Life Story Work', *Adoption and Fostering*, 32 (2), p.43–9, London: Sage (for Coram BAAF).

Betts, B. and Ahmad, A. (2003), *My Life Story* CD-ROM, Orkney: Information Plus.

Bhreathnach, É. (2006), *The Scared Gang*, Belfast: Aldertree Press.

Bhreathnach, É. and Breen, C. (2017), 'The Use of Observations of Arousal States and Heart Rate Variability Data to Inform Best Practice', *Treating Trauma: Key Interventions for Emotional and Physiological Regulation*, p.2 (Conference contribution), London: Centre for Child Mental Health.

Bond, T. (2015), *Working Online. Good Practice in Action 047: Ethical Framework for the Counselling Professions, Supplementary Guidance*, p.15, Lutterworth: British Association for Counselling Psychotherapy

Bowlby, J. (1969), *Attachment and Loss*, New York: Basic Books.

Bowlby, J. (1988), *A Secure Base, Clinical Applications of Attachment Theory*, London: Routledge.

Braun, V., & Clarke, V. (2019). Reflecting on reflexive thematic analysis. Qualitative research in sport, exercise and health, 11(4), 589-597.

Brodzinsky, D., Singer, L. and Braff, A. (1984), 'Children's Understanding of Adoption', *Child Development*, 55, (3) pp.869–78, New Jersey: Wiley.

Brown, B. (2006), 'Shame Resilience Theory: A grounded theory study on women and shame: Families in Society, *The Journal of Contemporary Social Services*, 87, (1), p.43–52, London: Sage.

Brown, B. (2020), *The Gifts of Imperfection*, London: Penguin Random House UK.

Burch, N. (1969), cited in Curtis, R.P. & Warren, P. W. (1973), *The Dynamics of Life Skills Coaching*. Training Research and Development Station, Department of Manpower and Immigration, National Government Publication, England: Prince Albert, Sask.

Butler, G. and Hope, T. (1995), *Manage Your Mind*, Oxford: Oxford University Press.

Cairns, K. (2002), *Attachment, Trauma and Resilience: Therapeutic Caring for Children*, London: BAAF.

Collier, K. (2019 February 3). 'The Five Pillars of Protection', *Self-Care Psychology*. https://www.selfcarepsychology.com/single-post/2019/02/03/The-Five-Pillars-of-Protection.

Dana, D. (2018), *Polyvagal Exercises for Safety and Connection: 50 Client-Centered Practices*, (Norton Series on Interpersonal Neurobiology), New York: Norton.

Denborough, D. (2014), *Retelling the Stories of Our Lives: Everyday Narrative Therapy to Draw Inspiration and Transform Experience*, New York: Norton.

Department for Education, (2004) *Every Child Matters*, London: DfE.

Fahlberg, V. (1994), *A Child's Journey Through Placement* (UK edn), London: BAAF.

Foxton, J. (2001), *Nutmeg Gets Adopted*, London: Coram BAAF.

Golding, K. (2014), *Using Stories to Build Bridges with Traumatized Children: Creative Ideas for Therapy, Life Story Work, Direct Work and Parenting*, London and Philadelphia: Jessica Kingsley Publishers.

REFERENCES

Golding, K. (2015), 'Connection before Correction: Supporting parents to meet the challenges of parenting children who have been traumatized within their early parenting environments', *Journal of Children Australia,* 40, (2), p.152–9. https://kimsgolding.co.uk/publication/journal-papers/connection-before-correction/.

Golding, K.S., and Hughes, D.A. (2012), *Creating Loving Attachments: Parenting with PACE to Nurture Confidence and Security in the Troubled Child*, London and Philadelphia: Jessica Kingsley Publishers.

Goleman, D. (1995), *Emotional Intelligence: Why it can matter more than IQ*, New York: Bantam Books.

Grotevant, H. and Von Korff, L. (2011), 'Adoptive Identity', in Schwartz, S., Luyckx, K. and Vignoles, V. (eds), *Handbook of Identity Theory and Research*, New York: Springer.

Grosvenor, T. (2017), 'The Supervisor's Power and Moments of Learning' In Vetere, A. and Sheehan, J. (eds), *Supervision of Family Therapy and Systemic Practice*, Switzerland: Springer.

Guber, T. and Kalish, L. (2005), *Yoga Pretzels: 50 Fun Yoga Activities for Kids and Grownups* (cards edn), New York: Abrams Books.

Hill, J. (2010–2020), *The Model of Non-Managerial Supervision*, NMCS Consulting, http://www.nmcsconsulting.co.uk/the-model-of-nmcs-training/.

Howe, D. (2009), *A Brief Introduction to Social Work Theory*, London: Red Globe.

Hughes, D.A., (2007), *Attachment Focused Family Therapy*, New York: Norton & Co. Inc.

Hughes, D.A., (2011), *Attachment Focused Family Therapy Workbook*, New York: Norton & Co. Inc.

Hughes, D.A. and Baylin, J. (2012), *Brain-based parenting: The Neuroscience of Caregiving for Healthy Attachment*, New York: Norton.

Jones, A. (2017), 'Project logic – Providing Services and Support for the Provision of Therapeutic Life Story Work', in Rose, R. (ed.), *Innovative*

Therapeutic Life Story Work: Developing trauma-informed practice for working with children, adolescents and young adults, London: Jessica Kingsley Publishers.

Kadushin, A. (1976) *Supervision in Social Work*, New York: Columbia University Press.

Karpman, S. (1968), *Fairy Tales and Script Drama Analysis. Transactional Analysis Bulletin*, 26 (7), p.39–43, CA: Regents of the University of California Digital Resource.

Keane, A. (2016 July 19), *What is resilience?* Changeboard. https://www.changeboard.com/article-details/16347/what-is-resilience-/

Keefer, B. and Schooler, J. (2000), *Telling the Truth to Your Adopted or Foster Child: Making Sense of the Past*, Westport: Bergin & Garvey.

Kolb, D.A. (1984), *Experiential Learning: Experience as the Source of Learning and Development*, NJ: Prentice-Hall.

Kuypers, L. (2011), *The Zones of Regulation*, CA: Social Thinking Publishing.

Leddick, G. and Bernard, J. (1980), 'The History of Supervision: A Critical Review', *Counselor Education and Supervision*, 19 (3), pp.186–96, https://doi.org/10.1002/j.1556-6978.1980.tb00913.x.

Levine, P.A. (2015), *Trauma and Memory: Brain and Body in a Search for the Living Past*, Berkeley, CA: North Atlantic.

Lloyd, S. (2016) *Improving Sensory Processing in Traumatized Children: Practical Ideas to Help Your Child's Movement, Coordination and Body Awareness*, London and Philadelphia: Jessica Kingsley Publishers.

Lucas, J. J., Velik, J., Matthews, L., Brady, K., Breguet, R., & Parson, J. (2022) Therapeutic Life Story Work Barwon Pilot Program: Final Report 2022 (Research report). Geelong, Victoria. Available online: https://www.mackillop.org.au/about-mackillop/publications/therapeutic-life-story-work

Maddox, L. (2012, January 6), 'How can adopted children be safeguarded in the Facebook age?' The Guardian: https://www.theguardian.com/global/2012/jan/06/adopted-children-facebook.

REFERENCES

Mauro, T. (2009), *50 Ways to Support Your Child's Special Education: From IEPs to Assorted Therapies, an Empowering Guide to Taking Action, Every Day*, MA: Adams Media Corporation.

McCloud, C. (2006), *Have You Filled a Bucket Today?: A Guide to Daily Happiness for Kids*, US: Ferne Press.

Mellon, N. (2019), *Healing Storytelling: The Art of Imagination and Storymaking for Personal Growth*, Stroud: Hawthorn Press.

Morrison, T. (2005), *Staff Supervision in Social Care* (3rd edn), Brighton: Pavilion Publishing.

Nicholls, E. (2005), *The New Life Work Model: Practice Guide*, Lyme Regis: Russell House Publishing.

Oaklander, V. (1978), *Windows to our Children: A Gestalt Therapy Approach to Children and Adolescents*, New York: The Gestalt Journal Press.

Orlans, V. and Edwards, D. (2001), 'A Collaborative Model of Supervision', in Carroll, M., and Tholstrup, M. (eds), *Integrative Approaches to Supervision*, pp.42–9, London: Jessica Kingsley Publications.

Pennington, E. (2012), *It Takes a Village to Raise a Child: Adoption UK survey on adoption support*, Banbury: Adoption UK.

Perrow, S. (2012), *Therapeutic Storytelling: 101 Healing Stories for Children*, Stroud: Hawthorn Press.

Perry, B. (2001), *Bonding and Attachment in Maltreated Children: Consequences of Emotional Neglect in Childhood*, The Child Trauma Academy.org. V3.0. Texas.

Perry, B. (2009), Examining child maltreatment through a neurodevelopmental lens: clinical application of the Neurosequential Model of Therapeutics. *Journal of Loss and Trauma*, 14: 240-255.

Pike, (2020), *Identity Explained for Children*, Pop'n'Olly video Identity Explained for Children | Pop'n'Olly | Olly Pike [CC]

Porges, S. (2011), *The Polyvagal Theory: Neurophysiological Foundations of Emotions, Attachment, Communication, and Self-Regulation*, New York, NY: W.W. Norton.

Prochaska, J.O. and DiClemente, C.C. (1983), 'Stages and processes of self-change of smoking: Toward an integrative model of change', *Journal of Consulting and Clinical Psychology*, 51 (3), p.390–395, https://doi.org/10.1037/0022-006X.51.3.390.

Rees, J. (2009), *Life Story Books for Adopted Children: A Family Friendly Approach*, London: Jessica Kingsley Publications.

Rogers, C. (1957), 'The Necessary and Sufficient Conditions of Therapeutic Personality Change', *Journal of Consulting Psychology*, 21 (2), p.95–103, https://doi.org/10.1037/h0045357.

Rose, R. (2012), *Life Story Therapy with Traumatized Children: A Model for Practice*, London: Jessica Kingsley Publications.

Rose, R. and Philpot, T. (2005), *The Child's Own Story: Life Story Work with Traumatized Children*, London: Jessica Kingsley Publications.

Rossi, P., Lipsey, M. and Freeman H. (2004), *Evaluation: A Systematic Approach* (7th edn), London: SAGE Publications.

Rowling, J.K. (2000), *Harry Potter and the Goblet of Fire*, London: Bloomsbury Publishing.

Ryan, T. and Walker, R. (2007), *Life Story Work: A Practical Guide to Helping Children Understand Their Past* (new edn), London: BAAF.

Shohet, R., and Wilmot, J. (1991), 'The Key Issue in Supervision of Counsellors: The Supervisory Relationship', in W, Dryden and B. Thorne (eds), *Training and Supervision for Counselling in Action* p.87–98, London: Sage.

Siegel, D.J. (1999), *The Developing Mind*, New York: Guilford.

Siegel, D.J. and Bryson, T. (2011), *The Whole-Brain Child: 12 Proven Strategies to Nurture Your Child's Developing Mind*, New York: Delacorte Press.

Stahl, A. (2018, July 25), *Here's How Creativity Actually Improves Your Health*, Forbes. https://www.forbes.com/sites/ashleystahl/2018/07/25/heres-how-creativity-actually-improves-your-health/?sh=1e8b951213a6.

REFERENCES

Stewart, W. and Braun, M. (2017), *Mindful Kids (Mindful Tots)* (cards), MA: Barefoot Books.

Stokes, A. (2018), *Online Supervision: A Handbook for Practitioners*, Psychotherapy 2.0 Series, Oxfordshire: Routledge.

Sunderland, M. (2000), *Using Story Telling as a Therapeutic Tool with Children*, Milton Keynes: Speechmark Publishing Ltd.

Treisman, K. (2018a), *A Therapeutic Treasure Box for Working with Children and Adolescents with Developmental Trauma: Creative Techniques and Activities*, London: Jessica Kingsley Publishers.

Treisman, K. (2018b), *A Therapeutic Treasure Deck of Grounding, Soothing, Coping and Regulating Cards (Therapeutic Treasures Collection)*, London: Jessica Kingsley Publishers.

Treisman, K. (2018c), *A Therapeutic Treasure Deck of Feelings and Sentence Completion Cards (Therapeutic Treasures Collection)*, London: Jessica Kingsley Publishers.

Ulleberg, I. and Jensen, P. in Vetere, A. and Sheehan, J. (eds) (2017), *Supervision of Family Therapy and Systemic Practice*, Switzerland: Springer.

Van Der Kolk, B. (2014), *The Body Keeps the Score: Mind, Brain and Body in the Transformation of trauma*, New York: Viking.

Vetere, A. and Sheehan, J. (eds) (2017), *Supervision of Family Therapy and Systemic Practice*, Switzerland: Springer.

Vygotsky, L.S. (1962), *Thought and Language*, Cambridge, MA: MIT Press.

Watkins, R. and Kontomichalos-Eyre, S."Community Around the Child" Report, (2018). Victoria Police and Department of Justice, ANZSOC Conference, University of Melbourne, Australia.

Watson, D., Latter, S. and Bellew, R. (2015), 'Adopters' views on their children's life story books', *Adoption & Fostering*, 39 (2), p.119–34, Sage Journals, https://doi.org/10.1177/0308575915588723

White, M. and Epston, D. (1989), *Literate Means to Therapeutic Ends*, Adelaide, South Australia: Dulwich Centre Publications.

White, M. and Epston, D. (1990), *Narrative Means to Therapeutic Ends*, New York: W. W. Norton.

Winnicott, D. (1971), *Therapeutic Consultations in Child Psychiatry*, London: Hogarth Press.

Wrench, K. and Naylor, L. (2013), *Life Story Work with Children Who are Fostered or Adopted: Creative Ideas and Activities*, London: Jessica Kingsley Publications.

Subject Index

5, 4, 3, 2, 1 grounding exercise 65

acceptance of child's feelings 273
access to records 8, **32-4**, 36, 49, 235, 294
   delay 236-7
active listening 93, 127, 268
adoption 6, 9, 33, 40, 44, 48, 129, 142
   teams 7, 13-5, 259
   outcomes research 308
Adoption and Children Act (2002) 3
Adoption Support Fund (ASF) xv, **7, 12**, 13, 17, 157, 210, 218-9, 238, 277
'aha' moments 114, 260, 271
air balloon journey **81-2**, 98, 145
'all about me' books 22, 59, 144, 187
Anger, birth parent 42, 230, 237, 254
   child 50, **87-9**, 114, 151, 175, 205, 243, 256, 261
   iceberg/volcano 88
   parent response 228
argument between child and parent 223, **225**
attachment 3-6, 29-30, 59, 72, 101, **132-4**, 161, 166, 173, 189-90, 192, 216, 279
   strengthen 171, 264
Attention Deficit Hyperactivity Disorder (ADHD) 56, 201
autonomic nervous system 91-3, 189

bar graph/chart, preoccupation 83-5
behaviour tree 30, **112-4**, 271
belonging 6, 20, 69, 110, 114, 118, 126, 161, 176
bias 63, 111 (*see also* unconscious and implicit)
birth details 146, 299
birth family
   communication 45, 32, 229, 232-3, 254
   contact 24-5, **35-51**, 124, 237, 257, 294
   culture xiv, 25, 29, 181, 173, 181, 209, 217
   current situation 24-5, 36, 43-4
   history 3, 5, 29, 41, 127-9, 145-6
   interview 36-7, 41-4, 235, 254, 298-301

loss 3, 6, 15, 82, 85, 99, 113, 166, 193, 204, 215, 230, 283
   tree 145, 147
   view 39, 41-4, 49, 132, 146, 214, 298, 300
black lives matter xiii
blame xi, 42, 44, 46, 132, 172
body language 60, 98, 126, 188, 268, 281
   memory 91, 127-8, 192-3
   movement 190
   outline activity 84-5, 98, 106, 111-2, 145, 295
bond 55, 68, 69, 114, 194 *see also* attachment
boundaries 48, 83, 123, 130, 194, 224, 257, 258
   online 282, 284
box of hearts ending exercise 140
brain and attachment 4, 6, 216
   development 4, 6, 184, 186
   early life experience 4, 89-91, 114, 132, 186
   learning & trauma 97, 184-6, 192, 200-1, 294
breathing exercises 65, 255, 294

candles ending activity 140
carers *see* parents
casework files *see* access to records
chaotic household 224-5
child definition of use of term xvi
   engagement *see* engaged
   history 5, 6, 23-4, 61, 115-6, 145, 152, 185, 219
   view 3, 21,-3, 25, 47, 63, 98, 100, 103-4, 147, 157, 163-4, 170-1, 174
child & adolescent mental health services 20
child permanence report (CPR) 23, 34, 214
child's pace 10, 55, 80, 98, 115, 135, 181, 196, 203, 227, 259, 264, 295
Children Act (2004) 3
circle of feelings 93

co-creating 31, 204, 210, 217, 220
complex needs 18, 65, 179, 180, 186-9, 198, 259
concentric circles 97-8
confidentiality 8, 38, 66, 76, 170, 258, 262, 282, 296-7
connection 15, 24, 57, 62, **67**, 69, 72, 80, 172, 173, 190
   in supervision 251, 261-3
conscious competence 265-6
contact 24-5, 36,-40, **45-51**, 124, 129, 229, 230-2, 233, 237, 257, 296
containment 3, 30, 36, 58, 60, **62-79**, 93, 205, 212, 224-5, 228, 271, 281
   in supervision 251, 255, **256-61**, 266, 279
   online 284
continual professional development (CPD) 250, 262, **287-92**
contract 26, 66, 76
creating therapeutic stories xii, **207-21**
   training 290-1
creativity xiii, 6, 11, 55, 76, 117, **199-206**, 208
   in supervision 251, 266, 269, 275
cultural safety xvii, 172
culture xiv, 103, 173, 181, **217**, 248, 249
curiosity 135, 203, 217, 230, 273
cycle of change 133-4

de-sensitising 102
developmental trauma 6, 30, 184, 186
diploma in Therapeutic Life Story Work xii, 7-13, 17, 202, 246, 263, 287-8, 290
direct work sessions xii, xiv, 5, 8, 21, 294-5
disengaged 132, 226-7
diversity 18, 29, 214, 217
   in supervision 247-8, 256, 265, 274
Dobble **72**, 79, 197
domestic abuse/violence 166, 215
dorsal vagal state 91
dots and boxes game 67-8
dyadic developmental psychotherapy (DDP) 20, 30, 258, 264, 273
dysregulation 185, 191

early relationships *see* attachment
eating 9, 189
electoral register 39
emotional literacy 61, **79-98**, 115, 1983, 294

emotional regulation 79, 157
emotional support 5, 228, 245
empathy 30, 114, 132, 139, 183, 203, 209, 223, 248
ending letter 155, 304
ending session **139-41**, 149-55, 227-9
engaged child 21-2, 50, 58, 68, 74, 76, 124, 129, 135, 172-3, 188, 189, 226-7
ethnicity 19, 22, 128, 274
evaluation 157, 159, 160, 171, 173, 176, 305-6
explaining why 117, 120-1
externalising/externalisation 5, 212, 221
eye contact 59, 67, 197, 277

fact, fiction, fantasy and heroism exercise 103, **106-8**, 207
family history 3, 41, 61, 116, 136, 145
family time 43, 45, 47, 175
   see also contact
family tree 145, 147
fear response 130
   see also flight fright and/or freeze
feedback from parents and children xiii, xi, 157, 174-6, 220, 305-6
feelings work/activities **79-98**
filial therapy 30
finding the warrior within 104-6
flight, fight and freeze 87, 89, 192
footprints exercise 138-9
foster care 43, 97, 172, 215
foster carers, xiii, 8, 12, 31, 105, 108, 117, 122, 152, 163, 188, 194, 225, 289
   see also parent
freeze response 222-3
future hopes and dreams 61, 106, 136, **138-9**, 146, 207, 278, 295, 300, 304

games 67-74, 79-80
gender 23, 63, 103, 247
genogram 145 (*see also* family tree)
glasses exercise **132-3**
goals 100, 103, 116, 137-8, 145, 150, 228
good & not so good of looking at past 115, 145
graph for scaling feelings **85-7**
grounding 64-5, 102, 197, 223, 259, 275
guided fantasy (air balloon) **81-2**

hand model of brain **89-91**, 145, 294
hand activity interests 74-5
   pride 101
   safety and support 75

SUBJECT INDEX

healing trauma 4, 6, 43, 47, 73, 100, 111, 114, 127, 132, 133, 141, 151, 173, 194, 205, 208, 212, 219, 255, 279, 281, 307
hearts ending exercise 140
health records 5
secure and insecure attachment 132, 133
heritage 111, 181, 209, 214, 298
history of child 5, 6, 23-4, 61, 115-6, 145, 152, 185, 219
hopes & dreams *see* future hopes and dreams

identity xiv, 3, 6, 18, 20-1, 38, 49, 61, 100, 103, 111, 145, 166, 170- 3, 211, 213, 216, 295, 307
imagery and metaphor **83**, 87-8, 91—117, 122-3, 135-8, 205
implicit bias xiv, 111
independent therapeutic life story worker/practitioner xii, 12, 13, 16, 17, 32, 40, 143, 239, 251, 254, 290, 302
information gathering/bank 5, 19, 24, 26, **31-5**, 56, 116, 123-4, 209, 210, 234, 235, 236-7, 293-4
internet/social media search 39, 47, 294
information sharing 34-5, 50, 61, 74, 122, 166, 204, 295
narrative 3, 4, 22, 34-5, 113, 122, 143, 147, 204, 207, 209-10, 211, 212, 216, 295
historical 32, 61, 115-6, 145
timeline 34, 61, **115-135**, 145, 146, 197, 206, 260-1, 295
metaphorical stories 215, *see also* therapeutic
stories
parenting wall 117, **122-3**, 145
initial meeting 25-8
inner qualities 104 *see also* qualities
insecure attachment 133
integration 4, 61
internal working model (IWM) 4, 100, 103, 114
internal and external world 114, 118
internalisation 4-5
internet/social media search 39, 47, 294
interoceptive system 192
interviews 36-7, 41-4, 235, 254, **298-301**
introduction/welcome booklet 59, 67

'Jenga' 58, 72, 73, 199
Just Right State programme 20, 66, **186-91**

lack of privacy 223-4
language 45, 67, 105, 137, 191, 214, 272
body 60, 98, 126, 188, 268, 281
later life letters 23, 33, 34, 142, 294
learning journey 60, 119
learning needs/challenges 123, 172-3, 180-98, 201, 203, 259, 270
see also complex needs
legal parent 25, 26, 36, 43, 144, 148, 214, 230, 231, 232, 294
legal status/special guardianship order 7, 103
Lego 128, 172, 199, 203-4
life journey 117, 206
life story book 5, 6, 19, 35, 59, 141, **142-8**, 231, 238-9, 294, 295, 301
life story work vii-iii, x, xi, xii, 4, 7, 8, 10, 12, 13, 60, 67, 158, 301
forum 289-90
listen 10, 30, 31, 42, 51, 60, 76, 93, 102, 127, 210, 233, 228, 253, 263, 268, 269, 270, 282
loss ix, 6, 5, 15, 82, 85, 99, 108, 113, 150, 166, 193, 204, 209, 213, 215, 230, 243, 264, 270, 279, 283

magical circle 106-8
maternal/paternal brother/sister xiii
memory 9, 125, 128
body memory 91, 127-8, 192-3
earliest memory 117, 299
memory books 23, 33
memory sticks 144
mind/spider maps 76, 115, **117-8**
minoritised ethnic background xiv
'More About Me' book 22
movement, body 190

NAIL it acronym 245
narrative theory/therapy 87, 212, 216
neglect 6, 66, 103, 113, 131, 185-6, 215, 271
nervous system 91-3, 184, 189, 192
neurodiversity 172, 180, **193-8**
neuroscience 89, 190, 192
non-discriminatory 63
non-verbal 14, 79, 265
noticing and naming feelings 91, 101-2, 294

onion layers 97-8
out of home care 32, 171-2, 176
outcomes measuring 156-176

PACE (*playfulness, acceptance, curiosity, empathy*) 273
parent thing exercise 117, **120-2**, 145
parenting wall 117, **122-3**, 145, 218
parents, definition of use of term xiii
   therapeutic 19, **23**, 30, 228-9, 267, 273
   view 24, 36, 174, 294, 302
person centred approach 248-50
photographs xii, 41, 143, 147
physical abuse 186
placements 156, 170
play 4, 20, 55, 61, 70, 79, 95, 193-194, 200, 203-5, 215
   ice breaker 58
   importance of **73-74**
   therapist xii, 7, 8, 14, 138, 181, 264
playfulness 68, 72, 200, 273
play therapy 9, 12, 21, 30, 207
Polyvagal theory 91-3
post-traumatic stress disorder xii, 83
PowerPoint 143
pre-occupation bar chart or beaker 83-5
privacy 17, 47, 223-4
problem solving 61, 73, 117
proprioceptive system 190-2

Qualities 104, 110
   child 35, 99, 101, 104, 110, 112, 136, 145, 147
   supervisor 250, 272-3
race 23, 63, 103, 247
rapport relationship building 61-3
referrals **19-31**, 152, 179-81, 186, 190, 196, 198, 210, 244, 259, 293
reflect difference 128
reflective journal 287-8
reflection process xii, 35, 114, 128, 143, 176, 233, 239, 247, 287-8
   supervision 239, 247, 251, 261-2
   267-72, 275, 279
reframe 93, 100, 216
refugee and migrant children 120-1
regulate, behaviour 260
   feelings 20, 93, 189, 270
relating to others 73
relaxation exercises 64-5, 294
religion 103, 217

repair, emotional 127
   relationship 129
   sense of self 111
   trauma 100
repetition 212, 295
resilience 61, **100-1**, 107, 295, 307
   see also self-esteem
re-story 93, 216
retraumatising 137
rewire brain 91, 216
rework/rewrite storylines of identity 100
routine, consistent 15, 62, 64, 66, 196, 294
rubbish bin treasure chest imagery 96-7, 109-10

SACCS 67
safe environment 6, 8, 36, 79
safeguarding 13, 34, 66, 129, 214, 251, 254, 262, 272-4, 297
safety creating a sense of 62-4
   consistent routines *see also* routine
   creating a working agreement 58, 66-7
   hands of safety activity 75, 145
   importance of 20-1, 30, 37, 47, 58, 62, 261
   see also supervision
safety of worker 234-5, 254-5
scaffolding questions 133-4
scaling feelings 85-7
security 118, 120
self-care 242-79
self-confidence 98-103
self-esteem building 61, 101, 107, 112, 115, 191, 295
self-regulation 22, 87, 101, 114, 184, 189
sense of self 4, 6, 61, 84, **103-14**, 171, 271
sensory integration 66, 184, 186, 190, 192
sensory processing needs 66, 179, 184-9
separation and loss 3, 6, 83, 99, 113, 150, 215, 279
sequencing and reframing 115
serve and return attachment exercise 145
session chart 67, 78
session plan 10, 56, 78-9, 260, 269
sexual abuse 67, 186
Sexual Abuse Child Consultancy Service (SACCS) 67
sexual orientation 103, 247, 274
SHANARRI outcome-based measurement 158-71, 307
shield of shame 117, **130-3**
sibling, use of xiii

SUBJECT INDEX

social media search 39, 47, 294
social workers *see* workers
special guardianship order 7
special needs 183 *see also* complex needs
speech impairment 181-2
spider maps 117-8 *see also* mind maps
squiggle drawings 68-71, 118-9, 195-196, 270
stop sign 119
stopping the work 127, 129, 151
stories, metaphorical 208, 215
   see also creating therapeutic stories
story cubes 72-3
strategy cards 102, 112
strengthen attachment *see* attachment
strengths and resilience exercises 101, 104, 110
stress 73, 168, 200, 236, 243
suitcase exercise 108-10
supervision 127, 152, 154, **242-72**
   culture 264-5
   importance of safety 251-5, 266, 272-3, 276
   reflection 239, 247, 251, 261-2, 267-72, 275, 279
sympathetic state 91-2

tangle of feelings 93-4
team manager 14, 236, 275
telling the truth 123-7, 130
therapeutic life story work outline 3-11
therapeutic life story worker/practitioner xii-iii, 4, 8, 17, 32, 36, 46, 47, 258, 264, 286, 289, 290, 291
therapeutic parenting training 30, 228
therapeutic stories xii, **207-21**, 290, 291
Theraplay 30, 185
thoughts, feelings, actions tree 112-4
timeline 34, 61, **115-135**, 145, 146, 197, 206, 260-1, 295

trauma impact 6, 126, 174
recovery 173
treasure chest imagery 96, 109-10
tree of life 135-8

unannounced visits to birth family 232
unconscious bias xiv, 16, 18, 32, 63, 111
unconscious competence 265
unplanned endings 227-8
upsetting a parent 228-9

ventral vagal activation 92
vestibular system 190-2
visualisation technique 108

wallpaper work xvii, 116, 139
weapons 98
welcome/introduction booklet 59, 67
wellbeing 257
wheel imagery 120
window of tolerance 74, 188
withdrawn permission to contact birth parent 229-34
witnessing the child's story 114, 116
word exploration exercise 110-1
workers creativity **199-206**, 251, 266, 275
   getting things wrong **222-239**
   knowledge of trauma impact 7
   support 15, 26, 129, 150-4, 179-8, 239, 242-79, 282, 288-92
working agreement activity 58, 66-7, **76-7**, 145, 196, 261, 294, 297
working in the moment 127
working with adults 289
warrior within exercise 104-7

zones of regulation 101-2

Author Index

Ayres, J. 190
Anthony, K. & Goss, S. 277

Baynes, P. 4, 158
Betts, B. and Ahmad, A. 12, 219, 289
Bhreathnach, É. 189
Bhreathnach, É. and Breen, C. 192
Bond, T. 277
Bowlby, J. 4, 100, 103
Braun, V., & Clarke, V. 307
Brodzinsky, D., Singer, L. and Braff, A. 3
Brown, B. 131, 149
Burch, N. 265
Butler, G. and Hope, T. 285

Cairns, K. 6, 274
Collier, K. 244

Dana, D. 91, 92, 93
Denborough, D. 100, 135, 216
Department for Education 159

Fahlberg, V. 3, 121
Foxton, J. 215

Golding, K. 207, 208, 216, 261
Golding, K.S., and Hughes, D.A. 130, 131
Goleman, D. 88, 89
Grotevant, H. and Von Korff, L. 46
Grosvenor, T. 260, 272
Guber, T. and Kalish, L. 65

Hill, J. 268-9
Howe, D. 6
Hughes, D.A. 30, 132, 188, 265, 273
Hughes, D.A. and Baylin, J. 62

Jones, A. 156

Kadushin, A. 250
Karpman, S. 267
Keane, A. 100
Keefer, B. and Schooler, J. 47, 130
Kolb, D.A. 268
Kuypers, L. 101-2

Leddick, G. and Bernard, J. 247, 248
Levine, P.A. 62
Lloyd, S. 66, 184-6
Lucas, J., et al. 61, 171, 173, 176, 307

Maddox, L. 46
Mauro, T. 182
McCloud, C. 216
Mellon, N. 208
Morrison, T. iv, 250, 267-8

Nicholls, E. iv, 4, 34-5, 120-2, 145

Oaklander, V. 81
Orlans, V. and Edwards, D. 249

Pennington, E. 6
Perrow, S. 208, 213
Perry, B. ix, 4, 189
Pike. 103
Porges, S. 91
Prochaska, J.O. and DiClemente, C.C. 133

Rees, J. 4, 6, 142, 144, 289
Rogers, C. 248-9, 275
Rose, R. viii-x, xii, xiv, 4-7, 10, 12, 15-6, 22,
    30-4, 55-6, 59, 61, 67, 72, 74, 76, 79,
    81, 83, 85, 87, 95, 106, 112, 115, 132,
    139, 141-2, 145, 147-8, 158-60, 165,
    170-1, 173, 187, 210, 238, 245, 271,
    274, 289-2, 307
Rose, R. and Philpot, T. 4, 76
Rossi, P., Lipsey, M. and Freeman
    H. 158
Rowling, J.K. 115
Ryan, T. and Walker, R. 12, 15, 219, 289

Shohet, R., and Wilmot, J. 249
Siegel, D.J. 74
Siegel, D.J. and Bryson, T. 89, 91, 145,
    188, 216, 253
Stahl, A. 201
Stewart, W. and Braun, M. 64
Stokes, A. 276, 277
Sunderland, M. 208, 215

AUTHOR INDEX

Treisman, K. 80, 87, 102, 112

Ulleberg, I. and Jensen, P. 256, 264

Van Der Kolk, B. 4, 91, 127, 193
Vetere, A. and Sheehan, J. 251
Vygotsky, L.S. 134

Watkins, R. and Kontomichalos-Eyre, S. 308
Watson, D., Latter, S. and Bellew, R. 158
White, M. and Epston, D. 87, 212
Winnicott, D. 68
Wrench, K. and Naylor, L. 4, 60, 61, 65, 75, 98, 215, 245, 271

www.ingramcontent.com/pod-product-compliance
Lightning Source LLC
Chambersburg PA
CBHW021818300426
44114CB00009BA/228